THE INTENT ON

Collected Poems, 1962–2006

ALSO BY KENNETH IRBY

The Roadrunner Poem
  (Placitas, New Mexico: Duende Press, 1964)
Movements / Sequences
  (Placitas, New Mexcio: Duende Press, 1965)
Kansas—New Mexico
  (Lawrence, Kansas: Terrence Williams, Publisher, 1965)
The Flower of Having Passed Through Paradise in a Dream
  (Annandale-on-Hudson, New York: Matter Press, 1968)
Relation: Poems 1965—1966
  (Los Angeles, California: Black Sparrow Press, 1970)
To Max Douglas
  (Lawrence, Kansas: Tansy/Peg Leg Press Publications, 1971)
  (2nd, enlarged edition; Lawrence, Kansas: Tansy/Peg Leg Publications, 1974)
Archipelago
  (Willits, California: Tuumba Press, 1976)
In Excelsis Borealis
  (Cambridge, New York: White Creek Press, 1976)
For the Snow Queen
  (Lawrence, Kansas: Tansy Press, 1976. Issued as *Tansy 1*)
Catalpa
  (Lawrence, Kansas: Tansy Press, 1977)
From Some Etudes
  (Lawrence, Kansas: Tansy Press, 1978. Issued as *Tansy 9*)
Orexis
  (Barrytown, New York: Station Hill Press, 1981)
Riding the Dog
  (Greensburg, Pennsylvania: The Zelot Press, 1982. Issued as *The Zelot: # 4*)
A Set.
  (Lawrence, Kansas: Tansy Press, 1983. Six oversize sheets in portfolio)
Call Steps: Plains, Camps, Stations, Consistories
  (Barrytown, New York: Station Hill, and Lawrence, KS: Tansy Press, 1992)
Antiphonal and Fall to Fall
  (Boulder, Colorado: Kavyayantra Press, 1994)
Studies: Cuts Shots Takes — a notebook sequence, August—December 1999
  (Lawrence, Kansas: First Intensity, 2001. Issued as *First Intensity Chapbooks #2*)
Ridge to Ridge: Poems 1999—2000
  (Ann Arbor, Michigan: OtherWind Press, Inc, 2001)
In Denmark
  (New York City, New York: Published in *No: a journal of the arts*, Issue 2, 2003)

THE INTENT ON

Collected Poems, 1962–2006

KENNETH IRBY

EDITED BY KYLE WAUGH
& CYRUS CONSOLE

NORTH ATLANTIC BOOKS
BERKELEY | CALIFORNIA

Published by
North Atlantic Books
P.O. Box 12327
Berkeley, California 94712

Jacket art: painting by Thorpe Feidt, *Red Earth: The Ambiguities 334,
to Sam Feinstein and Barbara Crawford, 1998–2004.* Image by Ailecia Ruscin.
Jacket and book design by Jonathan Greene.
Title page art by Lee Chapman.
Printed in the United States of America.

The Intent On: Collected Poems 1962–2006 is sponsored by the Society for the Study of Native Arts and Sciences, a nonprofit educational corporation whose goals are to develop an educational and cross-cultural perspective linking various scientific, social, and artistic fields; to nurture a holistic view of arts, sciences, humanities, and healing; and to publish and distribute literature on the relationship of mind, body, and nature.

North Atlantic Books' publications are available through most bookstores.
For further information, visit our Web site at www.northatlanticbooks.com or call 800-733-3000.

Library of Congress Cataloging-in-Publication Data

Irby, Kenneth, 1936–
   The intent on : collected poems 1962–2006 / by Kenneth Irby ; edited by
Kyle Waugh & Cyrus Console.
      p. cm.
   Summary: "This collection of poems by the influential underground poet
   Kenneth Irby is the second volume of a new series of beautifully designed
   literary hardcovers celebrating central yet underappreciated figures of
   modern American poetry and literature"— Provided by publisher.
   ISBN 978-1-55643-833-2
   I. Waugh, Kyle. II. Console, Cyrus. III. Title.
   PS3559.R2I58 2009
   811'.54— dc22

2009022205

1 2 3 4 5 6 7 8 9 [SHERIDAN] 14 13 12 11 10 09

This book is dedicated to the memory of

JOHN MORITZ

(1946–2007)

Poet, printer, publisher, critic,

friend, companion, encourager,

all without measure

ACKNOWLEDGEMENTS

First and foremost, the author wishes to thank Cyrus Console and Kyle Waugh for the immense amount of work they have done, absolutely crucial work, in every detail and at every stage, in preparing this text, and repeat and underscore those thanks again and again. Without Kyle and Cyrus, I could never have managed it, never at all. Should any errors remain, they are entirely of my own responsibility, none of theirs. I would also like to reaffirm once more all the acknowledgements and dedications in my earlier volumes, and further as well warmly thank those who have more recently first published many of these poems. To name everyone I am deeply grateful to for their friendship and assistance, for their heart-felt generosity and hospitality of place and spirit, would constitute a list far too long to include here. Only to specify those that follow does not in the least diminish the great debts owed to all the others: Lee; Cyrus; Kyle and Jacquelin; Jeff; Howie; Ed; Paul and Chris; John and Sharon; Stan and Judy; Mike and Anne; Steve; Roy and Marilyn; Pradeep and Jessica and Max and Krishna; Mark and Janice; Jim and Sue; Ken and Caryn; Tom and Denise; Bob and Helen; James; Dick and Virginia; Billy Joe and Susan; Keith and Deborah; Joe and MariaAna; Don; Paul; Jim and Marta; Simon; Kyle; Gerrit and Deryk; Patrick and Ariane; Thorpe; Helene; Charlie and Nikki; David and Lisa; Jim and Ange; Mike and Tania; Dan and Kate; James and Amanda; Geoffrey and Barbara; Rob; Jonathan and Scott; Elie and Nona; Paco; Joe and Molly; James and Amanda; Richard and Lindy; Stephen and Virginia; Don and Marge; Pierre and Nicole; Robert and Charlotte; Chuck and Megan; George and Susan; Clayton and Caryl; Peteris; Pat and Marla; Rich and Martha; Ben and Ari; Bob and Barbara; Jed and Suzi; Marty; Anne; Ed and Jenny; Andrew; Anselm and Jane; Dale and Hoa; Nathaniel and Janet; Larry and Lenore; Bob and Susie; Donald and Joanne; David and Cecelia; Duncan and Genie; Robert and Jess; Monica; Ted and Timotha; Shep and Diane; Daniel; Steve; John and Kristin; Bob and Eileen; Larry and Lyn; Christopher; Curtis and Mary; Ruth and John; Gary; Lowell; Fred and Anne; Jerry; Rob and Vic; Robin and David. To all *who know the tone — whereby life is here sustained.*

Lawrence, Kansas
March 2009

CONTENTS

a rapid shadow from a slope of grass

— Percy Bysshe Shelley

and the unseen is proved by the seen,
Till that becomes unseen and receives proof in its turn

—Walt Whitman

(Shall I make my list of things in the house and skip the house that supports them?)

—Walt Whitman

arise and unbuild it again

— Percy Bysshe Shelley

THE ROADRUNNER POEM

April 1964

O saisons, O châteaux!
Quelle âme est sans défaut?

— Rimbaud
Une saison en enfer

1.

The roadrunner that crossed my yard
and the roadrunner my neighbor kept as a pet

And the grain I am sunk into
staring into the wood, the bole in my hands, the window sill

The glaze that would be left
and the smoke

Catch me as I go out along the ploughed fields
and stare there, back at me as I

at them   went in   come out
stroke the flesh

as I would of your body
who are not here, and inhabit,

flesh gone up in ovals, circles, grain,
all the running on the other side of the yard

we walk beside
the opened fields

2.

Does not end there

These are not fields we have ploughed ourselves

And you are not even here, the here
I am not in but to see it, say it

so you could come here?   Or even own the land.

The wood is grown
here, the cottonwoods in the front yard
the window frames are made of

And let the ownership go to hell because
I do not — O Spaniards who took it
because they
came here
O Mexicans   O Americans
O Easterners to this
west
claim — till the ownership is over the hill
and gone into the mind to see and believe relief
to ever live on,
before it's real

Roadrunners come home to

And the house can sit on

3.

        So there is no
        way to say how
        I came here — the accident
        or past, fragile —

        are all the familiar paths to take, no matter
        how fragile, but *did* come here, not broken

           to this.
           land, seeing it spread

without ceasing, in the imagined
spread of the mind, and under foot

    and to you
    with whom I
people here the country
because you are not in it

    — as shadow off the leaves
    of these cottonwoods. Committed,
    loved, placed
    in this love till

    the soul's, body's
    history
    does not matter, only
    this place, only

    its coming
    to this moment,
    clear, seeing,
    unhesitant the sight

4.

There are only the two
cottonwoods in the yard, and the backyard
bare dirt, artemisia, burrs, but stretches away
toward the Rio Grande, across the road the fields
cultivated, the trees past them
go on to the river bed
     where hovers
green
     above the air

Smoke there
today where
logs are being burned, a sawmill
going, that is even fall, in this far
country where the fall of the sap
is so slow in the trees
I forget there is a fall at all—

smoke glazes the panes of the window
And from across the street a roadrunner stops,
lost at the edge of Albuquerque where is
no space to run these roads

and goes on across the yard toward the river,
and I go into,

walk beside these fields,
and forget no one I have ever known. O

come home, o
run nowhere

but to this quiet

5.

My living here is incomplete
empty
without someone to live with
Live with you, marry you, have you

but I can only in this vision
out a window, only
hardon in this empty bed

It would not be here
if you were here
what is here
in imagining

What is remembered
is love.
                    What is not

till later

is the old failure
my own
despair
all over again

                    •

The land is incomplete
without someone to live
into it. There
it is — in and out
the juice and sluice of energy
from letting nothing be gone
from it, of us, to it —

rests in a line of sight
glowing there, out the window,
into the compounded vision
that has to buck the street of houses and cars
going on back into Albuquerque

to last

What I remember
is the farm west of Plains
is the family on it.
                      What is not

till later

is ruin,
is that care
does not make it theirs

6. Recollections. Parallel Texts

for Robert Kelly

There were full corridors in the upstairs
of the house, side by side
of different times, the same
corridor of flooring and walls
over and over — not years — which ones
do I remember the year? — but instance
down to the last sash of color
on tin soldiers, wooden logs
are not burned to the ground
in their outpost, light goes
in and out of, up and down the walls,
to the floor, through the curtains

There are the two, parallel halls
in the upstairs hall. Any time
before this time, any movement
before I speak now
races, shunts, has to come and go
in that corridor.

    Where I walk now
    is now
           O seasons
    I cannot savor

blowing, my hair blowing
at the window, that tear
their sound but do not ever leave
the hallway — this all, remembered,
re-smelled

if I go back to each time
I go back to
that corridor, that house,
or even remember
them —
nets?   caught
in?
or growing
them —

The bloom that
never comes
when expected,
but comes,
question
as fruitless
to what core, to what calm,
as of the flowers
on the desk in front of me
or the flowers
always out that window
that hall
I walk, walked down

Where is the tree growing
or where open
the bloom

Except that I go / am there

past you
to come back to the flowers
and furnishings of my life
except such footsteps

go side by side
or straight on out the wall
into the air over the driveway
into the lines of telephones

cut all the old looks at the neighborhood
into *emptiness* (of voice)
authority (against me)
relish of beds in early morning

(I fucked myself by myself).
Rise up!
call out for the house to *fall down*
to get out

Those voices of myself I can hear
in that hallway next to this
I walk down now —
                              it is a dull thing
if they do not meet

if we continue to care
and cannot get out

7.

(Artemisia
rabbitbush
saltbush)

Sand drop-seed
Prairie June
Needle-&-thread
Green needle
Bluestem, (western) wheat
Blue grama
Side oats grama
Hairy grama
Bottlebush squirrel tail
Big squirrel tail
Pine blue
Sheep fescue
Little bluestem
Buffalo

Three-awn
Porcupine
Switch
Nodding wild rye
&
Cord

                grass
(buffalo
jackrabbit
whitetailed deer
prairie dog
harvester ant
pronghorn antelope)

Andropogon – Bison – Canis

Andropogon – Bouteloua – Bison – Antilocapra

Andropogon – Bulbilis – Bison – Antilocapra

"No line on a map can be drawn to represent in any realistic manner the actual conditions found in nature. Isolated hilltops, slopes and lowlands exhibit the transitions on both sides of such a theoretical marginal zone, and only in the broadest sense could insistence be made that, even in the zone itself, a continuous zigzag line could be drawn to outline the dovetailing or interlacing of ridges, and valleys, and slopes growing the respective species of grasses adapted to them."

—James C. Malin
The Grassland of North America, 66.

8.

The charges
      of fall

are of the plants
lived among now — the change
of that vegetation
each year, as I have moved
place each year —

and so keep track
of all the movement
I am in, around me, till it is
into me,
     the sap
that rises and falls

9.

And the seasons to change me
may come back only
to the same metal as they began

Why should I even
care further? Possess
the quiet, know no gold

to go to
that is not
here

10.

Where do you even, collect at night
all the ways home it would look like you could go? —

stranded downtown drunk without a car
the highway?
if you hitched the 20 miles to the turn-off
a path?

rises with the moon
and is orange as it sets, the orange mountain
side orange in the light
off stones off polished dirt

off the sky
Three horsemen come down the close hill
at 3 a.m.   The moon
in you, drunk?   that comes

close to the earth
and makes men mad.
Till there is no way
 to go home

and he lay drunk
on the kitchen floor
beating his head
against it

"I want to die.
I don't even know
where I am.
Go away, go on home."

When home
is where the path
must lead? Did I register
nothing, keep nothing I saw?

So that the moon did not move at all?
Or the horsemen leave the highway
and move down where they willed
across the rough ground.

◆

And tonight it is into the moon
light I must go, as it enters
my room, or my windows under its
color, I am in, I look into:

all things revolve and reflect
there, I, in them, in the glare
glaze across the pane,
of focus. Into the moon? —into:

the *night*, the *light*, the *stare*
air gathers around, cold, around me,
warm, to become warm — and I'm
around, into

the yard, the earth, the treed
spanse, I look toward. Here
is the world
of all things.

Walk
in that wet grass
bare foot
toward the mountains
and past them
the plains

                    ·

Home, o
rivers to run
flush across our upper
vast plateaus, the mind's,
the body bleeds and shits and loves
with that close in inside
where rivers might run
to water —

          Faisal said all Arabs loved
          not the desert, but water,
          but green, but trees. But home
          is not past us

Where do the people go
in that landscape? Where do they go
in my room, where
do I go in the moon,

the light across the. floor where people
might walk—
                    There
is the clear body, luster of parts

translucent to the nipples and hair
Where the body parts or thrusts
to be within itself
O where they cross and recross,

the whole journey into the moon
into the plateaus where only
water rushes that we loose, see, find, go on
ourselves

Who comes
to those streams
to drink? Who lives
in the moon?

                    ◆

            There is no one here now.
            There is only the recollection

            All over again, an hour ago, and now again
            The friend fallen drunk and slobbering vomit
            on the kitchen floor, pounding his head,
            wanting to die.

            There drink the few
            loved ones,
            at those streams' banks
            in that plateau.

11. VARIATIONS

Until there is no place else to go

A)

Redfield	Moran	
Uniontown	Bronson	
Garland	Mapleton	
Xenia	Blue Mound	Lone Elm
Trading Post	Iola	Pawnee Station

Where the railroad has left them
again as alone as they were
when it came

       The highway
is local, or tourists, but the other world
does not come in
           to touch the land

     O I've got my radio
      and a tv set too
            but

and the wheat goes off to Russia
or the cattle,
         and we know exactly where,
see it, even, on that screen, read
of our own extensions

but the town
that fronted its own earth
itself

does not now

Turned back alone
it does not, as a man might do,
turn to the land, aloneness, embrace,
but looks back
along the sporadic tracks
back to a Kansas City
or Chicago
or on past,
                    ah, juggling the attractions
in the air above uncertain hands

o the twine that breaks or snaps back
                                        home

        & you go there some Sunday afternoon
        but you do not stay

B)

Even money
will not bring ownership. Love. It is

the body in front of me. Ecstasy marks up
the body
            but is not satisfied, hangs on

hangs there in front of the stare
O god, that I want you here

That to know at all is of the body, and the body
yearns to be joined: that to know

the land in front of me at all
is to have to sleep with it

and cannot

You walk caught on fire
every time the foot hits the ground

C)

So I do not know
how I came here
that was direction
in me

Love, if I am
caught by it now,
is almost unseen
under the woodwork

(a person 3000 miles away
I thought), in the mountain
or shape of land
scape settled and caught hold

unawares. Dust blows
by. How many people
in those scraps
of paper.

Having been here
in the Army, having
given body and blood into the dirt
it is the unvoidable

mud in my bowels.
As if that
were the charge of fall,
as if the hanging

between flubbed anger
and peace,
the drunk quiet
hangs, lasts in this easy chair

till some sodden flower
blooms — wait, hell yes, wait
long enough, weeds even
will have to come up, bloom, seed,

die off. There
works the charge of fall
and spring
just as well. I am in. My

sap, too.
            Which is love,
in this woodwork? Who I see
each night walk in

out of the dark kitchen and circle
the rooms, walk to the walls, and look,
looks at me, and goes off —
tracks in the dust —

That is *myself*. Stares back at me,
the look out there in the air at me, searching,
plaintive. How many years old
ago? Where did I come from?

Or slung that look around
over the shoulder, time
after time and stop and turn
before going out, drip

the soggy fatigues greased
and wet come in off K.P.,
looking for beer.
                    Who talked
then, in that silence?

Myself, crossing the room
where I sit, watching myself,
nothing to say, the blood
all over again, gone lank
back into the grease and dirt

land sweat shit
and that *look*
                    Here, *there*, out there,
are the only paths?

    Cross and recross across the room,
    in the moonlight, in the dark

    I cannot speak to myself or tell
    anything, but carry
    with me

                    ◆

        There drink the few
        loved ones,
        at those streams' banks,
        in that plateau

12.   *for Ed Dorn*

There is snow in the mountains today, certainly,
cold behind clouds come down even here
falls. Open where I walk, even, footsteps
are in a forest across the Pan American highway
and downtown Albuquerque an old grove
of oaks. My own snow falls down,
I am in — till even the city
is our own, every person I walk by
glitters there, in that snow, in their eyes

O friends that are not here
why do I live in these empty ravines? —

track wild animals across the snow of this place, winter,
there is that distance of compasses and rocks
where deer leap over or rabbits on past bushes
where what few friends there are are in the distance,
walk, almost seen, almost talked to
where the traps put down
are to live by, love, yes, even,
love by —
where the distance is endless to trek
where snow has fallen, is with us, lummocks the footsteps

No echoes in the distance
or news

I stand on the edge of the Pan American highway where my car
        has run out of gas, hitching a ride

East, where the snow grows in the mountains

West, that there may be distance
        to go into

23

What else is here? O in this city where the groves
are full of snow, and habitable then

      the winter of this year
      come down, entered, sighted
      across, there the walk
      that is not ever lost

13.

      Roadrunner's tracks cover the grain I left but he didn't eat,
glaze of sun rays going down catch me
in the smoke as I go out where were ploughed fields
but are now housing developments
stare back at me as I glare
back, in and out of me, at them

The air strokes the flesh, as I have
of your body, who are not
here or anywhere but
in my mind to inhabit, have —
                      houses
never to inhabit with that much intensity

flesh there gone up in ovals, circles,
grain of wood and grain of ear of corn,
and running that has left tracks
across the yard —

where we do walk beside the opened fields

and the bloom of that intensity
blooms, is the flower

The moment
that is full of the earth

is full

— 17 Sep–30 Oct 1963
Albuquerque, New Mexico

MOVEMENTS / SEQUENCES

this selection of poems from 1964 is for Sam Spencer

PREFACE

The sea is shining as the light — beyond the Golden Gate the space is dazzled in its bands: horizon, line of bridge, the bay — into the headlands at Marin. And in this room, looks out directly on that expanse, come now toward sunset, afternoon spent cutting vines and grass, the music from the phonograph shines, even my hands, the skin and hair glistening, give their lustre, and the cat sleeps, head turned upside down, beside me. This flesh I am enters and returns, focus and in blur, the presences the day has, makes different, gives. Where I am, wherein the body and the anguish flourish, is then *demanded* to be said — to preface even this preface, to record even the first thoughts of words here, sounds begun: it is the setting then, the area where growth takes place, this orchard. So that ecstasy is not a movement to leave the body, but a movement of the whole body to join that which surrounds it — the literal mulch and stalk, sap and resonance everywhere around. That is the people there, as well — as surely growing there as the phloem and xylem of the vegetation in the yard. And all the movement of me, that moves as it can toward that ecstasy — Love's reality is to *love*, not to understand or change, only to love — comes, in the discrete moments it can be said or even perceived, to be said, shaped still in working, *in* the movement, no other place, way: given. The energy does not ever cease. Thus in the sequences as they piece by piece go and return, the quietnesses, the pauses, the spaces between, are toward regeneration too. Accumulating what sounds and words, meanings and relevances, attach themselves, not ever intended or thought before hand to be there: as now the cars' sounds out these windows and the clouds' unknown movements across the sun and bay, determine along with whatever thought ahead of time, the music being listened to, this being written; what moment I am in: this 5:23 pm of Monday, the 15th of February, 1965, 1436 Spruce St., Berkeley, California.

In that process Robert Duncan has called "the dwelling of the imagination in the speech," what means I have to participate at all are in the shifts and twistings of syntax. I would follow Duncan in what he shows me of that process, as best I can: following my vines of twisting movement, blind but certain, wherever to go. The wisteria. The roses I trimmed today. Even into the colored patterns of texture visualizations on the cover of the *Scientific American* in front of me: grass in patches. Finding a way in what shows no way: so, blind: but with the confidence that even to set one word down or speak at all moves in meaning:

so, certain. As the runner that has grown through the dining room window and started now up the curtains — where will it finally go? or be cut, and shift, grow, and start again. "Pause — and begin again," Patchen said so long ago. Following the textures and wrenchings of how words follow each other, the flow.

◆

Whatever *me* my poems give is as much myself as any part or notion of me that I have. The poem is an offering — as the intensity of conversation is an offering — into understanding, acceptance, love: not those generalizations but the whole person in its specifics of those – and beyond. As it is the space made to live in. In both cases the address is *beyond* me, however close in that still may be. One does not create a poem that is any more or less intelligent than any other poem one has written. But the area in which the intelligence (the *all* of it: the whole body) works, is to be constantly extended and enlarged. Who we are accumulates behind us, pushes on into the space before us. Blind and certain, as the vine's tendril. "The likeness is to nature not to these tempestuous events." Men, man, a man: myself, wherein all men stain and touch. And the touch, back out, to them. The poem as the intensity of speech, of the one person speaking it, past himself, the enlarging and cohering.

◆

"Once more on the prairie we experienced a feeling of relief, for the jostling on the uneven pathway and the cold and snow gave place to rapid and easy travel. The weather was more genial, and hares, starting from the sage bushes, enlivened our progress. We made camp before nightfall, on El Rayada, a half-mile above a party of men whom we did not go near; they, supposing us Indians, corralled their animals in haste."

— Lewis H. Garrard, *Wah-to-yah and the Taos Trail*

"For a man's problem, the moment he takes speech up in all its fullness, is to give his work his seriousness, a seriousness sufficient to cause the thing he makes to try to take its place alongside the things of nature. This is not easy.... But breath is man's special qualification as animal. Sound is a dimension he has extended. Language is one of his proudest acts. And when a poet rests in these as they are in himself (in his physiology, if you like, but the life in him, for all that) then he, if he chooses to speak from these roots, works in that area where nature has given him size"

— Charles Olson, "Projective Verse"

15 Feb and 13 Mar 1965
Berkeley, California
Ken Irby

The Space Made

Rain that would fall without any care
is months away.
Go out and get drunk in the moon
for wet.

*

The land, that has love in it, stretches
west, where the ocean lies that is still
to go into, out of this continent, or NW,
past the mountains, between them — where stand

in those trees, or barren bowled hills, or by
that west sea, the few endless friends the face
and faith and mind forever fasten on, magnet
in the ice cream eaten swings, all old beer

once down in the flesh, lays out in those
permanent lines. It's all over the cold night lines
out of doors here — so that I can't even think
of those loves except the land runs, goes on

through them. Here is our skin, this brown dirt —
I ate potato skins of, dug out of that Idaho,
wine, out of those valleys down to the Pacific —
and the relinquishment is impossible.

— 13 Jan 1964

Bandelier

for J. & R. L.

West as we turned off toward Los Alamos
the Jemez all were white, caldera, old
volcano up whose fingers dome down this far away
we drove, behind us the Sangre de Cristos
white behind Santa Fe

Saturday, sun, in the canyon of the river of beans
where beans still may grow,
an orchard irrigated 50 years ago
still in lines below the cliff ruins,
beans grown here 700 years ago
at this wide place
in this narrow canyon

What did we come to find
except that people could live here?
if we walk on another half mile,
another cave high up on the cliff —
here is our own movement to live here,
living, go out under the firs
in ease —

that the flesh, the belly
is too fat and pooches out
over the belt

would melt away here,
and in the eyes —

The distance from those holed cliffs
to this meadow beside the one stream

There is no distance
that will not fit in here

❖

And after we've seen the ruins
sit and eat the picnic brought
cooling the beer in the river,
a squirrel with immensely long ears
comes and goes, approaching
and running away, standing back to a tree
watching, not giving up

and the beautiful punch line of Ron's joke,
"My child, what do the goyim
know about fancy fucking?"

spread, where the heart
will always spread, in the shade
and half in the sunlight on the table,
where what few people there are
to love, what few places
we can live together

here, this tight canyon
like our own muscles
flexed and relaxing,
the space, the gush
of water and the mountains behind us,
we carry in us

❖

If we feel home
in these ruins
of Bandelier — the body
does not lie

35

its ease here — not all
the energy of those
Pueblos of 1250
is lost —

Handed on,
enter
this canyon
and be given it,

undoubted,
unswerving,
the whole body, love
and nerves

open, and stand back
to look at themselves —
men, men
we *are* men,

living,
we come here
the same
as they did,

shit,
and pee on the ground, smell
ourselves, eat
in this same

City of how many? 100
in three stories of adobe,
and in the cliffs above
more

We do not leave the world
at all, if we only
walk
in it

The centuries,
to be in the presence
of all our kind,
and know them.

◆

Above us as we go home
the mountains white
in all directions

no matter where the sun
will set tonight
it will turn red
against that white

—25 Mar 1964

For William Frederick Kimball, Born 15 Apr 1964

1.

The moon is full tonight, come up one hour now
over the mountains, east, hangs over the pass
that goes away, travel
is what we have,
as it to west
will pass

and in the air, that light
proliferated
holds us, thoughts' waves and energies
as that light's
thermonuclear energy,
reflected,
we are reflected
only as well

stare at ourselves in the air,
only ourselves!

or if we can, if we lose
the idiocy of that composure
the one moment of clear, certainty, it takes,
see, and our blood flow with,
all our kind,
neighbors, friends, loves in the distance
that give some knowledge
to know anyone:
the 300,000 people
in this city,
the brothers, the
blood

       the moon had
coming up
       and goes down in

The son the Kimballs have had
in Seattle, come with blood
from his mother, into this light,

pulse of blood under the skin,
light in the eyes,

the pulse that shakes the air

And the few people walking along north 4th Street
here, almost out of the city,
vibrate the air they go in,
north, in the moon, rocking the street

I drive home

        The blood pumped ascendant
        past all misuse

2.

And last night the moon was almost at this pitch,
I didn't see, under the clouds
that were the wind, all day long today,
I hadn't even looked for

    2 am Friday morning Cummings called me up
    "Come on over Saturday, I got a pony keg
    and you *know* somebodys gotta
    help me out, I just don't
    drink" who's been drinking
    since he was 5 yrs old —

                 old Army buddy
    we talk about
    over and over

    I got to his apartment about 3 Saturday afternoon
    His wife out of town till June, he could
    screw now in the open he'd screwed in close all along
    The door was open, no one home, the keg there
    I sat and drank and waited, put a bottle of aquavit in the freezer
    to lap the beer

We ended eventually at some girls' apartment —
Susy, Ruth, who else?

                           $175 a month, The Metropolitan Arms,
with a swimming pool Macey stuck his foot in
to see if it was water
was in it

And while the girls, finally, got ready to go
somewhere else (not to our beer bust, where Cummings told me
they would be), the records going, the easy slides
bumping the movements on, in the slow background drinking
out of the gallon milk jug of beer we brought,
I ate their hard boiled eggs and tuna salad, drank,
shifted their records to Ella Fitzgerald
which they straight away took off

The wind blew straight out of the west,
and raised the swimming pool water to waves that broke along the bank,
the dust muddied

Cummings went off with some neighbor girl
come in with a pie, and I followed after —
sat bullshitting as he dried her dishes
and she washed and I drank at the bar
kitchen — and she, with a date coming,
cooked dinner for us and talked about
the bitch she'd been living with, had to, move,
outta *that*, and having to go to Belen
tomorrow (Sunday), and the old man
(27, my own age, and she kept asking me how old
I was) she was going out with that night

till we left, as she was getting in the bathtub
and her date was already due

Tomorrow was Sunday. Cummings said, I'll take you to Belen

And we drank, the 5 or 8 of us left finally,
till 1 o'clock in his apartment

and even then driving home in the light there was,
I didn't see the moon

                              The blessed names,
                              the kindnesses

3.

That we came together at all
not just that we got drunk

                    I would stake even the soul
                    for even a grain of that

                    we swirled in the mouth
                    to savor

                    and gulped down

4.

                    Your father and I got
                    as drunk,
                            Will Kimball,
                    the drive is not hidden
                     behind the scudding clouds

                    He was a burning cocksman
                    in his time

                         To you

Fruit of the loins
we wish to have

are our beauties

are the whole movement out of ourselves

Here in the moonlight we go in

You will go in in your time

5.

O Lamb of God, Who take away
the sins of the world,
grant them rest.

Let eternal light shine on them, o Lord,
with Your saints throughout eternity,
for You are good.

Grant them eternal rest, o Lord,
let perpetual light
shine on them.

                        Give in this morning past
                        the sunlight kindly
                        to wake them

                        this moonlight softly tonight
                        to turn no one
                        from his sleep

We give, ourselves,
even in the stupidest words

or we are assholes

— 26–29 Apr 1964

For My Brother

I.

The rain moves in circles, blown, tonight,
trying again to write you for your birthday, 2 days ago

3 years ago your birthday I spent all day
drinking beer in a grove of cottonwoods near Belen,
in the Army, the Saturday afternoon on into a bar
in Torreón that night

and the next year, in the North Pacific
testing atomic bombs, on Johnston Island,
still in the Army, I hadn't heard from you
for months in Mexico

as this spring, again in Albuquerque, I have not heard again
that the months are you have been in,
and know the silence won't do any good
to cross whatever continent, to New Jersey

where this rain smells
up the air if it falls —
and where we have come from, what
all we have come through ourselves, looking to be

our own selves, still
knocking the blood on
to find that, who
we are,

have we spoken about that to each other?
I want the words
to follow the blood
and tell it all

ratchets of distance,
slipped in attention,
wondering what to say,
the core of memory

But birthdays are lousy times
to bring it up at all

＊

Some neighbor comes to the door, wanting me
to be quiet with the phonograph
and in the house the smell of wet pine trees
is blown down from the mountains

If I turn away from the window east
you will still be there, past the distance

2.

As we started to land, the tail wheel locked, and we spun around
off the runway, digging into the soft dirt, ending up half turned over,
the left wing tip and stabilizer crushed, and halfway back
the fusilage bent to one side.
None of the liquor we were bringing back from Juarez
was damaged.

We got out and went after a tow truck
and watched, as it came out from under the bank of yellow clouds
all the way across the sky,
the sun go down

       The feeling of helplessness inside the plane

       The wonder, now, how much of the world
       we carried in us

3.

From Sandia Crest to Tijeras Canyon
the Crest Trail is 14.5 miles long.
It should normally take about 8 hours to hike,
though it would be harder
going from Tijeras to Sandia Crest (mostly uphill)
than from the Crest to the Canyon.
                In May
there was still snow
along the upper reaches.
            It took us almost
10 hours, having spent
5 climbing the trail to the Crest
from Juan Tabo Canyon first.

Behind South Peak there are mile-long meadows
covered only with stonecrop and short grass,
not seen at all from the roads,
and the path through them
cuts down into the soft black dirt
till the track is a foot below the pastures,
lipped with the soft turf

There the sun went down on us
and we stopped and put on sweaters

…as if crossing fields in the plains
at sundown, headed for the creek bottoms…

We made the last 5 miles down in the dark
and reached the highway about 11 o'clock

         At the point the trail doubles back
         and starts down the canyon
         the whole city is spread out its 20 miles either way
         — the carpet carried in the back of the head
         lit

4.

I thought next to write about:

the vacant lot at the corner of Franklin and Hancock Streets,
the blackberry vines in one corner
the pants and legs got torn climbing through
to get over the fence and down the block the back way home
my last year in Cambridge

and added then:

         climbing down 200 yards of wet
underbrush in Portland, Oregon, to get to the highway out to the zoo,
through blackberry vines tore hell out of our pants,
the week I got out of the Army
and went North

         and the patch of blackberry vines
outside Alan Kimball's house in Seattle, across the street
on the corner of a vacant lot, we kept wading through
to retrieve the plastic saucer we were throwing around —
was the first time I knew they were blackberries

46

5.

The air in the windows of the Reserve Center
is March, but the smell
is of early evening in July, would be
from shadows in the street,

to walk on off in,
run and slide across the farthest home
plate, slide home in the dust,
slid in, with the people there, you love

Wanting to get up and leave the endless senseless
Army meeting, all day
                              where that plate
hangs in the air

                    Paulinus' answer to Ausonius,
                    in an agony of love
                    that gone so long without a word to say it
                    breaks in itself,
                    tears, gives itself
                    a thousand miles away

                    "living, remembering, to eternity"

                    in the endlessness
                    of that bondage

Who is standing there, where I look off
to slide home? even to turn and try to look that far,
what eyes look back? really? even
someone I have not met at all yet, to know,
no limit at all where love may be —

and in the flesh, now, the fibers
bonded, of the names, bodies, skin and eyes
already known, strands in the same muscles,
Ron and Joan, Sam, Elie, Jim and Angela, Ed,
Bob and Bobbie, Alan and Martha…

                gone down a thousand years
                all over again, reading,
                the wrench, the bundle
                of those fibers
                in the flesh

                turning and singing,
                bending and alone, sore,
                ecstatic

                where we know no place to go at all
                they are not there —
                              smell, and turn of air,
                              and fall of light

                            —Mar–26 May 1964

For *Round Dances*

                  "it is the
          body
              answers"
                  — Robert Kelly

Albuquerque, July, the month of rains,
the rains begin again

today, begins —

and from this photograph
of ecstasy, of stone
two thousand years ago,
Skopas' *Maenad*
turns in the mud in the yard outside

                O the head thrown back
                and run naked in the rain

                her hair run down in sop
                across her crotch

                and crotch wide open
                run against the trees

                the mud across the toes
                and in the loins

Sluice the body —
              mine, come out
from under its own clothes,
                  body curved
in the wood grain of the door, dark
haunches lines groan dark with wet,
                    the yard

The season down next day and days, on
to August, runs to autumn

Albuquerque will flood before it's out,
floods already now, from this one hour of rain

                The head turned up
                to the sky

holding the wet she gives
and the rain wet back

together in the juice and meat
turning in mud across the ground

silted in flood
away, sopped

up to flow away
in autumn sap:
the ecstasy!
the face is up

to open to —
and the feet

we cannot even see
for that light

As 2 years ago tonight
I stood on the deck of an aircraft carrier
at midnight
and looked up at the sky turned bright as day

at STARFISH PRIME gone off 200 miles away above,
a million and a half tons of TNT-worth
of atomic bomb, so bright the flash of detonation
lit the deck light as sunlight
through our goggles almost all-opaque

faces turned up, across the sky
the band of aurora wide as the Milky Way
turned red as the light faded red to the south
and after 15 minutes
was black, and night again

                              turned up,
                              and did not dance

                              the bodies, twist
                              in ecstasy, or even move

Beer spills
on my pants
as I look up
and out, the rain,

drizzled, all day
at work with weapons
dulls, come home
to a post card

from Buffalo, from
Robert, I have not
heard from
in months,

the grateful words —
and on the front
Clyfford Still's
1957-D No. 1, beside

in ink, marked
"Very Big"
The orange comes out
of the blackness —

And Skopas' figure
dances from the photograph
in the rain —
Land in the brain,

seasons
of how to live on it,
of where to go now,
city, another

try, or here, on
again as first
thought possible —
Love comes

on letters, words
start off again —

The light
thought only possible to burn
these 2 years
carried in me,

comes out, up
from within,
shines
from within,

in the face,
in her body
wet across
the ground,

hurls itself in light
alike, around the room —

Sit here, stare
into the postcard,
and meet again

the parts she danced
and carried in her

O the head thrown back
and run naked in the rain

> The orange and black
> were painted on her head,
> the eyes,

> I have not seen

> The center of this year has been
> how difficult it is to live
> alone

> the crack in the body —
> light, wet, and remembering —

> the cracks in the wood

> Where the light shines
> at all

Circulate in the blood
ascended in the sap
now flood at peak
before fall in fall
   work of the day
   no ascent
   only the walking
     and alive
       pumps

—9–14 Jul 1964

The Move

1.

Eyes light up?
   no eyes
light up — only the light
   back down the road
north from Los Angeles — still

   now, at this sunset, light,
days later. And in the memory —
   lines, layers
in the air, fog — shines, goes down
   these clouds to sea
and set —

   ·

What the hills are
   in California — what
landscape strikes to, come to
   the first time, this time
the first I have ever
   seen California — and come
into the land, on it, here,
   to live —

   What was San Francisco
vegetated with
   before any settlement? where
I stay on 48th Avenue
   a meadow, to the beaches?
the headlands
the hills

        where
the trees?
          "those hills, that
I think of most
when I think of California"

                   short grass and yellow now,
                   rounded steep, and the trees,
                   live cork oaks —
                          I thought
                   were most like what I thought
                   Spain must be

And those who came here first,
with some like past, past landscape in the brain,

what did they see, striking
   here, struck into?

  ·

Open the door
where in the backyard
the sunlight flows

Out of this dark apartment

And the grass blows

  ·

The ecstasy
        to *see*
such land!
        seeing where one knows
the heart goes: land, at all,
        and here, most fair, even
away and no kin at all
        of what I home, my plains, of Kansas

Where does that ecstasy
lead?
      as where did it lead
      those, each *one*,
      before me, 400 years
      or one
              into
              whose
              flesh?

              even what street
              to live on

                            questions
                            the race and out of breath

                            of heart
                            are left with

2.

      Eyes light up?
      as they could not yesterday, only see
      light down that road from Los Angeles,
      come here — and in the gloom

      afternoon of the room, know
      nowhere to go, ignorant
      of San Francisco, lost of a job,
      clodded, ineptitude,

      see what? what
      eyes shine? the despair,
      to see where
      I might go? of having

no skill to saw the way
away through
this gloom even —
with words, come up from where,

to save and help, turn tools, turn
way itself?
                    Movements of despair
never cease, move now

under the joy in the memory of this day's
sunshine,
                    but turn
out the gloom again, as well,

as it did the light in the room —
save for that glimmer
held over the road,
the eyes could not ever miss or let go

3.

Did I want only to see the body
pass in front of me, naked, to sleep with?
          Out of the dream, on this air mattress,
          in this sleeping bag?

Whose? Even of my friend, Sam, known
so long, to come to, fuck? how
          hold? the embrace in the head.
          It was of a man this time

returns? and then, where turns
each woman? Elie still wet on me
          after a year. The eyes
          close. Light shining like the sea

shines on them from the flesh.
The fibers of love: give all,
     fold over that — glow on,
     even after waking up, turn the body warm.

The eyes light
with the glow —
     love, flesh not lost to resolve it?
     I wake up in a strange apartment, another city,

     and shine in the darkness.

4.

Speckles of light
lodged in the eyes
like flecks across the eyes
of gold

             like gold across the scales
             of the piranha I saw
             placid in the aquarium in Golden Gate Park
             their eyes shining

             and ferocious

Despair, its
curdles and turgid knots
lead me, I lead
them —

     literal in the room
     they mount,

or in the sea
go down,

but move,
rancid and become sweet,

sour or insipid
carry down

these hills and earth
into the blood,

the old job
gone, too, or

the new, unfound,
lank despair,

hair lank,
in the mirror

of my open
cigarette case

go gold
across my face

.

Even to die, goes that way —
or failure, flows
on away, becomes another thing
altogether. Die. Flow quit, but
only here. Light
gone out, is gone
on out, another
side to shine on — behind the eyes, or
behind the life.

How simple that seems now. Not consolation,
only simple

Weeks later than I started this,
wondering even how

5.

I find from my old teacher, Andrews, in Walnut Creek,
 the peninsula originally was mostly sand, hills and trees
where the Presidio is, bogs along the bay, and all sand
and grass here, even till the late 30's, early 40's,
when these houses were built. Some still lasts.

But the first imagination of the land
as meadows, by the sea, down, waving, to it,

persists,
in its on imperative, empire,
moves back and forth between the light and dark

As in the moving shadows of those redwoods
he said once grew behind the Berkeley Hills,
were so high, coming in the Golden Gate
sailors could see them, above the hills.

  •

Writing, this Friday night, October come,
the blood, rich, with all the accumulations in the mirror of the cigarette case,
goes out to play, across the land, across this peninsula,
just as my hand across flesh, my pants leg, or this paper now

I think I'm going out for a walk,
the air's so rich tonight

— 20 Sep – 9 Oct 1964

A Set Series for Roy Gridley

If you go out of Fort Scott south and then west toward Pawnee Station
you get completely different country
than if you leave north and then west,
or east, or go on straight south.

Incursions of the prairie — Pawnee Station,
or north, near Hammond, toward Kansas City —
upon the hills and trees' covering
come in from Missouri.

Or due west, out the country roads
behind Gunn Park, toward the pasture airport,
is so wild a hill and hedge and rock,
like wilderness, condensed intensity —

there is no sea near —

witches come out, the anguished dead, into the mind
to breathe it even

Last year's beer cans thrown away
clank against the ones thrown out
tonight, in the same places always travelled
to get here, and all the spirits

dead, in this place,
start, and surround, and wait.

.

Sunlight on those
brief, half prairies

even if the sun
is not out

light in the head
two thousand miles away

or that there are no
restless dead there

only the sunlight
on their shining hair

.

It gets harder to talk about Kansas
the farther away I get from Fort Scott.

Or that I'm now brought up these last two months
against walls of myself, fucking up, not going into
any one, the loss of love = the love not given at all, or not taken —
people — look home

town because it's known? or more,
because it's me, and only there

can I go in —
the circle to focus

comes narrower,
the land

presses up
like flesh

toward the hand.
Turned away on through highschool

from any one my age to know,
to know any one I turned

on and on head long against
the buildings: everyone who'd

ever lived or passed through
Fort Scott, the residues, the

identities, the
identity.

Till now, having absorbed
of that search

so little else, so few
people known, women

finally
entered,

wondering
where to go

It is against the same
old buildings that I go.

The farther away I look
from Fort Scott, the harder it is to see it.

•

The flower that is the Imagination, that we live by, blooms
from the flame the eyes burn down the very town we live in
in all our light
to know

and then build up again
to give,

to live
in

．

Till I feel, brought in the movement
of looking home, past the multiplicity of field's
physiognomies, against

Till I feel brought
to the edge of love —

that much to give
that opening to receive

Till I am brought to the edge of
loving this town

— and giving or not giving
make no difference

．

Love that invades everything — till it is
        part of the body, not its object —

        and when that part is gone? —

even into the eyes of the photograph
that look past me, beyond my shoulder —

        and there is no way for it to come back? —

．

White honeysuckle on the one white trellis fence
        beside the garage
goes into the night
        to offer
all the odors —
        only at night

You can see all summer
        in the half still light
hours after the sunset
        and then the streetlight

the trees opened
        and gives them shadows

Who will emerge
        from those openings?
and who will reenter?

        So calm
only the odor, that is
        to open and enter,
only the opening
        and entering,
only the warmth, and light
        almost gone,

move,
are where the body
endlessly comes back to —

faces there, now, the line of hedges
to go through, to come to

love, love
for this town,

to fall in love with,
as surely

as the loved one
in the photograph before me

.

So that the whole effort to go out of ourselves,
was first learned here for me —
crossing 8th and Judson, in the vast houseless lot on the
corner before me, beside the Sample's mansion, there was a white
pavilion, a summer house, a garden arbor
— it is as if I walked there in the darkness
and it alone shone out

or mornings, out of the mist,
walking to school, it came.

There is nothing, then, that does not
contain the divine —

in us, from us, into the
        sight

only to find
    it, only
to know it's there

                Pencil lead broken off under the fingernail
                    trying to clean it, I
                looked up and saw the whole green tree
                    out the classroom window,
                moving the green crystal craze in my veins
                    I felt, was there, but
                could not ever see till then —

freshman year in highschool, I
have never forgotten it, nor doubted
what it was —

.

So that if you enter our yard, when you are very small,
through the front gate, and turn left, into the half lot yard under the pear tree,
it is another yard completely
than if you go right, around that corner of the house, under the 3 maples
And if you enter the back yard from the pear tree
through the gate in the trellis fence,
it is always unknown land. Where the sunlight
always shines

Until it is not just Fort Scott
    to come to to love

but that house

.

So that the lands
    to either
lead up —

so that I have not
    yet fallen
through into love,
    through the separation,
joined

but wait now, poised, I know

Oh, God, I do not even know you
till then

eyes turned back, inside,
blind, stumble

on, into the love
I cannot come to

any other way.

— 30 Nov–1 Dec 1964

Three Variations (to follow the Series for Roy Gridley)

The banks of fires of leaves
along the gutter, I have been thinking of
all afternoon, go out, glow dull, it's dark
outside the house —
and in this literal day
much later in the year, December, snow
is there along that house, its fence —
or the eyes behind it, going
about their work, how ever so, much later,
hours than here, years than mine —
I only now come to see them, mother
and father, in any peace in my sight —
they have or do not have, but move
and glow there, snow across, as those
old autumn fires I saw all day
glow across, heap coals far into the dark,
before all vision. Start, flicker. Or grass spears
of green might push between the snow
and sidewalk, spring and summer, autumn and winter,
endless, synonymous —

                              their eyes
all carry
into mine.

    .

Christmas, then, in the heart's
plains, in the plains
blizzards blow toward home,
grain elevators stick up
lights on, blinking,
have made cathedrals
in the sight, bells rung
wreathes hung on
are silent,
but there, if you look up
4 am driving all night
home at Christmas time, the mind
will decorate, ever
green, and the sounds
toward the dawn, changes rung
on and on

    .

Gordon said to me as we left his parents' house Thanksgiving,
"They're good people." Knowing them
as good people he'd come to know.

Density of speech, overlay of memories,
felt without speech, ease even to be there.

Come to, Mother and Father,
at this long distance, some times

the look up and the ease
to see you are so great.

                              —9 Dec 1964

Sequence

for Larry Goodell

Rain, flatulence from pasta, strained
calf from dancing all Saturday night, lights
out, into the street the eye lights go, light
points on tire tracks, wet cars, tarps
from someone moving in upstairs, thuds on the floor, door
bangs, shake the phonograph, lapse now
into quiet, I go wet
into the street

  •

Strained pasta from flatulence, rain
Lights night, Saturday all dancing, from calf
Light go lights, eye the street, the *into*, *out*
Tarps, cars wet, tracks, tires on points
Door, floor, the on thuds, upstairs in moving, someone from
Now, lapse, phonograph, the shake, bangs
Wet go I, quiet into
Street, the *into*

  •

How did I get here? how the hell
did I end up here?

sounds, half
ass importances, go

where loves
drive. Go west

from Albuquerque, then north
from L.A.—

as my family
went west to Texas

and then north
to Kansas.

The slow
shift of continent

underfoot. The tides.
Feet lead the blind, blind lead

Dark is the night

   .

the blind feet that lead
on to this coast, land, the hand
full carried

of what other
come, born out of,
love, the body turned

this compass how long,
since Fort Leonard Wood
in the Army, Fort Riley

and bare dirt, from childhood
eaten, no times remembered, smells of,
rites repeated over and over

without knowing,
only it was
dirt each time,

love, the body
turned to come
here, only

to come here, and be
lavish, rich, relish,
only the coming, here, only

the love, the body
sopping from it, caked
with it, beaten,

flubbed in attempts, almost
no heart to go on, but
relish the earth,

glorify,

praise
it, be
praised,

simply
to walk
on it

•

the efforts
to know home, to learn
this city come to, to know

have nothing to do
with why the come here,
tell nothing

of the body's decision
Rough shod, ideas, how much
they are important

but have not yet
ended into the flesh
to tell more than they knew

•

Well, what have you done, no matter
what you've fucked up?

Just as turning the memory's seeing of Fort Scott
around, looking at those houses

from the back,
down other streets.

•

Lineaments
Slime

Slides

•

So *that's* what you're doing…
I haven't danced this way
since, God? the Junior…
…1945…

•

You know he was queer —

he kept asking me and finally
I said alright, the need
was so great

•

I wouldn't care
if you were trying to grab my ass all the time

•

geraniums

a groundhog

gulls
in a spiral

sunlight

•

You're a great man, I don't mean fame

…well you *oughta* know

•

"Only the heart remembers
and records in the words"

•

Marsh flats in the south bay
where they farm salt

Wrecks in the rocks
below Fort Point

Tide rips
Eyes skinned

in the redwoods at La Honda —
until there are

no people? One block
of leaves in the gutter

beside the football stadium
in Fort Scott. Buck

Run. Cut
in the hand

from last night's
beer can

Michael's child
asleep in the next room

kleenex box next to her bed, because
"I sneeze in the middle of the night"

Where Gunn Park opens in the back
into the whole open country, without distinction, no fences
into the woods —

come down
on top of the head —

                   .

              it makes no difference
whence they come, the instances,
what home the mind
or liver carry, live in, heart
demands, encompasses —

to the kick
when they come

One, then, image
to the other

or persons? enter? enter,
in whatever entrances

the times of understanding
make

—6–14 Dec 1964

KANSAS–NEW MEXICO

Lawrence 1965

The land itself is a survival

—Walter Prescott Webb

I.

All day there have only been scenes in the air —

> west of Plains, southwest of Liberal
> the bluffs cut from the Cimarron
> cut the plains out from under
> the seen space floats away
> like a river, like the river
> cuts below it, where the prairies suddenly
> are made sure, I had forgotten they were
> they were so long and constant
> all the land
> rolls out from under

> > 3 months ago: the endless photograph
> > the caught body my body
> > the car door pinched
> > and the woman, Charlie, picked up
> > at a noon across the Oklahoma panhandle
> > scratched
> > seat across my bare back

> > where the body falls away
> > beneath, cut out
> > from under

> the trip
> gone in a line, there are always
> dots, towns,
> after dots,
> connect, that I thought, or saw, on the map, to go to
> — and sure enough, come to

Firmer than any other line —
her unlined body or mine
bear and connect, go where
we thought all along ahead of time
to go

No firmer —
tree? to go under
to pull up under in the shade
out of the noon across Texas

> 1953, was Ellis Kansas
> "the birthplace of Walter Chrysler"
> out of the disk of the plains,
> that fired and was the sun
>
> into the trees, down, across
> the bridge, dry stream, into the trees
>
> and out. The dark
> scar
> on the retina. Flashes, in the air
> turns, and goes out

2.

out the windshield for 50 miles ahead
the mound over Tucumcari
breaks

> has the blood broke
> and you come west
> she said
> my blood is broke

she said, you'll see it for 50 miles
ahead

and in Nara Visa at the gas station
it was there

3.

Fort Scott
Chanute
Augusta   Bourbon
Wichita   Neosho
Kingman   Wilson
Pratt   Greenwood
Greensburg   Butler
Bucklin   Sedgwick
Minneola   Kingman
Meade   Pratt
Plains   Kiowa
Liberal   Ford
Tyrone   and the counties   Clark
Hooker   Meade
Guymon   Seward
Texhoma   Texas
Stratford   Sherman
Dalhart   Dallam
Romero   Hartley
Nara Visa   Quay
Logan   Guadalupe
Tucumcari   Torrance
Santa Rosa   Santa Fe
Clines Corners   Bernalillo
Moriarity
Albuquerque

Some
only seen
    at night (Dalhart)
or only
     drunk
(Moriarity)

4.

The fields around Plains come right up to the town
Across one road the trees end, there are rows in the earth
We turned there at sunset, the sun already down,
till the light faded, driving roads dividing fields and not links of towns
The land flat there, really the flat of Kansas' images,
the trees out past the town only around farm houses,
only there the only lights on in the dark,
and across 12 miles or 5 south the grain elevators up, blinking

There is no other place to go there
but into the earth
there is no other color
but black dirt
there is only the smell
of that earth
cow shit, catalpa trees

dark and gone out
the light of the earth is gone down in

5.

My mother is there on those same plains
that are at sunset
all they are
Sheltered in an asylum
where she does not belong
but on those plains where she does belong,
or where the earth is close —

Break down, that is in the mind
so fragile, half here or half not here
Does not belong there,
without any control of herself at all,
without being able to be seen in public,
does not matter, makes no difference at all next to that
is forever better than that
shelter in that
asylum

Let the plains
take us home. Let the earth
be where we
belong

        in the yard,
        or in the fields
        where she grew up

6.

And the picture of the farm in the dark
hangs in the dark in the brain,
the days afterward in a motel in Albuquerque,
looking for a house

    Where
    have I moved to?

    What picture of the spirit
    of the house —

        is it
        a spirit? Point
        where the earth
        stopped, up into the man
        stopped,
        and the place to sleep

        mixed and
        indeterminate
        where each
        ends or begins —

    is moved up
    into me?

And I wake myself half from sleep
each time to say or see it
or write out, ride out
for 3 days from that motel

or now 3 months from the house found

to see it,
that falls on top of my head
each time I walk in
or out

And where the eyes go,
have gone all the way from childhood,
looking for that vision of home,
hangs in the air,
is fair colored and in light,
or in the dark, lights
across the dark ground

And will carry it, the sound right
in the wood, walls quiet
and covered, into

> The person
> there is
> to go with

> o old and silly dream
> that does not come true

> is endless
> I will go with

"We turned our horses' heads to the east; Atlanta was soon lost behind the screen of trees, and became a thing of the past. Around it clings many a thought of desperate battle, of hope and fear, that now seem like the memory of a dream; and I have never seen the place since."

and in the flames
of the fireplace
all loves, all persons
even touched

this was the highway
here

flare, buckle, and flare back
out of an endless city

of houses

burning

> — 21 Nov – 2 Dec 1963; 23 Sep 1964
> Albuquerque, N.M. – San Francisco, Calif.

RELATION

Poems 1965–1966

For Larry Goodell, Robert Kelly, and Lowell Levant —

friends, poets, loved ones,

sustainers of the spirit

My thanks to the following publications, and their editors, where some of these poems (sometimes in differing versions) first appeared: *Poetry* (Henry Rago); *Wild Dog* (Drew Wagnon); *Work* (John Sinclair); *Poems Now* (Hettie Jones); *Io* (Richard Grossinger)

PREFACE

I have denied all of these poems, in one way or another, at one time or another — and have also recognized that they are as much *me*, the forces through me, as any other act or notion of myself I have. The poems are survivals, then, as Walter Prescott Webb said of the Great Plains, *The land itself is a survival.*

.

Most of these poems were written in Berkeley, California; some also in San Francisco and Palo Alto; and others in Placitas, New Mexico, Lawrence, Kansas, and Princeton, New Jersey. So I was, in these two years, over and over at the concerns of travel (outward or inward) and domesticity — Núñez *Relación* and Coleridge's "Frost at Midnight"; Haniel Long and Martin Buber; James C. Malin and George MacDonald's *Lilith*; Edward Dorn's *Geography* and Robert Duncan's *A Book of Resemblances* — as I am still in them.

.

Being homeless, I was given a home by these friends: Sam Spencer; Pat and Michael Abramovitz; Mary and Michael Yeaton; Jerry Aistrup; Martha and Alan Kimball; Thisbe and Don Blake; John Friedman; Edward Grier; Larry Goodell; Angela and James Irby; my parents. Without them I could hardly have survived at all.

.

The *pastoral*, as a mode of poetry (out of the eight Sir Philip Sidney lists), seemed to me particularly of two concerns: a calmness, a quietude of the whole being, derived from all attentions and awareness; and a feeling of great closeness with the vegetation lived among — an ecological calm — poetry that *feeds* us (*pascere*), not just that tends the sheep. I know Pasternak (his Zhivago, that is) concluded that the pastoral nowadays is an artificial genre, a falsity, for *the living language of our time… is the language of urbanism.* It seems to me that classical pastoral verse was always the product of city dwellers hankering back to an idealized rustic simplicity (as Bruno Snell, for example, discusses the process in the last chapter of his *The Discovery of the Mind*), and thus the mode was, strictly speaking, always "artificial." But I am concerned here with the precise landscape wherever we are, here and now, as the "spiritual landscape." What plants grow in my backyard, 1614½A Russell, Berkeley, California; and how I am aware of them. For the pastoral mode, as I feel it, enacts a state of consciousness or awareness, eternally and recurringly common to human beings, every day, every life. Given the amount of shit we live in, it is also manure for all manner of living growth.

                The cherry and plum trees are in bloom again, spring come unbelievably early for a man such as myself, born and raised in the plains. A great lushness of the sclerophyllous landscape, and an accumulation of all our humours. As the land arouses the sensuality, so the corruption of the earth exasperates and frustrates, a hoarseness of the loins. The soft, green Berkeley hills hang down almost into Sproul Plaza, where once again strikers, for the same old silly (selig) demands of respect and the word, are beaten and tear-gassed by the cops. The irascible longing. There is always a poignancy, living here in California, in this land that should have been the most beneficent of all human dwelling-places. The poetry of this mild littoral clime is marked by many turnings, distracted and multiplied attentions — but centrally, in my own case, by the conviction that the landscape demands us, and reveals us.

— Berkeley
Feb–Mar 1969

There is no illusory world, there is only the world.

—Martin Buber

*the correspondence of natural things with spiritual
things, or of the world with heaven, is through uses,
and uses are what conjoin*

—Emmanuel Swedenborg

A true account of the actual is the rarest poetry

—H. D. Thoreau

January 1965, Looking On

Moss in the gratings
of a sewer vent

And past me have gone
a lady cop in a yellow slicker
ticketing in the rain
and those who have come in and out
after books

There is no image the flesh
does not take in, sink, the hook, there is
a weight beyond me all afternoon, into the drizzle
uncertainties of
how to look

A man comes in selling ballpoint pens
"I won't be back to bother you for a long time, not till April —
I'll let you have all three for 75¢ — they all write"

And in the dust on the floor of that used-book store?
So seared, the scars he must have had so long
any look back at him
is not even felt?

Moss
on the sewer plates

And on Clement Street
leads straight to the Pacific
men dead on their feet
come — back? home? down hard —
to die. The clod prim slickered copess

And there is no footprint
no print in the moss
the wet, sopped weeks of rain
does not take out of men, bodies
the bodies sopped
staining the filthy concrete

The rancors of texts and elucidations

And the quiet light down on the dust, in the windows, in this store

My God, my hands stuffed in my dirty pockets

— 11 Jan 1965

Two Fragments for Bill Dodd

The loneliness of West Texas
as Ed Dorn said, like the love of death

"the loneliness," the man had
cattlemen came on, wandering east of Las Vegas, in the Staked Plains

was not of the people missing
but of the endless eventless landscape

where what few rises there are
give only onto the same repeated vista as before

and to be born there
is what you look for, out any gaze

and the stretch clear on through
out the back of the head

·

Tulia
Mule Shoe
Dimmitt
Floydada
Levelland
Plainview
Whiteface
Meadow
Crosbyton
Spur
Lamesa
Bovina
Friona
Paducah
Dawn
Goodnight

— 12 Jan 1965

✪

It is almost 2 months since I have seen you
          Where the body can touch them
Light out in Berkeley is behind clouds only
          Geraniums
The least parts of the body thrive
          As into this light
Out to meet the great
          Do I go completely
The 3 circles of the stupa in the brain
          Into the fields there, S. Folsom St., the pastures where you wander
Morning lecture after, walking in the rain
          Out, past where I am

Puddles, carved urns, barbed wire
                 Are what I carry with me
Maybeck's gymnasium for women
                 Out, past these windows
I have not seen you anywhere
                 There is so little love, I mean
I have only wanted to see you everywhere
                 At 5 a.m. and dawn on
Visits to San Francisco, the surly unemployment dirt
                 I have awakened into the same light as all day long today
Even at 2 a.m. you were not at home
                 Gordon come, on to Los Angeles, not stayed
Gordon come, on to Los Angeles, not stayed
                 Even at 2 a.m. you were not at home
I have awakened into the same light as all day long today
                 Visits to San Francisco, the surly unemployment dirt
At 5 a.m. and dawn on
                 I have only wanted to see you everywhere
There is so little love, I mean
                 I have not seen you anywhere
Out, past these windows
                 Maybeck's gymnasium for women
Are what I carry with me
                 Puddles, carved urns, barbed wire
Out, past where I am
                 Morning lecture after, walking in the rain
Into the fields there, S. Folsom St., the pastures where you wander
                 The 3 circles of the stupa in the brain
Do I go completely
                 Out to meet the great
As into this light
                 The least parts of the body thrive
Geraniums
                 Light out in Berkeley is behind clouds only
Where the body can touch them
                 It is almost 2 months since I have seen you

                                          — 30 Mar 1965

✪

I am so tired tonight I cannot even see past this room
    into the next dark room, look up, focus to look there
past the map of Kansas look
remember any my old pictures of
old times last night too drunk to drive home
would I enter the wood desk, lie flat, return

o open gold
             bottle of elixir
fragile of one headlight busted and burned out and the left front tire shot

the arguments got into tonight with old friends
know better, I don't
             ram me head on
out the window at dark
             night wet lights from across the bay
and the talk still going on
             quiet let sights drum no loss be day
                        from each other

in the kitchen
             Here may I chew my cud
              it will be time to sleep
              soon enough let no
               zap slip through
                untouched
                the fingers

♦

So he's walking up & down all whichaway this & that jiggly
and this man come out the woodwork, cabinet, file drawers, green eyeshade
white spats old gold studs a roll two hole & three up turn down the corners
the eye lights & looks straight shot at him, roll me no cigarettes I'll light you no butts
        would I hang loose ends my sweet song along time
        never no ways & anyhow flipped up the pencil caught it
        wondered where to go & called it putting the piece

        back in shape:

        — of the hand
        — to do the required exercises
        — Supreme Headquarters Allied Powers in Europe

        now falls the memory to,
        the flow of,
        unhinge

"To quiet the mind and make it receptive to divine influences"

        that one may even sleep
        and fall like rain

                                                        — 15 Apr 1965

        The Journey Itself Is Home
                                — Bashō

        That is the mind's trip
        anywhere
                        as well as roads forever never settled
        stretch

If I do not come to rest
in me
there is no home not of the mind
more peace

Stations, way
places toward
the relish in
all things

the stretch out
toward that
— entrance —
resolution
*that is the
mind's peace*
love

•

Am I willing to be lost?
that is
a way as well

lost, is fuckup of the choice made,
realized? arrogance of intention, that we knew
from here? shown
vanity

When there is
no way
that is not
arbitrary in
some other way,
we stumble on

and survival comes back
to ourselves
who have so fought
to rule

—2 May 1965

Freedom Is the Unclosing of the Idea Which Lies at Our Root:
the Freedom of the Rose Tree Is the Rose
—George MacDonald

the flow of vegetation
        to know dissections of
                is not to enter

its flow—
            I would not impose
upon, myself upon,
                    but sit here in the yard, the continuities,
out of myself, into the sun, back again,
into the tangles of wisteria, the heavy smell,
the rhododendron bush alone, nasturtiums
up beside the dilapidated summer house, spread lawn
notched by bushes (camellia) of this yellow Victoria
's age's house, and where I sit the cottage behind
on Bonita St., Berkeley
                    opens us all to the bay

        we strive
    into around
    each other

104

•

and on the bed inside, Mary asleep
    who lay asleep against me all night
        after, where, we intertwined

and in this house look at each other smiling
    lit in the open shade, clear day
        is our open month the May

may all times for us however short together
    be — open, light — around us
        wet in each other, wet all over each other

as wet spray as the sprinkler Mr. Street
    runs where looks on off any look
        the bay lies, "sheeten metal," Michael said a day ago
            it is today
                    and seeds our air
                    with its endless wet

•

I mean, Mary, I enter you and I look on now
as I wake up, move
from my tangles
knots darks and shifts where the fence to next door
is so thick with vines only a few boards show
                            into the sun
you have now so opened
    where I lay
        simply to be here, at ease

           is world walk
           clomp clomp snick snick
           lengths of footsteps
           in the gravel drive

it is past any demand but what we take ourselves
        calm, in us, where we want to go

I grow beside you
        as your wisteria adds silently at night
            minute fractions of an inch

and the fragrance

                        I had forgotten that smell of a woman
we mix
            sounds of the evening approach
            as you wake and move
            the squeaking springs

    .

blue striped cup   tin pail   beer bottle
blanket spread   red plastic car   gray & yellow plastic truck

the children's aura   left in these   turned upside down
grow in the grass   as we   children in us
grow in the light   falls across   the face

what we have left   grows   behind us

faces in the mirror   swarm   blood in the hand

insects turn the dirt   wisteria flowers   blow

so heavy your sleep   the breath stirs   beside the bed
                              the curtains

                                — 3 May 1965

The Brief Connection

At another day minus four years I would have been back in the barracks, duty ended, locked
    into the indigenous landscape, liquor, listlessness out the window, Albuquerque,
    set into the Army out of time except eventual release—

that long country of flat perspective, and dry, I read of this afternoon again, Haniel
    Long's *Piñon Country* again, running a tailor shop in San Francisco, the years and the
    distance of hand to cover whatever land, crossed, matter not as much as landscape
    held in the head and incessantly crisscrossed as sunlight's different slant of fall is
    here down Clay St., half a block from Portsmouth Square the Sydney Ducks and
    whorehouses radiated from like spokes of a wheel—

it's the time of day I want a drink—there, from a hidden and illegal bottle if I had it, or beer
    brought back from the Picnic House across the street—here, I have sold nothing
    all day (no garters, fat ties, Harris tweed socks) to pay for, finance: lost high finances
    —as if near payday in the Army and bereft of ability to drink in company that
    paid, left to write angles in the windows out upon those mountains east—tonight
    I go home to Berkeley—there is the question still of cause

                                     —18 Aug 1965

Sequence

So we wait on the verge of—
                         the want to move on again
The pressure that becomes unbearable to stay in one place any longer

American history is the only history

107

Local history is the only history

               it is the
                              body
               answers

            •

P. came in this morning and told me
his wife had been raped Friday night — coming home
drunk from a party they waited over an hour for a bus
and arguing he got mad and walked home by himself — she tried
the people at the party and called a cab, and waiting
3 guys hit her —
                              "after 2 days of eating ourselves
apart over that, we decided to move — to Albuquerque,
Tucson, the SW somewhere like that"

And in the lunchcounter later, drinking coffee,
he talked about George Catlin — *everytime I go east*
I feel I'm going against an enormous tide

            •

I'd said when I came to San Francisco, the only way to go east
after you've come this full tilt west to the ocean
is north and then east again — the great
clockwise undercurrents of the continent

But we'll go the south route next month
to Albuquerque to pick up my books that are stored there
and they'll probably go with us

            •

That is, what makes us move?
                                This thing
for them—
                they'd been talking about leaving for months,
moving to a new apartment soon, anyway—

this rape

They tend no cattle in the sunned pastures
of these streets, not even a car
what grass flesh milk dessert sustains
past the regurgitation of oneself, and eaten all again?

it is the pressure cooker's lid blown off
of the lady who lived behind us in Fort Scott
her face and arms burned into scars

what dispossesses us
what we do not have to take
        sitting down,
                but move—

·

All day has been the necessary tedium
        to come to this quiet—
left alone as Mary's gone to pick up Michael
        and lost in Melville lost into Clarel—
put again by your phonecall
        upon the turn we move upon, where
pivot us, old throaty night quiet songs
        before we leave, tell us
where we've lived, here, sweaty
        drawers left, garbage sacks thrown out the window—

Mary come home asks me to take the garbage out
and in the yard the amaryllis' smell is thick, their pink—
so soft they turn in the dark yard the stamens clink
filter butts in the grass thrown out of the upstairs window
     roll cold against my feet

The important question of our movement
is how different it is to go this in & out I have tonight
and you to move that move to come to Albuquerque

— to come to this quiet

even Michael's shouts and machinegun rasps
do not disturb, garbage sacks or clock ticks

is from or to that same movement you move on now? all
lost shit necessary first to rest at all? what done
to come to whatever ease, lasts now, while it is, endless—last
fall in isolation on 48th Avenue, wandering Golden Gate Park
where groundhogs came and went and doberman bitches
to greet me, what pain of loving a friend I could not touch,
slow turn up and down night mattresses without, as rose and fell
the geraniums' saturation glow, the fog that came and left

we move, to lose the pain? I moved
to this yard, it took months, it's taken
months to reach this ease tonight—

the difference of the distance of the travel, the length of the steps,
    long time—

and then we wait on the verge of—?

as I wait on any step at all out there in the yard
for the chink, the clink, in the amaryllis, to open
or to begin to bore into—

as you endure the lapsed long pain of *where?*
and a weekend of rape and after eaten into and out again

to face any new place
and rechallenge the power of your roots
      to sink into

Let it come, let it come,
the age of our desire

I have endured so long
I have forgotten everything

                    — 23–24 Aug 1965

Gymnopédie

I get up to pee, and you
to take off your clothes in Michael's room, look
after where he lies asleep, come
then and piss after me, and then to bed

                    lapse into silence
                    is the night we have not
                    looked at
                    except the windows are
                    so dark
                    they only show
                    reflections back

and the moon hangs
gravy heavy
cloud full
in the redwood
shakes
beyond the hedge

day to come
in our fingers
we will fuck
into being

night
in the pit of the stomach
eases

Hangs down,
            Michael,
you start and snort now,
rustles its boughs
wherein the flute plays
carrying on its length
the 12 dancing princesses

lift up their skirts
to pee
stains down the walk outside
in yellow glitters
past your eyes

·

Fresh may we wake to
what we have made

—7 Sep 1965

Series — 4 Oct 1965

step out this evening to see the constellations
sought nights before and light too light across the sky here,
Berkeley bends toward Oakland and glows, to see — that I wait up
late now till darkened, and at the west horizon
the Scorpio to rise before this month is out, that is my birth's sign —
look in the evening before the bay is dark, for the evening star,
Venus, come into the house where whips his tail
my sign, my flesh, the opened and then tightened countenance

Anger's movie is of this season?
                       All Hallows' Eve
in the flesh, the sky turn bends to,
                         that in the aftermath of,
November, I was born —
                  may the year leap again
as the child from its mother
                    into the light —
tail coiled and sprung
             the sharp sting of light
             to come

   .

the house, all houses
to be roofless, then —
the yellow sky that
Stan and Coleridge and Crane
demand, and the stars,
canopy me if I
walk where they open
continually — may I —
for it is all prayer,
that we go past even where

we want to be, fail
at — be so open
that no other
house's roof will do
but this — this
none, this all, this
endless spread of sky

.

acceptance give us, where before there was none
acceptance, even before we can love —
if I came down onto the bed to you
and we fucked the whole afternoon — sweat rises from,
mist now at dark, drifts through the eucalyptus on the hills
east toward Orinda, west along the bay,
what we have given back into nature
as taken — it is the anger yesterday, shout
and I called you every kind of bitch as you sat on the toilet
trying to piss, Michael between us —
come back, opened up and split open, talked about,
into some ease, some, whatever little, taking of us
as we are — acceptance, acceptance give us,
even before we can love — living together, live together,
where before there was none

quiet as you sleep now
the gas hisses in the stove, and the moon
covers into blue the empty beer cans on the porch

.

so we have lived together here five months now — the yard become
our courtyard, our portico of the sky's covering

the major portents are
arrivals past the hedge and garage:
    Frosty the white samoyed
    friends
    the landlord in bib overalls

  ·

in the flesh the flower blooms
of the freeway from Oakland to the Bay Bridge
and off it toward Emeryville three vacant lots like parade fields
eucalyptus still grow in along one side

is in the hand turning the tub's faucet
water out, as the cars' flow on the freeway,
in fits and jerks before it runs, twistings
of the vine's stem, before
the flower's come to, and the tendrils
turned in upon, out around
where the light falls

as I turn to you in the dark turned away from me in bed
cup my crotch to your buttocks, flatten my hand
across your stomach
the flower bursts
the petals flow as moving lines between the skins
along the ridges where the sweat is
into bloom

canopied flower, skin
full of stars, yellow
light shining
back into our eyes
the gloss of eucalyptus leaves
our loving's fetor
reeks of

and shakes, trembles
in the winds
as leaves, as curtains
at our windows

    •

and the portents that come, lead away:
— the landlord who snoops,
    mowing the grass in the morning looks in the windows,
    and won't let us stay
— the white snow dog
    who endlessly wants to go away, anywhere, waits,
    lies sleeping beside the car so no one
    can leave without him knowing
— the friends, already moved,
    John and Gail gone

they are so literal, the signs —
       tides, ephemeral, go far away

—4 Oct 1965

Moon

We have entered the dark stretch of night just before dawn
as we have entered the dark stretch of land
before the home's come to

It is not anywhere an ease of meeting anyone we come upon
distrust is natural as want of companions
and we who have entered into such closeness with the land
less and less crave anyone

I have said, "O Moon, my wife!" and again tonight
as the moon is full over the imagined, fabled city
the pitches of the body are turned to her, are hers

"Rich weeds!" Only the treed and then blank land
is city for us — to approach the western mountains
hold stones of moon as promise — but she dwells here
spread upon the grass, to plow into
our cocks as shares to turn the earth
sweat and come, light and light
sink into, planted here

What noises we have heard in the night
are those who guard her jealously

We come
new
to wed her

        •

That is what the dream tells, wide awake
under the full moon has risen an hour ago
over San Francisco — I am in the fabled city
and the mind goes backwards into Kansas, come there
naked and tired and two hundred years ago, new
and explorer of the plains
home came to be —
                    there are no dreams of now
                    there were not then — to push
                    into the new land
                    was not to plant there
                    new cities like the old
                    in every heart — as I
                    have wedded in the time old thoughts
                    the moon in full tonight
                    did they
                    who came there first

·

In the back Tim and Jerry are building on the new room
The chair I sit in is a camp chair. The beer is Colt 45
The ground the self can see at all now
is so complicated, so many levels, so thick
conglomerate, so dense the trees
I do not even know the names of —

                              may then the welter
                              of such facts the gaps cannot
                              snap and crackle fast enough
                              to hold — give way
                              into such ease, the face
                              lets smile, even the back of the head
                              rests and lets the breath out easily —

Jerry came in and left the stapler
There is the moon
's light around his head

The painting of a wheatfield in South Dakota
lapses from its sunlight
into this moon

We have approached the fact of this land
as body as alive as our own

and then seen beyond us
into the ground
is simpler —

                    In the moonlight
                    the explorers have lost
                    all sense of self

                                        — 8 Nov 1965

✪

Now may the light
night sky bend down with rain
into the cups of our sleeping heads
dreams make us into days of ease

There is not fought a war
we are not in lost in
looking for light moments even one moment
the ease from makes

There is no pain the photograph's pain
may make us equal to
only our own to come to
not hatred but the flowered march

The burn of self outside a union
no one is in but to burn beyond
the face out of
consumes to light

Night sky bend down
that no particle of all
you cover be lost —
excoriated   burned   shot open

Where our heads like cups
wait
where the fire waits
for what day of ease
dreams
do not make

—20 Oct 1965

✪

What colors are there
in your hair?
        I didn't see
past the red, gone brown
by dark, red hairs around
your cunt — that is the word
we said quietly
in the dark, cock, hard, come
not quietly, but to
quiet
      The long filaments of hair,
of us spun thin into the air, yours
I still find stuck in books, mine
are with you, all over the house?
Bind us
       Your hair, your red
and russet hair, fair winds in the dark
never desert us, the air
of Bach's suite lifts gently
in Palo Alto toward the night slips
west toward the ocean, as east
toward Berkeley and your sleep
the earth turns, runs
before the sun

We who fucked night after night
linked the earth to earth,
               I think
we made the sun rise
for us, day after day —

the hair, the red
lights of strands

last to

                        — 11 Dec 1965

✪

Dream Children — A Reverie, Lamb called his discursion
into the darkness beyond the lamp, into the back
calm and always present regret — regret   regret
lost intentions colored in the cardboard paper book
at the edges of the room. They recede from him
as he tells
                    how it was to be a child himself
to himself —
                    We are in a dark room
and the children gone to bed now
are my friend's, not mine — and the road stones' glitter
is golden in the half light toward their bedrooms,
footsteps on as we would go there in our thoughts
or they have already gone on, the marks
of their small feet cut in the gold bricks.
                                        Recede from us,
recede from me among my friends
lending me without knowing their eternity.

                                        — 9 Dec 1965

Relation

Mesas, erosion —
who was it, Dutton, Hayden, Gilbert, or Powell, said, it was
the *least* eroded country in America? The rest
all more worn down, long ago, to a nubbin —

Bryce's "hell of a place to lose a cow in" canyon
rims its amphitheater open toward the south
the river there, way south, roads its way
toward lower California, sawn —

  the year the fathers rallied
  round the bell in Philadelphia

  the fathers west crossed
  the crossing of the fathers
  now silt and muddy water
  backed up over the whole long canyon

  toward the home
  stretch, through
  Moquis and Navajos
  toward Albuquerque

  having circled north from Taos
  into the Colorado gorges, west
  through the Uintas, south along the Wasatch
  and across
      looking for California
      and the way thither

· The sun is out here in Palo Alto, and the flame red pyracantha
 clacks its berries against the clapboards, windblown
 as the clouds blown simultaneously show and recover
 the direct sun
     such elements as only lately
     eroded those flats and ranges
     — the "Plateau Province" Powell called it

It takes such soft wool
as Escalante and his fathers wore, such
pain and ease among, such
care to even see
                    to live in that land

                    —on any land, the care, that the wear
                    is of our feet across
                    not inundations planned

Cabeza de Vaca and Escalante
went through the trek, into the land traversed, the heavy
foot lift, over old and used again tracks—
          Sauer and Hallenbeck traced the trails Núñez used, still
          visible and followable today, from the Texas shore
          to the Guadalupe and Sacramento mountains,
          south along the road to Cíbola—

through the land
is its own experience, care for
what care the land demands

And the interior distance,
the brain pan, the heaviness there

                              —for Escalante only came back
                              where he had begun, a great
                              circle without touching California
                              or that western sea—

the plains in the mind
eroded to the Ground
the self lost on off
in those steep and wandering canyons

while the soft wool robes, the soft
touch of the
hand of the
naked bearded
wanderer

       created them anew
       who touched

                  — 21 Dec 1965

The yard of the house at the corner is full of oranges
A dwarf lives there — as in the fairy story
lived under an orange tree, his skin orange —
as here it is his wife, or mistress,
who is orangey

        Don't let your deal go down

        I love the gamblin' man

        O Lord, honey, take a drink on me
        .   .   .
        Two old maids a-sittin' in the sand
        Each one wishin' the other was a man

But the orange tree is in no desert, as it was
with the other dwarf —
              but here is on
the eastern slope of the coastal range, toward
the south end of San Francisco Bay, whoever lives here
who does not have to, has money —
but the backyard of my friend, a teacher,
is full of what richnesses other climates
aspire to with wealth and ostentation —

lemons, gardenias, pomegranates, roses
in December

This is what we came west for

But I have come south from San Francisco
for these friends. Here it is the day after Christmas
and we listen to the New Lost City Ramblers
waiting for the chickens stuffed with peaches and mushrooms
to cook —

       west along the ridges separating
Palo Alto and Los Altos from the ocean, through
the redwoods at La Honda, down those then open
and now with rain green round valleys
toward the ocean, the afternoon drive
uncovers the land from its piss-ass tracts and highlines
and brings us the old closenesses again
— stopped in some drivein in the last noonmeal of summer —
heights again, they are anew, a new
and other order, kids crying and hollering in the back seat,
get out to pee by the ocean, sand flats awash, a plover on —
& other order, as if it all
were all a new and never come to
meeting of each other, finding ourselves
suddenly among such people
we could love, could face
all shit and waste against us
and survive
into yet another order
of the closeness we had found

    •

It is an orange tree the kid there
plummets with oranges to shake down —
past the dwarf and that dark, orange-brown mistress,
his tow head beside the pyracantha berries' red
turns toward the other corner, where two
teenage kids are married, out in the yard working on their car

Rain tonight
and in the morning the streets awash, the sun comes out
as it was yesterday
we said we'd run and laugh in
naked

—26 Dec 1965

Rose Street — January 1966

Now it flowers,
                    the car out in the street,
the black Volkswagen with the right rear tire flat,
                                        flower
of her I lived with half that year
love does not come by intention, even the lost tries
trying to give space — let it be —

the threads of its back
the threads of our nerves
strung and not let up
fuck into the dark hole over which
the one last nerve between us strung
lapses or straughts — straightens, taut —
breaks in two and snaps back on the bedstead

126

the sweat sopped into the sheets
into the mattress
                        and that flowers too, another florescence altogether

and the fuck of us
both is in the body's memory
cells of the hands, tits, cock and ass

is five feet out there in the air
that remembering

   •

I wish we had fucked in the street

or in the bathroom, standing on my head
eating you sitting down, legs spread, my cock
in your mouth, legs across your shoulders

   •

The flowers are in the street to come up or for us to wander in
the streets should be left open to all people, the meadows flowered
ways into sunlight or the dappled shade
once creek beds to play in, now these streets

marching to Oakland in the half fall light
                        one tendril
singing on a dark porch in the summer night sidestreet
                        one tendril
turning the corner crossing the street at the sight of a friend
                        one tendril

the flower that blooms out this window
can only bloom in the street if we walk there, each footstep
planted opens land beneath

those who walk in the middle of the street
        are completely different people than those who walk on the sidewalk

127

and what was only in the dark before
    now moves in incessant colored movement
    down the intense sunlight

the flowers are *here* and *now*
    either there is one where you are
    or the space of you lacks you

I have come into the room, and weeds

Your life and your death are with your neighbor

and the sexual act in the street
    or on the bathroom floor
    goes on out of us, way past us
    till we can see it without any us in it at all

.

Your car sits in the half-moon outside
one tire flat, where you left it a night ago
We have been apart now half the months
we lived together
The hills above Berkeley
hang in the moonlight
the wind carries over the hills
as if the smell of calm
the summer night might bring
But I look up and out
and only the streetlights glare between me
and the dark rise beyond —
it is winter, and they
are cold as winter beyond this mild clime
Not that we long for each other now or want us back, pining,
but that we made it together —
calms, leaves the inner organs
eased to come again,

as calm, eyes shining and the hair,
as this light, as the rise of land
and fall, beyond the eyes
toward morning

— 12 Jan 1965

Let This Time Have Its Canto
— Robert Duncan

Toward Oakland in the night streetlight glare
the open ends of cars go by,
kids, highschool kids, it's Friday night
and in some distance the diffusion gives no direction of
a basketball game lets out, waves
here to the backporch wash on

                        They and their cars
are flowers in the streets —
                        and from this notebook, my own petals
drift, fit to their own —
                        We will be calm
or we will be gassers — *the Beatles are gear*
written in passing
on a billboard

                thrown open

flowers, flowers of us, flowers because
we open in the air

.

The fuck we all get tonight, or think about
incessantly, goes past us, is always more
than we are in it —
                    that is why
we enter it again and again, keep coming back, never tired
to make it again and again—
                              that is why
we go off in the streets,
                          drive and ride,

sing this song and shout, shake
it on out and stomp about

But the last line is not
where the record ends, or where
the car's broke down and the wheels fall off

                                        baby

    it is so quiet the cars go by   like harps
        or guitars blown hard through
    even stars fall down and crinkle on the ground
    daddies
                To *hear* each other, just to *hear*
    the other

    the songs we put over ourselves   because we're in them

    and then give up ourselves   into the others there

    sweet chops   pussy cat sweetie   hang loose

the last line is not anywhere we are not willing for it to be

                                        — 14 Jan 1966

★

The flesh of the woman
idealized in childhood
without knowing, idealized and wanted
after in highschool, without ease
O her flesh. The dark brown
dirt under the fingernails
She was not idealized. She was
unknown country to come into
Men fuck women
to go beyond themselves, utterly, out
into that night or such heady light
nothing is known at all. Feeling the way
Men fuck men
to know them, to
sensuality of oneself
to communality, walking off together
across the near plains. The flesh is very near
Only rarely can men
endure the presence of gods

— 22 Jan 1966

Richland Cemetery, Wakarusa Township, Douglas County, Kansas

the poetry of accomplishment   the reckoning of attaining
fierce reputation   vowels, muscles in sunlight
dead inchoate   restless compassion into contemplation
what union here   what ease is possible   what exaltation

beyond the yellow broomgrass   Blasdel turns his camera
toward where we talk   away from the gravestones
the sky smoky into spring   the green rising in us

the goods that can be held   without possession
the leap of mind   without compulsion
where the intellect sparkles   the grass rustles

late afternoon   toward Happy Valley
wondering of the land   to live on   to come to

the leap of body to its knowing

— 10 Mar 1966

✪

The hills beyond Lecompton west
rest as Virginia, mountains, Tennessee, alone
the farmyard driven to, wrong road taken
a dozen dogs run up, barking

mash smell almost in the air
the river working at the hills' edges
the flat flood plain half a mile wide
left into the valleys roads do not end

— 16 Mar 1966

✪

The road to the cliffs at Bodega Head
is grown back to grass again
There are no differences among us
as we walk back from the sea — green
fly us against the wind

Along the San Andreas fault
the poppies furled are on the verge
of opening — green
bend against the wind

There is no speech equivalent
to the distance crossed

But this

— 20 Mar 1966

Three Geographical Variations
for Ed Dorn

North out of Lawrence we turned
east before we had to a back
track to Valley Falls and Ozawkie back
roads north into Hiawatha
Old trips of the past will not save us
Noon meals in or out of a calendar
picture quiet and readdress the east
turn into White Cloud and Iowa Point
to reach toward the river and where
the river's urge in us eased us a little
That is the flow the urge toward
each other links hand in hand as
word in word driving drinking beer all Sunday afternoon
I have come west and at the far ocean remember
It does not matter loose specifics of whose
the linkage matters the flow
the closeness possible the intimations of divinity

as intimations of the dreamed spread land
spread before the eyes of those White Clouds diddled sooners
even the willful wily promoters
looking west at the land's run
out from under them

    .

I will not let blood and I do not know
if there is any turning back upon the land
to traverse, how much
traversing now will reopen
what spaces seem nowhere
ease us together — it is not different to go past
the endless misuse of landscape
here in Berkeley or there in New Mexico, what space
is open beyond is open across the whole world
Looks past whatever salvations of individuals
realizing salvation is only to pass
into the space all people live in

    .

There is no need to substitute any world for this one
in order to come into any wonder or more
enter the open imagination. Good and evil
seem kindness and indifference   at each footstep
At the other edge of each tree   another pasture
the shade fallen on each face into the sun
Into each lit house dark street we walk home
The stories where we are all changed
beyond the wardrobe's back wall   pass through
The eye is blue wonder brown opener the horizon
shines through upon the toss and fling the ring glints
head up in the air   grass goes by   like starlings
iridescent in the sky

— 16 Apr 1966

Placitas Poems

blackheaded grosbeaks in the box elder
toward Jemez the high clouds linger
over the river and drift on —
that is all blue in the distance, haze
as the hand lifted to shade to gaze
out from the sunlit terrace —
close at hand the silver salt bush
and across the red dun hills green
dots into gray of scrub juniper
aroma where the fingers crush it lingers
fingers run through the hair leave on the hair
the pomade of such wandering around
chiggers on the ankles bite to

    •

the sunlight is in a thin line along the river valley, the high
stepped bluffs along the west stretches
highlighted, the fall of eyes to light
as naturally, looking idly up and down the blued haze stretches
north into the Jemez — all mountains and all ground
grown luminous behind the clouds and shadows, light
beneath and in all landscapes seen, whatever size —
down to these stones under the feet, leaves and samaras
blown across the table, box elder bugs
spin in quadrilaterals above the road
as in circles earlier today, before the rain, gray Canada jays
wheeled settling and rising on, moving eastward
through the gap toward Golden

    •

the light falls across the room from my friend's lamp
gone to bed in the other room he sleeps or tosses around half-asleep
under the fall of the light here, the record going on the phonograph —
come to visit after two years almost — it is
into the light night air all goes, our
touching hands again, my staying here, the long
disjointed conversations — into the land's light, the dust
blown up in circles before the rain again tonight
the gnats in disjointed turns over the terrace — the light
that comes up from within the land
and down to us, part of it, from the sky

way north there are faint lights in the river valley, a few
where Los Alamos sits against the Jemez, faint
lines of snow on the peaks above Santa Fe
shine in the moonlight — behind us, out of sight
the tv towers on the crest blink red and off
as the heart beats and relaxes

·

apricot nectar, a flour can full of peyote buttons in the kitchen

·

the old what few songs few ever sang less sing now
late at night, one man, walking home, drunk, against
the dust rising from his footsteps, against one
fence and then the other, sings a Mexican
borracho song heard first a dozen years ago my brother
brought back from Mexico
78s scratched with dust

they fill, his phrases out of the song's
disjointed, as his laughing, stumbles
kick the knees out dancing down the road
poorwills churble in the piñon off the highway
swoop the small nighthawks by the cottonwoods off the hill

threads of an old song tie together
as string ties together his shirt falling apart

.

Martin sits crocked in the Thunderbird telling
how to work off too many hot chiles
's to get on a woman and work away and when you come
they're gone

riding home at 2 a.m., the moon
sets brick red toward Cabezón

— 29 May – 1 Jun 1966

Point Reyes Poem

The fog moves in across the bay in combers strain out the sunlight

.

We climbed the path to Mt. Wittenberg on a clear Sunday
over the ocean the low clouds moved away from us
Reyes' spread hills spread away on every side
the sea into burned so bright we couldn't look straight at

The path to the sea
goes down gradually
miles of forest, onto
grasslands, let down
to empty farms, the steep
last hill, the pastures
flat a hundred yards
along the cliffs

The grass rises and burns
light, back lit and side
in the last light hours
lupine in, paint brush
slides a little, rides back up
the wind down the trees' gap
fans

.

There are only two ways onto the beach or back up
one down a stream's gully, steps cut, boards back up
the other through a blow hole, another stream's fall to
                                        caught us
ankle deep coming through from the sea side
tide up, wave backed
up the pants, sopped and socks squished in the boots

we stopped over the cliff rise to wring the socks out
poppies like earrings in the grass, over the cliff's edge toward China

.

The trail back is a road left over from the dairy farms, so gradual
no rise is felt at all, through bay trees showing
eucalyptus on the hills showing the sky in scattered patches white beyond

As we turn into the first of meadows in a string before the trail's end
a boy and girl rise from the roadside and start on ahead of us
Debussy's *Syrinx* playing on her radio
our dog in gazelled leaps chases deer along the hills above them

having come to the last meadow
      seven deer in three families move contrarywise in short directions grazing

having come to this meadow
      there is only the uncertainty of all purpose

•

And drove on, fog dark, sun set, north
        into the coast hills and redwoods
to Occidental, "wide place in the road
        with three enormous Italian restaurants"
fivecourse duck dinners, stuffed before the duck ever came
        rolling pebbles from the beach around on the table
offering to pay the waitress the final odd dollar due
        in quartz white stones

•

Frozen seafoam, petrified jellyfish
purpose but to wander, too rarely here, too often
mind in, locked gaze out
onto the splendiferous —
        as here the spread coniferous forest
o city, where all our meeting is —
not what buildings we have built
but where we always live

•

And with the duck in us head back —
        across the swamp flats below Napa
the lights in the bay float and waver
        "Goddam, coming through Sonoma
just to see the square"
        the black dog in the back seat shifts
cars mesh and pass the radio light rises and floats
        into the directions home

over the Berkeley hills eucalyptus sway in the breeze
wind carries the smell of miles down wind, over the oceanbound air

•

Now in this room weeks later dill weed smells up the air
the rug's meadow light falls across —

                                room of the world
this is the room the eyes start out from
birds fly through the look on out
as gnats and flies fly through the room here

    •

The space between the trees we enter holds us
the calm, light down into, over eucalyptus boughs
       the point the afternoon has met us
and we stop, the sound of our feet in the leaves
       leaving its echo past the ears

so we have brought our meeting with us
       carried as one room of air around us
to these trees
       and suddenly stopped into the light
they merge, all spaces merge and fall away around us

o enter the splendid city!
       where all our meeting lies

                            — 28 Jul–28 Aug 1966

Our Conversation is in Heaven
—— St. Paul

The friend who came to dinner has gone home
late night the streets full of sycamores holds all the spaces
held in our speaking—— the conversation in the room
gone into the yard's opening, the long now pauses
between the phrases remembered, the alterations of cells
the body's answerings, long off echoes felt halfway to speaking

farting getting up to go upstairs to bed

New Jersey stretches away all trees out the attic window
only able to see the streetcorner's lights
only nearby, scattered up through the leaves
shifting slightly in endlessly connecting directions

as all the turns, half bits of thoughts started
abrupt, talking to John tonight, Jim and Angela
held and encountered, relaxed and begun again
laughing out in the middle of the living room

the light would break in all the windows of the house
if we looked at it once, would break in our eyes like window panes

that as we turn disjointed and uncertain
at even the next word, to make any connection
connects everything

—— 11 Sep 1966

✪

There is only one world, and it is everywhere around us

　.

The fog in the trees drips,
　　　　　　　　　　over the hills
and far away the sun in the valley
shines where the snows above in the Sierras
rest early

We are not at home if we are not at rest
going and coming in —
　　　　　　　　　　home is the bed's
stead, where the rest takes place
all the circulations, out and in
that lead to sleep at last and back, to calm

as　　drip　　drip
calms the traffic's sounds
into their own and granted, widening orders

　.

That is the incessant writhing movement
we have seen upon the walls

the light in the dark parts of the house
that does not ever leave us
eyes closed or gone into this dream's
other dream,'s sleep

careful of us You are

we have seen that care
move with us everywhere

till it is even brought to face the contorted hatreds of misorder
      their own misnomers
faced across the table or across the interval of sidewalk
drafts, armies, police of imposition
impossible offices of even the most benign appearance
      hateful

only the human, the human is broke
in them

where even on *their* faces swirl
the endless curves and revelations of the light

Wrath is the breaking down of all relation

  •

That would be anyone met in the forests of these hills and fog
not known before, only this meeting
the possible transcendence of all preconceptions
and the self given over out of isolation

now, only now, *now*
                  the   drip
    drip   of the fog
                      counting
    this eternity

  •

The green man covered with his vines beneath his suit
around the corner of Cragmont Park toward the fall of rock away
we said only a few words, looking out toward the bay
where the words met in the space around us
dark tendrils in us grow carried in us now
      out toward the space, who comes toward me

is not the same space, changed, she comes from blossoms from the grass

across July, Tilden Park a hill once, or
Shattuck and Vine, her flowers from her hair
in the laundromat, halfway into evening, leaning
against the change machine, the odors of us
mixed and smiled at in the air, we knew them

flowers, flowers of us

you who pass through this poem
and out the other side
                                        counted
by the eternity
of the words

.

They would have us forget the eternity of the music
that the music is there at all

they would have us only be angry at them
or be quiet in desperation, submission in no other terms
than theirs

not *hear* the music, the flow of all movement

.

The sun has set squarely in the Golden Gate
into the bed of clouds come up just before

We are the last first people, Olson said
and this is our West, the *cloud-capp'd…palaces*
left *not a rack behind* —
but recognizing that lost, this ungot-at and still held, West
over and over again in these sunsets
these vistas, this down and home again to ocean, start
up and never seen before province
revealed its inner lights no clearer time than sunset
can we see where we are before us

145

come to this ocean and this gate
the clouds give name to
silence is golden

•

The friends that did not come, the enemies
that did and not known to come upon
new land come into —
                     this old swell of elegance, San Francisco
the assuager of all such loss and loneliness
or dust washed off and liquor made in place of water
as if the gold were
in the liquid

movement of the eyes

•

Ravagement. War gone on
abroad far west of here and with no
vision of the light across us, we are in, but
spilt blood's light

Already in Vaughn Moody's time
his soldier face down in the sand in the Philippines
An Ode in Time of Hesitation
is clear now has been
uninterruptedly hesitated upon
to this, no longer hesitant, full given, plunge into
       darkness

dark at the heart of the nation
that has no other light to see by but spilt blood's

But the city, Charles Williams said,
we can found, at any moment —
the nation can only appear

146

and what the city is
            between us
is as we choose and let loose
from our sluices of the divine
what pitches and currents caught in us
cross to the person
facing or turned even part way
toward us

the sunset in the air
as our light in the air
between us

            ♦

And the music flows
that out of this unknown country into the sunset ruled it all
overcomes, regulates into another order
the ravagement made
out of tossed up and not kept promises
— inhabitants and use of land —
out of unsaid, held in, secret, and most kept promises
            with only inward gods

But the music, the music!
I *hear* you, I *hear* you
said against all fears of paranoia
to the person across from us

Sam across from me in a bar in Torreón
half a decade back
thinking I was putting him down
I pleaded not to turn away
away from the spread out top of table's
place where all our meeting lay
not back, into the lost
dark self's involvement
no place touches onto

and he is gone now from me, I from him
but in regret and rancor, ravagement

Bound upon the wheel
as we are, the lama
said to Kim, be not
angry with the man, for he
has already repented, and you
have only a Red Mist
before your eyes. Let it
wash away in the River
that we all seek

       •

But the meeting once held
is not ever gone or let forgotten
The love held and acknowledged
the fire flow of each person
letting through him the fire flow
of all movement

still vital in the air
the cells of the body changed by it
permanently

as against such transformation
the ravages against the light
wear down the body
clog up the sluices through

       •

Sam, I have learned to love with you
and not expect return, know
the love flows on unimpeded
given back or not
but loosed—

and that there is no
seeing the returning, your holding of the heart
's movement beyond yourself
— that is always love —
hidden from my
foil-ridden, sunset and tree-within
ridden mind

.

There is only one world, and it is everywhere around us

— 5–6 Nov 1966

Strike (UC Berkeley, December 1966)

All that is unjust leaves us impatient with eternity.
—Robert Duncan

Vaughan saw Eternity in a great ring of light in the heavens. I have seen it this afternoon in the swirling fog through the trees and houses on the hills above Berkeley — looking out the great east window of the library reference room, the strike on, thousands standing in the rain in the plaza at noon. Only as we are at ease to move among each other, as the rain and fog move among us, are we free. The place from which we move toward Eternity, move to perception at all, depends for its being open on our acts between us.

.

Now as the rain gusts west, wind out of the valley
toward the open sea
                    the dull gray in the brains of men
blows leafless, stuck in the mud

149

Strawberry Creek rages bank-full and brown
west as well, we who are anchored

                                    only by our feet
wander to intents as well as these

    •

Protesting the use of the campus
given freely and with all commitment
to recruit Navy for the war
when other nonstudents, protestors of the war, had been denied

students sat down around the Navy's table
rather than leave that crux of use
loose, fluxed and wishy-washy washed away
in the old loosed promises
lap, the Navy breaks over and over in those waters
only that much war away

you can make such references in history
but in literature it is not so easy

Cheat asked for "imaginative and creative proposals"
and then rejected corridors of access offered through the human
community of space made on the floor around the doors to the Union bookstore
the human aisles the doors to the true union

proclaimed a riot in the midst of singing
and called the Alameda County cops and had them
pick out the 9 nonstudents as alleged only leaders

sometimes the same reference will serve —
such as personal names, and geographic names,
and names of corporate bodies

the use of *imagination*, the act of *creation*
being the wielding of inarticulate and sense-less
(having no means to sense but)
strongarm power

all references to this place
        are to all places
all references to these names
        are to all people
and this corporate body
        to all institutings of power
above the relation between each person and each person

censorship is the effort to — or the actual prohibition
                                        of communication

        .

Streams out of us, words, acts in silence, singing
from the land under foot
from the common land held inside us
Strawberry Creek carrying to the Pacific tides
        these silts and erosions
the war west of here 10,000 miles receives slowly
but inevitably the directions of our weather

        .

STRIKE   COPS ON CAMPUS

DON'T GO TO CLASS   GO TO THE LIBRARY AND STUDY

MAN THE PICKET LINES

the leaflets drawn hastily and printed overnight
        a student being dragged off by a cop with
        arm raised wielding the campanile as a club

keep time in hand
and beat those down
who seek what smidgen even
        of eternity, justice
to see it by

or say it is not time

We are told that unless Heyns gets faculty support…then Somebody Worse will take his place…Somebody Worse is in Sproul Hall right now.

the *time* is not right
                ripe, fall off the tree and rot
                        before ready?

too *young* to make such decisions
                        STRIKE
and answer now an eptiness
between the strokes of the campanile
as opening and limitless

·

The rain is so heavy in gusts umbrellas are flipped inside out
and the cover brought against the direct weather
is blown away

the picketers at the end of Telegraph
circle the center the restless movement up and down the avenue
leads to

at the point you look at the center
into the rain and fog beyond
at the point the center of the look is
each person at each person passing
eyes now up directly to eyes
every face is the surface on which we *see* the light

STRIKE against the dull gray in the mind SPARK
HERE held out in the eyes held out in the eyes' look back

      •

Face the rains again, falling to flood
all night on new asphalt
up washing clothes past midnight
in a laundromat on University

the revolution will go on
whatever suppression of this attempt
kept in the active underground
and passed on to each new year of students

      •

The strike over, voted out of fear down by an old academy of faculty
and the threats made, better never do it again
the conditions from which all discontent grew, no different
only the threat clearer, unequivocal the lines drawn
solidified, the stick up the ass of power

if it is not here now it will be here again
the names of *California* and *university*
gone on into another relevance than guessed at first

every day the struggle:

let not the given conditions of each day
drag down the first moment of waking
and keep dragged
no goods finally ever enough
even when the few goods got are got

— no, not even this exhortation —

if we *see* each other

we make an eternity
in the weather

Light is the result, the rubbed two sticks
of all relation

—1–8 Dec 1966

★

results from my book:

Robert reads it in the morning and says its lovely

Duncan says, "Irby — beautiful book," and wants to buy a drawing

Richard also mentions mostly the drawings

Roy says I'm wise and tells about revolutionary tactics in Lawrence and what's
     been learned for next time

Marilyn asks about the chicken stuffed with mushrooms and peaches recipe
     and how to go about cooking it

Clayton finds the sexual positions "ambiguous" and cites "a lovely line"

Larry says you give us more than you think

Lowell writes that he hears the line of continuity of the whole book now

Lyn gets my address from the preface and writes for the first time in seven years

Serendipity sold out is first order and got another; Cody's still has 6 of the
     original order of 10

Shao remarks from the photograph on the back that I'm reading John Buchan
     and that my arms are bigger than anyone else's on the beach around us

Jim has not written

Ed G. as ever says something in praise and something in criticism, citing, curi-
ously, the one poem Duncan had liked most, as too flat and prosy

In Berkeley Telegraph Avenue is being destroyed in order to save it

The campus under "reconstruction" is back to normal: tired and quiet

It is election day 2 Jun 1970 party primaries and constitutional revision hot
     and smoggy

Relation has been published 6 weeks

I sit on the terrace of a northside coffee house at the lower edge of the redwood
     belt if there were redwoods left

On the interface of the summer fogs and the summer heat

Facing the pastoral characteristic of the nation coming up the street toward me

156

THE FLOWER OF HAVING PASSED THROUGH PARADISE IN A DREAM

Poems · 1967

(As a Preface — March 1967)

The Western Union

                    might be

      The Pacific Republic

neither of which are dominions

      of Rule

          Power (except That which

             is Within)

      or Control

but of

      Relation

& of that City

      where all our meeting lies

As has been said:

      the Nation can only come into being

      but the City we may

found

        Between us

        Here & Now, as we read

these words

✪

Whoever lived in this house last, left
some razor blades (good ones) and a persistent
lingering of woman's powder, rises now
each time come in the door, blended with lemon yellow soap
off the sight of lemons hanging at the porch
light, skin bruised, washed clean, oil of living
in and around, the traces on all things, these
shot spare words as if the spaces left between
and where the words were, dropped out
shone always, on and on, along the house roof
edges of eaves, morning light between leaves
slight haze where the nose knows between
the air outside and the powdered, lemoned air at waking
opening the door a crack without getting out of bed

.

At dawn, almost all stars gone, the hills
        hang under haze, into light
Even less visible as the sun rises

And at night, late after sunset, stars
        all started out, out of the hills'
single, silhouetted trees
        the moon returns the sky to

        light upon the floor of the house
        the door is open through its glass

As if the powder shone that lies along the cracks
as if the moon were in the powder, powder of the moon
lemons of the waiting hanging fullness
for the unintended sudden look up —
caught and brought to knot across that looking
light and all the person, moon

and all its darkness, leaves and
all the slight recurring, shifted
movement—
                    the endless instant
the turning lasts—
                        and the head drops back
ringing

✪

Looking quietly for the place
to go in by

and in the quiet, lasting miles to sea, hours
        inland over the hills to the valley

realizing to be here is to
have entered the whole—

There is no illusory world, there is only the world

•

Heads of lovers below the hill
show above the hill, their bodies
together in green unseen

and the live oaks' leaves move
very close to each other
whole branches taking their leaves
in directions the leaves move contrary to

below the walk white shirts and skirts
lie on the grass, only shift slightly
to keep the circulation going

blues and reds
without heads

(the trees'
leaves
keep)

walk by

the buildings move only
as their pigeons move

            •

So the sight at any moment
is complete, needs nothing more
to come into being

the whole entered, as pleasure
is full not in extension
but in being

            •

The girl at the next table
whose eyes' green is her sweater's
moving toward her ribbon's,
                        half between,
her gaze, lost at the sea she thinks of behind her,
reflects
there are such moments
as only the bound-up movements
of the eyes and fingers together
can come to

there is her face, after all, her hair
and body showing above the table

— these words are a body
to move about the moment
after she is gone —

it is not light to say that
but heat as well, kept well
below the visible bands, felt only
in the body's rise to pitch again, she gets up
for the first time, I look up
and see her legs back and forth away
the slip slight movement together
and the heat her thighs leave behind in our air

live oak leaves blow between the words
as they blow along the table from the door
someone's left open

    ·

Light that has no other place to go
burns in the mind years waiting
to dance again — along the hillside
faint lights in the dark bob —

bursts as brilliant as the sun
light up the midnight sky
thousands of miles in every direction seen
carried inside waiting for the light again
that carried *that*
and fell as calm and common to us
as the sunlight —
it is *this* sunlight now, and the look
up and out into it

easy to think
this moment that the revelation comes
is where the entrance is
when to be here at all is to
have entered the whole world whole

The Flower of Having Passed Through Paradise in a Dream

What did I bring back? I can't even
        remember the dream, but I
              did dream. We fucked, twice.
You're still in the bed beside me.
The body *seems* the same…does it?
        The cells slightly changed, I don't
            see the same, as after
touching you over and over last night
        I don't feel you the same — that,
            gone into the eyes?
I have swallowed a seed
        and it has blossomed everywhere inside me
            even digestion…new, short rivulets

But I am *here,* on this verge of a bed
        looking out through the door into the almost red, raining
and you are buried under the covers next to me
        and if we have come into
            new? even *changed*
                     world?
we have been brought along together
        and all the familiar shapes
            lying, still, just ready to reveal

But the *flower?*
and what did we *leave* there?

—I don't even remember the dream
   I don't even remember how you touched
   before I touched you last—

equivalent to what we've brought
Brought? what is *here*

I hear your breathing bringing to
whatever I think, its quiet, moving order
and all these disparate thoughts with no connections I can make
are left connected in that calming motion

the gaps left, the covers torn up from our loving
    and you will make the bed again
        and we will tear it up again tonight

and we will wake *each* morning
    changed and shifting in the change?
and wondering *which* the changes are?
and thinking of each other in that, past what other else?
and this flower, what we have made
    between us?

"If a man could pass through Paradise in a dream, and have a flower presented
to him as a pledge that his soul had really been there, and if he found that flower
in his hand when he awoke — Ay! and what then?"

                    —S. T. Coleridge
                    Anima Poetae

A Birthday Poem

for Doug Palmer

There is the one light
and I have wanted always to talk to you in it

Here it is your birthday, and the night sky
the clouds over Oakland drift pink from the lights
The moon that is our sight by night
give you her light to hold your sleep to peace tonight
and wake nowhere diminished, into such heady sun
only the patient love you said you wanted always to see Ruth in
is everywhere, on everyone, you look

Birthdays hang us up
if we do not wish them, happiness, beyond us
Lousy times, I told my brother once, to talk at all
they still are *special* times

Birth brought us here
Celebrate that over and over, bound
upon the wheel we are, but the binding
is together — and all fears
of each other are fears
of ourselves are fears there is no
space between us we both inhabit
that there is only emptiness there

There is not
Look up, you wrote once — into this space now
Woke up, I have been in your house
when I thought there was no place to go, and came
coverer of ineptitude
laughing out of that same fear
drives us off into the night alone and wild

167

Think, that your own house
has been that refuge and renewal
even when all relation had fallen apart between you —
as I have never said the right things
to tell you "happiness"
never the incredible necessary things
— I mean, the belief is never full enough —
to hold up the poethood —
and yet beyond me a light has sometimes sustained you
you saw come in with me
I didn't know was there

So the place is more than we knew
or know even now
Light in your house, off my hair
relation broken between you and regained again
Think yourself of the places you both are broken and welded together
and if I touch those places now and grow stronger by them

think what you've made

.

When we moved the piano in
Ruth took the mirror off the wall
taking away the window of reflection
I look up into this window
and see the world beyond
as through your solid wall

.

So the birthday is every day
as the death day and the day of rebirth
are every day — going down into the dark
not even at sleep but in bright day
the look up and utter darkness, the look up
and only inside, all senses reflected
only in themselves

No. Stand at the door
and come out into the open, is in this room too
look up look up
look down into the ground, the incessant
life's activity thick in the grass, look up
into the sun beyond us, into
the faces, carrying all this too
who share that face of light
Where we may meet
so much better that we meet
than think each other enemies and stoke
only our own short fires, rage rage
to keep that close iron stove inside
lit up at all
                    Let it burn out here

For Gail

> And, at the outset, I call upon that Lord
> who dwelleth in my lady's eyes

— *Convivio*, Ode III
(trans. Philip H. Wicksteed)

Despair, then don't stay
        coiled in the brass wire of my notebook
where the look   fixes and returns
        fixes and returns without ever leaving
as long as the book   as long as the look
        are only here in front of me

come out and circulate in those turns
        and shine with me in the sun

or I'll carry you, the brass ringed book
walking, rummage the hill's grass with
    finger
            or I *won't* take you, after all?

                        cop out

As when the door opens
and she walks in, the look up
circles and reenters, light upon
her eyes
        there is no choice but to enter
the interchange?

Even of you I walk to now, Despair,
    would I be the choice —
               so silly to think so —
of your being here at all?

Turning around and around the look itself
those turns might be the circulations
to such entrance as her eyes
the light strewn suddenly and everywhere
the burst in the middle of the body
changes of despair ringing the brass
    into her gold

I would not choose the world, but have it
    come in everywhere upon me?

•

        This makes my face to change
    Into another's;   while I stand all dumb,
    And hear my senses clamour in their rout.

               — *Vita Nuova*, Sonnet VII
               (trans. Rossetti)

And at the window catch all the light
         on my own face turned up to yours
come in the door behind me
         light to equal light
until the room is filled with that sudden
         voiceless brightness
the soft glow that face to face
         carries the intense sunlight
into human shape

I cannot see my face turn into yours
         or yours turn into mine
only at the point the eyes meet
         both of us turned by the light
into *its* face, *our* faces gone
         from any *us*, all self
from any serving of the self

      •

It is not that easy, but it is that easy
         when it happens

      •

         So is recorded in my memory
            That I turned, looking on those eyes of light
            Whence Love had made the noose to capture me.

                           — *Paradiso,* XXVIII
                           (trans. Binyon)

171

Solstice Set

toward the bay only the sky and sun
on houses' sides, no San Francisco shore, show

we are very careful
so useless very often

when that line, irregular and lit
irregular, of trees and houses and telephone posts
hosts in the mind the communion of lines
toward linelessness, all other lines
lines do not know

a moment look up through the window
lets hear who's come in downstairs

  •

no easy route   at home
                at night
friends staying several days
pop corn downstairs

you enter the same window through that —
going downstairs, the smell hits you —

as coming upstairs, out of it,
the door to the porch is open
over, on the air, we would be careful
looking out over water
not to fall in

to create that equality
between us, as we are
to all eternity

•

we sit in the living room
in the evening of solstice, midsummer
midnight and only dark a few hours
imperfect custard cools in the icebox
carrying spices calm now dinner eaten
we have left off between us
not many lights, and they
not bright

           are there?

•

Venus hangs over the west shore
the moon behind us rises full to our cross
greeting
Balanced, hanging still and enmeshed in circulation,
moon and Venus in the parts of the body
swing at ease

✪

    The eucalyptus smell in the air
    turns the hair to hanging leaves

✪

I am accustomed to sitting facing Moe's
    till the revelation comes
then wonder where I ever was
    but here
no more entrance than an itch
    behind the ear
I am so married to the very
    flesh walking by the door

173

to make love hangs if we would talk
        between us in the air
fingers following to find out
        where the words came from

Coffee drops off the spoon
        back into the coffee
reflections and clear sight through
        off the window pane
reflect in the coffee, broken
        up in circles of the ripples
words between the brain and fingers
        follow

   •

and I scratch my head, trying
to get past the hair to the brain

lose my fingers in the thoughts
or the thoughts into my fingers

talking leaves the fingers free
to linger over other surfaces

your face in the mountain god's dark green
words we didn't say to each other
waiting in the fingers to be freed again
tongue along the tongue, feeling the words let go

✪

The light in each room of the house is different
but the light of the whole house
hangs suspended in eternal afternoon
facing south, the west stretches of horizon
playing out where the sun
moves north to south again
But the excitement is not in the light, disembodied
not moving but the mind moves to it, back, to it again
The returning recurring excitement
is to live here
the light in the body, the shadows
lightened into reflections but not erased
your face smiling up or looking out, clear-eyed, out the house
where the weather continues
we are this household of

what the body holds of
and gives back

your dream of the trees and pasture
out past the balcony, straight on into
the distance past the door
set with chairs and sofas
having come home to

.

Rising early before you are up
the late summer fogs moved in and no sun out yet
going down into the living room and kitchen
taking a piss and lighting the heater
to dry my socks out

before activity begins
bringing the warmness of under the covers
to the coldness of the house
filling the downstairs left bereft of person all night
with our presence again

We come downstairs into the currents of air and vegetation
that flow along the ground and circulate

having gone upstairs into (even during the day)
the intimacies of the mind into its dreams

.

It is not daylight or nighttime
the light lasts — in the memory
in the acts of creation of its presence
resonances given off, held in the old woodwork
the house as if a weekend carpenter's
part-time occupation

The light lasts on out of history or memory
in the face and turn of head toward the sink
that endlessness of everyday
that is precisely eternity

✪

Now we will speak with ourselves
and all those communicant unknown
possible endlessly in this farthest
inside address
that reemerges in the world begun from
thickly inhabited by the same
now certain countenances

.

I didn't leave you, only came out at night
in the flatlands, miles away where the factories
begin out of nasturtiums and geraniums
From this sunlight at midmorning
the turn of the world we can turn with
is half a world away to night —
so nothing moves but cats

the same vegetation in an unknown clearer wind
the certainty of faces in the places
just passed through to get here
simultaneous through those dark windows
through these windows out into the street
who comes in the door, last dregs
of too sweet coffee in the slopped-up cup
Quarter moon waning, fog along Marin the coasts of home
always known beyond exact sight
to enter and come again without difficulty
Known now the sight and thought of sight
no matter where the thought
can come home any time
once I have first entered that back
calm pasture of the mind
where all weather is,
               and begin again

It takes so long to know that
you have given me the gem for this day
in which all days re-shine and re-shadow
reverberate in noises audible
as these down the street outside
That is to say, I have lost no senses to come here
if anything, they all are sharper
lie without much argument for use
until they come in perfect unison
with the mind in operation

Reach up and touch the blue-eyed grass!
whose nod makes no sound we can hear

The fog reaches the Berkeley flatlands
and renders audible
fogbell sounds across the bay
impossible to hear when clear

✪

The sky lit orange at sunset through two oaks
as lace the pines and redwood thick as night
lace or screen against the water tower seen between
leaves themselves turned black at light along the line
telephones and Marin's shore the sun long since set
gives now slow to see through as wind through
the English walnut's dryness readying to drop the last
of nuts and follow with the last of leaves

rustles hang at the porch door open
the redwood next door a hanging woman
clown Indian leap frog over shoulders hidden
toward the Bishop pine a block away
leaning forever in another forever imaginary wind
south no seashore no palm no balm
here can take away the urge to

      .

Lords of the Light and Air
are Immanences, not rulers

and this the carry-on of hand and felt
intention in the lines
as if some phone call along
the silhouetted lines, pulsed the lines
shifts
            and gaps   where no intention
determined
            open

looking up to take a drink
the sky is black and the light left
is only the lamps', the record humps, over

spade kids of the neighborhood talk walking past
carrying the same rise and fall as soul music
on the radio next door
Boss to our souls the sky at sunset
hangs over us all oblivious
and enmeshed

✪

All the months lived in this house
without till tonight taking off all my clothes on the balcony
and standing naked with a hardon to the moon

In the tower of cock between us
the surf rises and falls, foaming up the shingle stones
beating on the shore we share between us

TO MAX DOUGLAS

It's crowded. No matter how much room there seems to be. And with all the conges-
tion there isn't anything much actually going on. But Irby can *sense* Delius across the
room, through all the bobbing heads. And what might have passed for the soundtrack
of a late 30ies light tragedy is revealed as a geologic fact, floating through the ruins of a
much earlier time.

One of my early notations, from Santa Fe, has him standing with a group of archers, all
army boys from Tennessee. In Irby's system, I have since thought, the zen cartoon is
real. He has the weight of a plum hanging over a plane surface. The archers bend like
hickory in the winde. Roots undisturbed. Santa Fe is just a pile of brown mud. They do
their time until the root pulls them back into the linguistic hole we call Tennessee. But
what does it "mean" to be from Kansas. Not grass roots. That's the broken wing drag-
ging across the cowpiles of the republican party. Aerial roots? Yes, if the mind has aer-
ial roots, having been in the air so long.

There is no placement but fixation in Kansas. It is true, there are those who can dis-
criminate her, and well. Malin's unsinkable dryness of attention has surveyed the sub-
tle differentiation of the counties. And we have had apparent features advanced with
their train of peculiar spirits. Flint and chalk, the bloody ground of Idealism, the au-
dacity of Wichita, the dumb torpor of Topeka, the mysterium of Emporia. The cow-
towns themselves were transkansas rendezvouses.

And Malin had reason with his own eye to be unsatisfied by models of early Kansas
Poet. Standards have been, in fact, rather lax for the whole region. We assume the
great have either migrated or gone to work in Chicago. Their minds have.

My mother, another native of the heart, used to speak quite a bit about "the wandering
mind." She was quick to notice when it did (where was your mind at then?) but her fas-
cination with its travels was intense. I always supposed, from other things she conveyed,
all the people in my prairie sub-region had quite special derangements. When I left
home I found that to be true.

Fixation. Irby has bisontine habits. No matter how far his body wanders, He never wanders. It is the endless rumination of the Big Vegetarians. It is this vaster length of service to the best earth ideas which gives nobility to the vegetarians. The habit is integral: the waving carpet of grass and the volition to movement are the same. He has made me see his example tho I crave false meat.

I asked an astute fellow-poet recently what one might discern about such work, frankly calling to any external markers. And the answer came that Irby had *Stayed*. Stayed with the materia.

I like the long line best, but the tightest work has been done with a derringer. Max Douglas, child of the crossing. From the Missouri bank, but imbued with a kansas tendency to flow out over the western swells, a grand inclined table. The diesels breathe hard going out to Denver, easy coming back. Max was quite saturn, full of the sensation of his own brilliance. In his short life he was able to modify Olson's procedures to fit his own situation. But he also had a fine ear for river-plain exactitudes, probably inherited. His creative psychosis came simply as his share of the normal meteorology of his homeland. His hunger for the power of language was his own. *To Max Douglas* is an address to native genius. Irby is a symphonic poet.

— Edward Dorn
San Francisco, 1 August, 1974

Did you walk
on your own unplanted self?

·

We hiked the long late Sunday afternoon
the Bloomfield downs of South Sonoma

David said, did you know
Max Douglas is dead, of an overdose

I was just about to ask you about him
anyway I said that was

right there so far away and lame
we stopped to get across a fence

and coax the dog through
under

West in one gap of remembrance
the sea was completely shining

under the coming clouds we cut
up an uncut pasture triangle, must

be I said unclaimed
headed for the highest point

so young, so unwanted, thought, so unknown
to himself — what's happening at home?

the downs of Kansas would be the Flint Hills
but that NE corner facing St Joe across the Missouri

is hummocked, bowled hills like these
but of a glaciation, high separate

from the plains, the secret of relief
leads to the river there

where I grew up SE it was
creek beds, Marmaton, mud

that is, catfish, gar
not transportation

we both, Max, face out
to reach the Great Plains in the back of the head

your high golden head the apple
roman beauty of your parents' single eye upon

queen, king, better
petit prince, uncertain, there

would be a needle for that
certainly, who knows

what virginities were lost
every time you met another person

shyness, as McAlmon said
of Pound and of himself

is high vanity

but the spurt to raise that
column of gold sand in the spring bed

some people can make it without drugs, you said
Ed told you, but I can't

where that leads

·

Where that leads, Ed Howe
at Atchison, leaning onto

a newspaper on bowled hills
above the river, thinks back

to St Joe and past and writes *The Story
of a Country Town, not* Kansas Ed

Grier said, but NW Missouri, a
completely different country, first

novel from the heartland
to reach East and make them

waggle, "Ours," was the
deep clarity, "Ours

was the prairie district out West
where we had gone to grow up

with the country," traces
of Lewis and Clark arc

between, their true portal
would be White Cloud, duped

ruined sooners, even
Iowa Point, if still

but the first bridge
was at St Joseph*

———————————

* [My mistake. In fact it was actually at Kansas City, I learned later.]

189

the wonder is, Max, did you cross
it first, going down to Lawrence

or was it Atchison, or as far
as Kansas City before you entered

the Bloody Land?

•

Lincoln came to Kansas once
Dec 1859, Elwood, Troy, Atchison

spoke from the hotel steps in already long
decadent Leavenworth

looking back
across the river to far

certain Washington, the day John Brown
was hanged for Harper's Ferry

one
of the crew of the good *Reuben James*

was from Troy

•

And Cy Leland
from the fabled towers of Ilium

ruled the state
for 40 years

·

Cy Leland
was all mastery

the closest poetry
stayed to that in Kansas

was Ironquill Ware

whose poetry "stinks"
said Malin, "yes, it stinks"

the smell was in my adolescent nose
I knew who lived in his old house

3 blocks on down my street
flapdoodle jingo verse, cut East to be

Commissioner of Pensions, wet
his wit flits yet above

some lunchcounter present
avatar of that high interview

the point is, *exiles*
and to reach from that, from your

St Joe to present Lawrence
is a cut as far

and continental as the reach
to California

you were crossing South of the Pony Express
North of the Santa Fe trail, askew

from the Oregon utterly and at
right angles to Lewis and Clark

in your *head*, poor
lost Missouri Max, McClure

was born in Marysville
you were still

in the whirlpool of the continent

.

Dear heart
dear heart   dear heart

the part of us gone out
in any weather

out on the Sonoma downs
after high October

"I cried when he drove off, even though
I was glad to see him go, I knew

he wouldn't talk to a soul
all the way back to St Joe"

the darkness through which the winds blow
all the way back to earth

and the lonely heart alone
hears   "needle
              ease

ease
ease"

as Jed Smith heard
"beaver
  beaver

please, without
greed, Lord?"   Lord

in *this* heaven
grant them peace who pass

beyond Leavenworth
West

following the circulations
of the continent

peace, that's not just
rest, but breath, a piece

of all the action
Laurasia, passion

running after
in the streets

Sauer was born
in Warrenton

you followed him back
to Ratzel

down the tracks behind that tavern
looking for a place to piss

alone

it must have been hopeless
and what do the hopeless

do but go on, to, "What's
on the other side of despair?"

hair
the air of October

blowing your spirit
back in my face

coming up the hill to winter
where

      dear heart dear
      heart dear
      heart

the roebuck leaps up
faultless manitou

we meet?

    •

What good does it do
to talk to the dead? — those who are

the removed from human communion, Duncan said —
a panel on a skyward passing truck

a Cooper's hawk
point North

this is the coastline of discovery, old
first tries here recur

Albion homestead, the return
against the North Pacific

the ratchet in the will
the redwood in the heart

not lost, the explorers of that
tiny space of intense reflection

and the signs of exploration
go on — where

will you live again?
what was your face

before you were born?   what
couple fucking will draw you down

between them, to be born
once more?

     — go on forever?
on up the hill, spreading

the downs of Bloomfield out
above the filled-in estuary

a man is made
of scattered images, a rout

before return
your death came

up the hill while we were talking
heading for the dewpond

to talk to those now gone
is natural, to you especially

who hardly spoke at all while you were here
a golden silence toward the ocean

toward the coming sunset
to *answer* the heart?

•

Between the cemetery of Nortonville
and the Rushville grain elevator

the grain falling through the glycerine
the mustard seed falling through

the Westward-facing heart
beat

germinates, the greenery
the crack left agap

to die out through
shows back, a flash of winter

intense green, after the first rains
out of the dun

does it?
in the space of a beer

swaller you held
your breath

in just plain desperation in
between those Sunday points of Northeast Kansas

that isn't home
it's what the heart is given

to make home out of
Cy Leland

also was a quiet man
White thought that of him

virtue, Malin said
he was only a local

boss, not
master of the state

he lived a long long time
all the glaciated past

of politics, he swore
to the Kansas City *Star*

not long before he died
it's all clean, the new era, I'm a

wild progressive now, the cigar
spittoons and dungheap days

are over

the camel on the back
can *only* come home

through the eye of the needle

O Maxie
what did you *do*

to be so sad?

     •

We only met one time
at Bromige's, talked of Dorn, of Ratzel and Sauer

before dinner, never again
I was off to Oregon in the morning

the line of that journey
and the poem of that line

are eternal, are what this still is getting at
the line of continent

Kelly's *Common Shore*, Grenier's
icebox door shots out the windshield

on, ground between Cascadia
and far Laurasia's Eastern tip

the febrile palpability
the breath on the edge of the lip

into the mouth, some
where the baseline of the heart

to jump on off
of love

this highest shove

    .

The survey baseline of Northern California
anchors on Mt Diablo

the survey spread of the hand
held out, the *nakwach*

half, leans on the line on through the eyes
what all trace you make

moving through one whole day
there is an equivalence of *hair*

for all those weeks Jed Smith
tracked North along the Sacramento River

      .

Surveys, land grants and survey
hoaxes, in the *hands*

Whitney and Clarence King (who
hated California, 's "unending

succession of same seasons"
making dull the brain), Muir

went up with the sheep
his first summer in the Sierras

as Hudson in Wiltshire
showed Salisbury Plain

in the spread of the left hand
the fingers rivers, the brain

is watered by uncertain courses
in this West, depending on the winter rains

and the head of *hair*
rolls on the plain

looking for its nest
looking for the true horizon once again

.

Which way did you come West
Missouri Max?

questioning the dead
because so recent dead

I wonder if you've met
King, will meet him yet, as I would greet

and question him if I were where you
see through the eye of your needle

where *do* the dead meet each other
or is it only here again?   needing

every hachure shade and contour
compost line of any mind of any

time to map the world line
of the fat

ole feet on the instant
do

    ◆

Interstate 80?   especially the arch
of Nevada

under the arch of the ribcage the redwood seedling sprouts
the years of living in California nurture *its* garden in the heart

as well as Kansas and New Mexico, all at once, as Freud saw
all the ages of Rome superimposed in one vision

as on the palm, or heart beat
strings across the belly pit of the Basin West

     ◆

"This is a time in which an edged fact
is more precious than an axe or a sword"

across Nevada especially, especially
as night comes on, in those hard towns

where in selected gas station johns
you get coupons for free casino drinks

on the verge of another time zone, another life
province, taking some bearing

from the redwood log in the courthouse yard
in Winnemucca, pointing Northwest, washed down

in the flood of 1964, branching a highway
into Oregon, separating Battle Mountain and the sound of slots

altogether from the things of time
in the vast isolation of all night across those coasts

·

Peavine Mt and Mt Rose
to Toe Jam Mt

the Santa Fe Hotel to Jackpot
Pyramid Lake

and its perfect Grecian shores
its flawless tone struck by the greedheads

from Fremont on, an old resonance
with the salt cave near St Thomas (now lost

under Lake Mead) Smith crossed to
licking his first cut to California

not even to speak of cities, Hughes
or the NTS

but just the *cold*, say
exactly the grip running out of gas

you wouldn't live past Ely long in that
without the Triple A?

the shores of Tonopah
after Boundary Peak

are peach
all these *grids*, Max

we travel on, we live
right on down to the lake

beneath the soul
o Bonneville of St Joe

even if you couldn't get laid
your open eye was finer than a needle's

to hang *loose* by
where did you put your great big *feet*

pissing off that tie
behind Wathena?

    •

Out of the splatter
Eileen asked why men

always piss standing with their legs
spread apart

facing the cross   freight
between the legs   back

shaking the drip
off at the moon

"he would have moved out here or San Francisco
but he loved that valley too much"

feeling for the
far

redwood weather, dark
women weather, woven

women trees of the fat
Queen Mother of the West's

black Amazon stocked paradise
the thick dark pubic fringe from Mendocino

North to Oregon

　　　・

Lying in wait for game
they hid behind stone blinds

"Heizer et al. opine, while others"
drove the quarry up the defile

made off the migration route's
direct path — the direct pass?

West? straight into the sun, the direct
home kingdom of the passing dead

they pecked on the rocks
conjurings notes annointings

visitations, the mountain sheep
prance spirit

whose horns are the coils of the ear
passing North and South

by season, East and West
by forage

by whole
intensity invoked

•

Sauer turned South
to Mexico when he moved West, and said

any Midwestern geographer who came to California
when he did, would have felt the pull

the deepest routes of movement on this continent
are North and South

the more because so hidden now
nothing will salve the Atlantic crossing's

guilty *Eastward* greed, not
still the *Flying Cloud* to China

so there you stood on St Joe
at the *wholly* crossroads centrum

of *every* whichaway America
underfoot

which direction now
does *distance* take

that aches in the feet?

•

The wind of a darker time to come
hangs in the dark

winter rain clouds, the Sunday
dark age as of ice again

of the quartzite boulders
as far South as Lawrence

driving the heart before them
into exile — the great

Pleistocene advancements of mankind
not proffered

in *this* offing? there is
in the air

the happiness of rain

                .

So a last
morning motorcycle in the Berkeley Hills

disappears into the gulf
a cold fucking, a cold

fucking speed, to the limits of curiosity, frozen
in scowling, humorless

deep sleep

                .

From the top of the world above
the School for the Blind, sight

stretches still for China, some
unknown clipper to break the line

crowned with boredom, crown
of greatness, investigator

of bleak time

·

The dark age, not from
violence dark, for violence lies

forever at the heart of things, but the cold
of the human heart

the *hsin* 心 the *heart*
that is the *mind,* as the Zohar

also knows them one, the organ of Eckhart's
intellect, the *intuition*

frozen
and scouring the earth

Ochwiay Biano told Jung
the whites are crazy, they think

they think with their heads
and only *crazy* people do that

how do *you* think, Jung asked him
with my *heart,* he said

do you believe white men
only think with their heads

Serrano asked Jung — no
only with their *tongues,* he said

"…which nonetheless
remains the Bestower of Praise"

                              •

Slow oxbows, bearing the weight
of instant millenia

                          •

O slow gut ache
Malin complained: "Instead of Kansas

being the mother of cranks and radicals
why not study Illinois and Iowa

in that ROLE"
straight to California…

                          •

…marginal culture drift
Sauer's long stretches of Pleistocene imagination

accurate to our time, "mosaic
of languages like the Caucasus," "end

of-the-line position, repeatedly used
for immigrant drifts"

hefts of exhausts mix
with the morning tule mist

"Patience, patience," to cut through
"Patience dans l'azure" etc., "possessing

only indifferent hunting skill…
depended more on stealth

and patience than on
prowess," hailing the sun

at the end of the continent
heavy metaphor

is the natural speech of those
sitting on top of tectonic violence

"mainly gatherers"
the most ancient and primitive people of the New World

pushed to the extremities of South America
and extinction, longheaded, shortbodied

Fuegids, also probably
these nut

stompers of Oak Grove
California, as far as Oklahoma

I came here first the same old route
the very first most likely used — 66

not too far off, Interstate 10
closer, that Blythe

cut — a spinoff off
the main migration route (South

along the Eastern edge of the Rockies)
West just

North of Mexico, into the Mohave
and on to the Pacific shore

— so Sauer opined — probably
from the North, past Shasta, too, though

that much harder, the sequence
of arrivals is not known, "in the southwest

California and northwestern Mexico differences
in cultural form and level cannot be

referred adequately to
lateness of contact or comparative

advantage of environment" some
were just thickheaded

so we rest today

.

The Berkeley climate of exotica
Sauer's home

these almost 50 years, Kroeber's
their houses just across the street from one another

Arch
and Rose

Grenier at one end
Bromige at the other

Max…
in between…

and that isn't enough, to leave it
at fixes

there is some wealth of person
of the bottom lands (you called your book)

that I will never know
if "men are known only in memory"

then here we are, tight
the only place we'll ever go

together — and, God, that's so *sad*
so fucking *hopeless* — *glory?*

to overcome
there's just this sunlight on the sidewalk

and no more?
or the smell of chili just now

from Pigg's in childhood
wafted in the door, to catch you

I will carry exact
to the grave

                    ·

"this is no
Road to Paradise"

looking, as you always
seemed to, West over the river

into Kansas, or along the Missouri shore
going that way — South

and West — the plat of settlement
is instantly more open

thataway — on the road map
all the mycelium mat of roads

stays in Missouri, East, behind the head
behind the eyes, before the river

the shift of more than half a century
from Thomson in Kansas City, looking East

indeed to Paree, and with the
Southern lees distrustful

of the Kansas freaks and sprees
of peanutbutter pie

border people are always strange
river people even more so

together, not just *unease*
of *edge*, but watery

deep inland introspection
subject to sudden inundation

and heavy mud, the boundary between
Kansas and Missouri is a zone

as violent of movement
as the San Andreas Fault

John Brown is still not a casual visitor
Border Ruffians still

wait above the flood plain
their clodhopper boots gunked with mud

stockpiling homemade shotguns
clubs and bombs, the high febrile

acid gorge rising in the blood
to break wide open this new *day*

the bright wild *blood* time coming, Quantrill
still waits to raid Lawrence, only from

within this time, the *rise*
is high tide *here* already

hard at hand

    ·

The woods around Osawatomie
are as wild, the thickets

on Potawatomie Creek just
as dense and matted beard

as John Brown's sons' farms
John Brown's grimeyed cutlass *hacking* massacre

a hundred years? anyone with sense would *still*
be scared *shitless* to go out there on foot at night

high, and knowing
what we do?

the underground railway now
is dope not slaves, runaways

of revolution, nutcrackers, unshacklers
of deep spirits

the dark gods
wait in the blooded underground

their visage is more shapeless
and more terrible than ever

.

So set out on the highest punas of the mind
or, now is January, across Wyoming

cutting South Pass for the dry
for the snow count time

the line of deepest need
blind and certain out between the feet

Stanley Baker 22
Harry Stroup 20

hitching in the Sur picked up
on some stolen car suspicion

(they hadn't done) once in the cop car
blurted Baker blurted out

"I have a problem —
I am a cannibal"

and showed the finger bones
they carried in their shirts

West of Sheridan Wyoming killed
a vacationing social worker fishing

Stroup from Sheridan, "we are all shocked
and surprised that we've got somebody

like that from our town," Baker from
Story, site of the Wagon Box Massacre, 5 miles

from Ft Phil Kearney where Red Cloud cut
the balls off the Bozeman Trail and stuffed them

decoratively into Fetterman's wide open idiot mouth
"he had problems ever since he was

electrocuted in a car accident at 17"
a deputy sheriff said he was "a nice looking boy till

he came out of the Navy and let his hair grow long and those
me-dalli-ons hang from him"

"they suspected he was stealing stuff
and we suspicioned he was doing something with dope"

they said they were members of a "satanic cult"
(fashionable LaVey of San Francisco scoffed at

too real and no money) killed the man
butchered his body

chewed on his limbs awhile
and ate his heart

then drove straight to California
where *else?*

he must not have been a brave man
or else they didn't know what way

to keep the courage
in the organ that they ate

it wore off so quick, so many
would have gone down willingly

if they had fucked them first
and kissed the cornhole home

in the polarized
cloud light Kali dances down the trashy

dust devil, in the balls
churning whirling

the thick crosscountry loam of skulls
wild around her neck, Durga

the Inaccessible, Kali the Black
Chandi the Fierce

mounted on a mountain lion, her tongue lolled out
slobbering, slavering her gnashing tusks

the blood of every sacrifice along the road
dripping off her lips and jowls and fingertips

shreds of the flesh of the butchered dead
hanging from her mouth

she dances thousand-armed upon the bones
demanding more

so at Mukelumne Hill where the sacred crystals grew
the Miwok stoned their own slow slow to death

o the Modocs
the Yahi children settlers

grabbed by the feet and beat till their brains
dashed out like cantaloups across the ground

sweet baby blood

"As a head only I roll"
"A bad song I am"

rolling on the edge of the nest
rolling on the knife-edge

of the bloodfouled West

•

That this edge of the continent
is a hinge

yesterday it was the blinding
Pentecostal light down over

Alcatraz, over the passage
between Alcatraz and Treasure Island

taking the ochred waters
Westward as the sight

over the fold before the Farallons
it seems as vital for Reyes

to have moved 300 million years to put
Bolinas abreast of Tamalpais this afternoon

as to see at all

Reyes, one of the kings'
crowns of the earth

out of sight behind Marin
vital, necessary, incessant

as sight, as old as sight, did
trilobites see? mud? certainly

the Jurassic longing saurians crossed
Salinia with their tiny nearsighted

foliage-ridden eyes, straining to catch
their tails across Laurasia, coming back

to bite, Ouroboros, across
the most ancient ocean

we are the inheritors
of that gaze

•

So from a rock in the Berkeley Hills
Lowell and I watched the door of light

fold under the mantle of earth
across the evening bed

as the low rain lanced in
below us, advanced

to the battle of the land
against the sky, not to be won

these distances of Paradise
as the step of airy nothingness

from Remillard to Cragmont parks
across the instant fault of happiness

to vault the jointure
of the continents to come

JESUS

The secret paths lead
South

I lost a feather off my hat
in the railroad mud by Holly Springs
when I was five
an item in the Indian trade between
Mexico and the Southeast
humid independencies, Núñez
is my crossroads of
carrying under my brim a view
through Texas before memory
up through the feet

So the Jews, we now
from Tennessee inscriptions
guess again the Indians the lost
ten tribes, may have run
that whole economy, the blood
line, equally black
say, under my fingernail
a crescent the fertility
of that ancient money touch
become the thread
of absolutely unambiguous
felt Direction

so to the Mystery:

•

When Jesus got off the train in Fort Scott
when I was 16, an Easter
greeting revolutionary
unseen, he came from the North
but was going South
as if a tracer through the Ice Age intestinal
dirt track, reaching down the Plains again from Asia
toward an absolutely other
Earthly Paradise

he clicked his teeth

asymmetrically, an offbeat
unexceptioned survey
of the heart, remembering
everything, Funesian
saying nothing

I thought he was reconnoitering
for the explosive
anonymous ways
to get there, hitching
would have been, it seemed
closer to the bone
but he must have felt as others did
the pulse of Lizzie Bowman's
Frisco Cafe
after the taverns closed
following a thread of smell along the railroad
riverlike, pungent Southward
in the silent age of America
1952, not ripe for any
second coming out, only to scout
if all the Mesopotamian
Siberian welfare trails were still
reblazable under the shit

I only had an Easter slideshow
single flash and poem and I thought
he *must* be a communist
walking the fuze line
checking if the plugins were still serviceable
but he wore a fish, not Japanese
more like a Marmaton cat
woven to be seen just in glancing
my attention was caught on a pocket flap
backlit, as if to return attention
to the returning leaves of Spring

taking photographs of natural events
was what I had left of his visit
for the rest of highschool
looking for the mystery
in, what I thought, the confusion of emotions
of adolescence

rolling between Jesus and arrival
and the insides of the hometown
numinosities

         •

Jesus was silent
Jesus was the natural
intent conspiracy
of my prick

         •

So Ralph Richards was Fort Scott's
production as historian
certainly an elegant stepper
show coming into Cohn's Coffee Shoppe
more memorable than anything he wrote

his wife was one of the most beautiful women
Southeast Kansas has ever seen
(and knew it very well, said Mrs Newman)
even in her 70s still
that slender Gibson girl fragility
colored faded roses from the beginning

the century cut
out West with National Avenue
at 4th, from under the elms
but the Richards' house stayed
facing Central School
the shell of World War I
the high life

I used to believe that Satchel Paige
had lived across the street from them
and maybe he *had*, in *back* of course, someone
told me walking around to the screen door with an old
true man's adventure magazine in hand
sometimes a scallop shell view
fluted of the Richards' corner
his sister Dr Hunter's wife
bent just as the hand would fiddle
by the solar wind, out of Texas
or a California summer hill
across the Kansas wheatfield stubble
his white suit and Panama
pointing behind him
into the dark hollow below Main
the Depression-ruined hospital never finished
some giant clam shell of a garden pool
scooping the mirror beyond memory
beyond melody back into earth

the Great Wheel of the Plains
turns under Fort Scott...

•

On the road into nowhere
in the dark just before dawn
the voice said
Your back and front
not your sides and legs
they're warm enough with fur already

all along the road were
men in glass enclosures
all becoming wolves
already more or less befurred
but no one's head yet changed

the voice said
These are your brothers
changing home

_____

O Ralph Richards
changing Spring!
your time of life!

that Jesus came to Fort Scott
like looking for a wife!

•

Ralph Richards' dream?

_____

the dark friend

the dark young man Thomas Vaughan
thought was the Devil?

out of the pits of Fort Scott
pounding on the window
3 then 3 then 3

    •

Jesus the revolutionary
the man of the wheel
standing beside the road
carrying a motorcycle flat
Tarot trump of the Hitchhiker
recurring wanderer of the Great Plains
keeping the lines of migration findable
wearing a jacket with a fish
that might be cunt and might be cock
pussylicker, hardon knife of the hard road
regenerator
reacher through the eyes
warmer of the heart

DELIUS

I.

Crapmusic on the radio
on Enzo's cold loggia
facing the morning
into Cascadia

"A Stranger in Paradise"
out of Polovetsia
out of highschool
a return to my uncharted Central

  •

prefaced by a dream
not of the church, but the dream
of marriage, not a lover
but certainly of love

I woke up hearing Delius
wondering why I'd forgotten
making the *walk* to paradise

  •

Sali and Vreli before the fire
        both dreamt the same dream: heard the choir
and saw the entwining cathedral light
        marry them, grownup and child
couples crowned together
and so awoke, and left, already
        on their way out of this world

passed through the fair of worldly
fair and wondrous things
and made the Walk
to the Paradise Gardens

that is all we ever hear from the opera
the Long Walk, nothing of the Caspar David Friedrich church
dream music, the Gardens full of whirling
dopefiend bohemians behind the Dark Fiddler
the lovers floating off in a coal barge, pulling the plug
and fucking into oblivion

was the world so full of pain for Delius?
then, in 1900, not later when the syphilis
already the ache of savored regret
the arch sarcastic sensualist beyond decrepitude
the never ceasing movement of the never repeating
delicate exactitude of parting

as of the girl's almost white blue eyes
looking up at me from the edge's table

"this is the most heart-breaking music in the world"

2.

Only a sensualist could *so*
trap the pain of parting
the endlessness of the moment of leaving
this world, this *only* world, for nothingness

the scent of a hopeless black pomade
on the wind, the curl
of left foam on a beer mug
along the terrace
                        yet *he*
haunts me, beyond his music, from
another realm than he believed in
sentient

"human life is like a day in the existence of the world"

3.

As there would be a Delius of this
Northern Pacific redwood coast

in the crossing of the sclerophyllous
into the fog belt
touch along the blind
immobile rapt absorption

as upon the keys
of the drifting skiff
while Fenby steered

but it would be the younger man
who hiked each summer over Norway
untiring on the trails of the Coast Range
in August and the hills gone golden brown

closest to the genius
of the region

…on up into Oregon, into the moistnesses, following
a *hearing* as if seeking a homestead
into music

•

...intent
upon the contours of the land

    "It was a long, long time
before I understood exactly what I wanted to say
      and then it came to me all at once"

Walt Whitman, along the Loing
      into blackberry thickets towards the Reyes coast
agonizing before the 3rd edition of *Leaves of Grass*
      along the North Atlantic shore
                      turning in the conversation
in the living room at Grez
      to the high hills, wordless

•

      "our job is to find ourselves
at all costs"
          "There is only one real
happiness in life, and that is the happiness of creating"

      "My whole life has been one
long struggle against ignorance"
                "If you knew the amount of music
      I've written and burned
you would be amazed"

•

      so that an eternal present
in his "refinement
      was a religion to Delius"

in the exact severity

before the piano, with the defects of his
        mediocre, his too long fingers, Fenby said

"When I die, I will *be* my music"

    •

lost in the night music of the Loing
        or in the redwoods at Hendy
in the noon wind, towards the ocean

California's climate, he told Heseltine
would be better for Lawrence than Florida

and if he had come to America in 1918
        as he almost, in that summer, even with the war
he would have come to California

                                the song *Hy Brasil*
of the Irish Western Islands of the Blest
        "where sea and stars meet"
Faralloned into sight
        further than Mendocino
as if on Tamalpais, exactly
        coincident with that peak in Norway
he was carried up to watch the last
        full sunset he would ever see

        seven miles in a litter
parting the surrounding fog banks with his focussed *will*
        exactly at the moment of sunset

    •

"In Florida, through sitting and gazing at Nature, I gradually
        learnt the way in which I should eventually find myself
but it was not until
        years after I had settled at Grez
that I really found myself
        Nobody could help me
Contemplation, like composition
        cannot be taught"

                •

somewhere between the rotting oranges of Solano Grove
and the date bugs of Lowell's cabin in the Indio palm groves

the direct line in whose gaps

                •

"A sense of flow is the main thing
        and it doesn't matter how you do it
so long as you master it"

                •

Hutchings ends his biography (1948)
        joining Delius and Richard Jefferies
The Hill Pantheist and *A Song of the High Hills*
        natural confluences of an English contemplation reached
intent upon the highest vista

        as on some prow into the South
following the shore   to the furthest reaches of the continents
arcing the ocean and the ice   by sheer and centered sensuality
        blown white

4.

These are the duties to find a new vocabulary

which if "Du musst dein Leben ändern"

enters the cracks between the natural and the cultural landscapes
    as "twilight is the gap between the worlds"

"voluptuous longing for the beyond"

seeking vision "with aggressive and adventuresome masculinity"

"to the limits of expressibility"

"the sustained chords in the high strings suggest the clear sky
    and the stillness and calmness of the scene…a seagull gliding by"

"the accompanying mood was one of frenzy and great physical activity"

"as on some mighty eagle's beak"

5.

This is the golden beech
in the last dream of morning
transforming by joining
the West Coast biome of the summer drought
as Vanamee digging his hands into his temples to call
up his dead darling, from the sheep fold
to Mexico and back
holds the one line of direct
the one girdle of the whole earth with
the beyond an ether of the dead to
as if even the hair turned
with the passing of the winter rains

.

Vanamee, and again Vanamee, what I imagine and barely remember
not what Norris actually made of him
sheepfucker
of such continence the strain on every hillside
reached to Chihuahua and back, cut his name on El Morro, followed Escalante
and kept on going, clear back to the San Joaquin
to call the flock up with direct telepathy

ravaging voices, wordless at the tops of mountains
Blackwood's hill spirits, Delian choruses
summitting the summoning
gut strain

.

that is, to join cosmology and continental geography
exactly simultaneous
Bradford no jointure to the stars Fort Scott

Vanamee wouldn't be herding sheep today, not clear
what loneliness he would be professionally deep in
Ed Abbey's *Desert Solitaire* alternatives
the "hopelessly corrupt" urban vastnesses as the moon
secret onion trails into the South hearing voices
carrying a cactus across the road just before noon

.

the stern aloofness that they shared, intent
upon a *current* in the world

                    Vanamee, between
one mind and another, even the sheep, even
to the dead

                    Delius listening, swaying, "a continued
reaching out of himself"

                    Jefferies
standing on the South Downs as if they fell away
8000 miles straight through the earth
into the universe

                    each of them
possessed by a longing so immense
it shot the wholly sensual through
with holes of an altogether other light

        •

this explains the secret trails
from Fort Scott into the South
the secret ways Vanamee followed
into Mexico with the sheep
the Great Circle back to California
the Florida fixed between Jacksonville and St. Augustine
by Delius and Conan Doyle, the deep trails
Buchaning over Norway, foot tracks poaching
Jefferies down nets and fosse
coverts crossing and recrossing
the natural mystery

into the withdrawal
                    "my balls rich as Buddha's"
burgeoning

        •

Jefferies had a wife and family
        it was not just himself he was thinking about when he said

"we are murdered by our ancestors"
                              but sought the downs

                    239

as Delius whored enough in Paris to finally marry Jelka
        as protectress of his Grezian solitude

                                    and Vanamee, that creature
of my California mind, fucked his sheep or beat off
        with his dead lover's golden hair in his head
circling the bone

their *feet* joined in some instant

triskelion wheeling beyond longing

        •

"I who am here on the verge
        standing on the margin of the sky
am in the mystery itself
                        There is no escape
from this immensity"

"Man's mind is the most important fact with which we are yet acquainted"

"I think there is something more than existence"

"I think there is much more than immortality"

        •

        "for did you not, once at least, speak with their voice
when you caught the smell of the moon
        and the cuckoo shouted at us, a strange definite message
out of the thicket in the marsh
        although night had long fallen"

        •

"I have always loved the far, wide distance"

6.

Percy Grainger was the first to say
        he heard in Ellington likenesses to Delius
outraging England — "is he *very* black, my dear?"
        that was 1933, Duke's first
continental tour — "the continent"
        still meant Europe
                        here at the Western edge
it means my own, behind me

                    Appalachia

   •

he really only liked to hear
        his own music, "Old Man River," "Old Black Joe," "spirituals"
"O Thomas, Thomas, what would I do without you?"
        swaying to the BBC overseas

                      the dance band

Ellington, Ellington, Ellington
        on the windup phonograph?

Reminiscing in Tempo the year after he died
        as if a memorial to that
Floridian magic fountain music, Griegish
        Germanic Yorkshirian Gallicized slavery chants, as melted
pot as America ever said it wanted

   •

a danceband sweetness in Delius

as though there were a Whiteman edge
        he counted on to come, a Ferde Grofé "On the Trail" in *Koanga*
to renounce

Bix Beiderbecke at Grez
nervous and a charmer, playing the piano
"In the Dark" in the dark music room
or the cornet
solo "Singing the Blues," "I'm Coming Virginia"
Hart Crane beyond Harry Crosby
pilgrimaging his way towards the Mediterranean
reading *The Bridge*
in the shadows of that room that smelled like childless parlors on the plains

restless, with Whitman
between them

7.

So Delius starting out over the Coast Range already carried with him the 30-year-later pale debility in the blood, hiking to meet at a crossroads cut with age itself, the point of turning wholly inwards. Altogether without bitterness or self-pity. Something in the stride equalled a continually demanded inner terrain only paralysis and blindness accepted with utter severity could bring to fruition. Having come Far West, the musculature reflected another climate than Old World or Atlantean, a shifting around of the magnetic poles, widely rearranging the felt directioned lines of force.

8.

A band of seduction, about to fall off the continent
certainly *not* the East getting home
beyond Sacramento is the *essential* roughage of the Western edge
unsettling a magnetic intestinal pole track
bloodred in the sky as the Spider Woman of the North and South
fades away, sustained in the, *only* in the
what man has matured as a creature of, ice
the Climatology of Attention is not the Extension of Empire
an Elephant palm we might say, nursing its dying with a nuzzling trunk to reach
    the stars
Deneb in the Swan over Bolinas the umbrella of an unquenchable reach
the drunken Strangers of the Earth stumbling into each other's arms
falling off the road to find their way back to that barely remembered home

in the hills the Leader of the Wind holds up a painted hand
pecked like a petroglyph into the rock
the Entry Sign upon the fallen shelf
down the stream bed of all many-colored rocks
leading the Wind that holds Direction

"to find a new vocabulary"
the Moki feather cloak
"hovering on the verge"

"so we must look not at the mound underfoot, but at the starry horizon"

for "the soul knows itself, and would live its own life"

CATALPA

23 September 1977

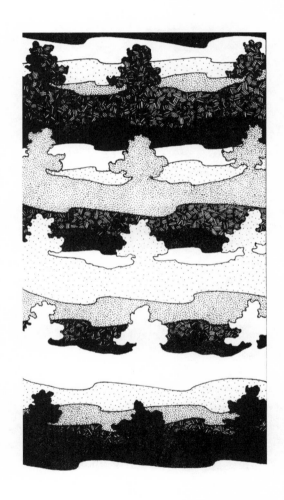

These pieces were written between February, 1968, and June, 1973, with the exception of "The Grasslands of North America," which dates from December, 1962.

My deepest thanks to the following editors and publications for first printing many of them, often in differing versions: Robert Kelly, *Matter*; Richard Grossinger, *Io*; Clayton Eshleman, *Caterpillar*; Ron Silliman, *Chicago Review*; Bob Grenier and Barry Watten, *This*; John Moritz, *Tansy*; Jim Willems, *Isthmus*; David Wilk, *Truck*; Larry Goodell, *Fervent Valley*; George Quasha, *Active Anthology*; Thorpe Feidt, *Red Crow*; Pierre Joris, *Sixpack*.

Three long poems from the same period may be found in the second edition of *To Max Douglas* (Lawrence, Kansas, 1974).

The drawing on the title page of *Catalpa* is by Lee Chapman. Other drawings are by the author, some based upon reproductions of petroglyphs and pictographs found in these works: Campbell Grant, *Rock Art of the American Indian* (New York, 1967); Peggy Schaafsma, *Rock Art In New Mexico* (Albuquerque, 1975); Forrest Kirkland and W.W. Newcomb, Jr., *The Rock Art of Texas Indians* (Austin, 1967).

for Gerrit Lansing

it is sufficient suffering to vanish never

·

But handle the stone

IN PLACE OF A PREFACE

(drawn from Webster's *International*, 3rd edition, and the *Oxford English Dictionary*, where not otherwise indicated)

LAND
· ME *land, lond*, from OE *land, lond*; akin to OHG *lant* land, ON and Goth *land*, OIr *land* open space, area, OPruss *lindan* (acc.) valley, ORuss *lyadina* weed, underbrush

-SCAPE
· = -*ship*, from a prehistoric Gmc word represented by OHG *scaf* nature, condition, quality; akin to OE *sceppan, scyppan* to shape

LANDSCAPE
· D *landschap*, from MD *landscap* region, tract of land (akin to OE *landscipe* region, OHG *lantscaf*, ON *landskapr*), from land + -*scap*, -*ship*

1. A picture representing natural scenery, as distinguished from a sea picture, a portrait, etc.
   b. The background of scenery in a portrait or figure painting.

2. A view or prospect of natural inland scenery, such as can be taken in at a glance from one point of view; a piece of country scenery.

3. In generalized sense (from 1 and 2). Inland natural scenery, or its representation in painting.

4. In various obsolete transf. and fig. uses.
   a. A view, prospect *of* something.
   b. A distant prospect; a vista.
   c. The object of one's gaze.
   d. A sketch, adumbration. outline; *occas.* a faint or shadowy represeresentation.
   e. A compendium, epitome.

f. A bird's-eye view; a plan, sketch, map.

g. The depiction or description of something.

Edgar Anderson, "The Considered Landscape" (1960): "When we consider a landscape, what *are* we considering? Is it just what we see or is it something more — if so, what is that something more? What we see is a view, most certainly. When we talk about landscape, when we try to have a meeting of minds as to its various problems, there is more than the view itself. We are *contemplating* what is before us. The eye is seeing and the mind is perceiving. What we think, what we ask, what we investigate will depend upon how rich is the experience brought to bear on that contemplation. It is not only what we see, it is also what we see *in* it."

Charles Olson, letter to Elaine Feinstein (May, 1959): "'landscape' — the other part of the double of Image to 'noun'." "By landscape I mean what 'narrative'; scene; event; climax; crisis; hero; development; posture; all that *meant* — all the substantive of what we call literary."

Carl Sauer, "The Morphology of Landscape" (1925): "a land shape, in which the process of shaping is by no means thought of as simply physical. It may be defined, therefore, as an area made up of a distinct association of forms, both physical and cultural." "In the sense used here, landscape is not simply an actual scene viewed by an observer." "We are interested in that part of the areal scene that concerns us as human beings because we are part of it, live with it, are limited by it, and modify it." "The content of landscape is found therefore in the physical qualities of area that are significant to man and in the forms of his use of the area, in facts of physical background and facts of human culture." "The content of landscape is something less than the whole of its visible constituents."

H.A. Gleason and Arthur Cronquist, *The Natural Geography of Plants* (1964): vegetation is the "general aspect of the plants of an area taken collectively and regardless of the kinds of plants which produce that aspect. It is based on the impression which the plants make on our mind through our eyesight, not individually, but en masse."

Alexander von Humboldt, *Ansichten der Natur* (1849), as quoted in Sauer: "However much the character of the different parts of the world depends on the totality of external appearances; though outline of mountains, physiognomy of plants and animals, cloud forms and transparency of the atmosphere compose the general impression; yet it is not to be denied that the most important element in this impression is the cover of vegetation."

PLANT   • (verb) ME *planten*, from OE *plantian*, from LL *plantare* to plan, fix in place, from L, to plant, from *planta* plant

                   (noun) ME *plante*, from OE, from L *planta*, probably back-formation from (assumed) *plantare* to tread the ground in planting, from *planta* sole of foot (also compare PLACE)

PLACE   • ME from MF, open space in a city, space, locality, from L *platea* broad street, from Gk *plateia (hodos)* from feminine of *platys* broad, flat; akin to Skt *prthu* broad, L *planta* sole of foot

Oakes Ames, *Economic Annuals and Human Cultures* (1939): "one point...is fundamental to the beginnings of agriculture, namely freedom from the overpowering environment of the primeval forest...open spaces away from the forest," "the evolution of the herbaceous annuals and the rise of man were coterminous." "The more important annuals... are unknown in the wild state. They appear first in association with man. They are as much a part of his history as is the worship of the gods to whose beneficence he attributed the origin of wheat and barley."

Sauer, *op. cit.*: "The facts of geography are place facts; their association gives rise to the concept of landscape. Similarly, the facts of history are time facts; their association gives rise to the concept of period."

James C. Malin, "On the Nature of Local History" (1957): "Every historical event must happen not anywhere, but in some particular place, at some point in space, in some locality or minimal unit of space in which its unique causal factors operate."

Karol Szymanowski (c. 1922): "The law has worked itself out in me according to which every man must go back to the earth from which he derives."

Arthur Darby Nock, "Early Gentile Christianity and its Hellenistic Background" (1928): "the rebirth is something done by word alone."

Osip Mandelstam, "Talking about Dante" (c. 1933): "Then the word turns out to be far longer than we thought, and we remember that to speak means to be forever on the road."

Bashō, *The Narrow Road of Oku* (c. 1689): "And the journey itself is home."

James E. Irby, Introduction to Ruth L. C. Simms' translation of Jorge Luis Borges' *Otras inquisiciones* (1964): "The *activation* of thought, shared by author and reader, miraculously effected over fatal distance and time by words whose sense alters and yet lives on, is the real secret promise of the infinite dominion of mind, not its images or finalities, which are expendable."

The Grasslands of North America

for Bob Grenier

Only a succession of far-reaching green prairies
the grass that is in
my backyard

As we moved down the hill in the grass
looking past the highway toward Hammond
our pants and legs caught thick in it
the same winds blowing

Where Pike entered Kansas
and drunk after drunk in highschool
we ended, the piss in the clover
the smell of clover so strong for miles
we stopped the car and got out
drunk in the roadway

That same country as entered
the first time it was ever seen

is entered again and again
each time I come to it
as I came here at three
out of Texas

was the New World

    •

There must be in the juice
and flesh a same plain
as these, the same moving
wave as this grass

the body comes back to
only having heard as they
only heard, by hearsay
and believed it

BERKELEY

We might say poetry
as accumulation of specific
but instead we talked about the mind
's a sixth sense, the Tibetans'
sense of it
          West in the mist
Tamalpais' top floated
the earth that was not connected
was ours clear up to the hillside
where Alexandra David-Neel spoke in Lowell
the scatterings of trees
on hills like our own hill
unpredictable
            "the dovetailing
or interlacing of ridges
                no line on a map
can represent"

but the greenery of grass
is fence

cutting even the heart away
with the brightness of the day

SW towards Orinda

The bell of a train passing
far off in the orchestra
sounds as a triangle in
Vaughan Williams' *Pastoral Symphony*

playing *these* fields, *this*
backyard, *here* the precise
moment of pastoral, quiet
accommodation of vegetation

Lowell said he wanted to
keep sheep, and gather
their wool for rugs
The malva, too tough

for us to eat, would
feed them now? Pastoral
from *pascere*, to feed
Pastoral poetry poetry

that feeds us, *pasture*
poetry, growing as these
long tickle grasses spread
and accommodating what

wind-blown, hoof-stuck, bird-shit
seeds will grow in *this*
plot of dirt and *this*
season's weather

On which we feed
take strength
return to earth
excrement of what we took

carrying elsewhere

Point Reyes Poem, 2

The poison oak on my leg still itches
I got at Reyes a week ago
climbing barelegged the Woodward Valley trail from the coast
up an old farm road overgrown with cow parsley and Queen Anne's
    lace, lupine and monkey flower
thick with poison oak
and in the woods' dark, still *green*

while in the sun, on hillsides down to
and on that narrow coastal plain
the grass is golden, wild oats mostly
and those a foreign plant, the Spanish brought
what natives left? what cover
certain, that Drake, careened
for six weeks on this beach, up
his estero, past Limantour spit
where doubtless his stone fort stood
or very near, up those Albion cliffs of Dover
what plants did Drake see growing here
that still grow here?

of grasses none I'm certain of
but Douglas fir
in almost unbroken stands, the forest
primeval, the black forest
and the Bishop pines on Inverness Ridge

and lupine? paintbrush? blackberries
poison oak certainly
his men must have itched from
infernally, though Albion

we share across 400 years
the haze of fluid, sap
the blisters raised and lymph

on equal, heedless bodies

Strawberry Canyon Poem

We followed the fire road up into the hills
for night time's sake, for smells of jasmine and of amaryllis
the faintest light register on the side bush growth
ceanothus? I said to Lowell would cover
most of any guesses what
not for the unaccounted registers of recollection, not
of tabulation *whose*
                    Lowell for the
distance from those lights of the Rad Lab and chicken farm
still lit our way
                    and I was off for
any, stripping off my shirt
till the mosquitoes
                    sensuality
of unintended impingements
                              trying
incorrectly as we argued and I lost
to place *this*
pace along *this*
fire road
with all the other times
a *here* that is the mappist's
fixed by what should be the necessary
lineaments of growing things

that nonetheless follow no
and will not be described by a
                         Sheer memory
the greatest adjunct only if
more important attentions
are incessantly at work
                         The path
back by the quickest
weight of the rut in the dark
only the feet to the contour worn
by the same
suspended searching blind
and certain as the vine
But it's clear our
                    (two, for Lowell
went first down the path
the last stretch)
                    way is polysemous
remembered and at
the fingers and the words
renerved

Equinox Poem

The sight at any moment
is as complete as the heart is
weight against that feather
in the balance of to-be, judgement
already, always, and after death

Thoth's measuring of time and soul
the body space within, these organs
that do not see but feel our way
by heat and rush of blood

down their dark

    .

The light rises in us, to the eyes
closed
as it falls aslant
a new season, the present moment
of the eternity of seasons
or in the leaves of the walnut tree
not just shifted by the wind

the certainty of knowing the slant of light
autumn
the certainty of knowing the physiognomy
Tibetan, in the photograph Eileen asked me how I knew
wasn't American Indian
                           to an afternoon
comes the perception awash

    .

Naked but for her panties
tits down on the porch
her body as I had always
stripped it in imagining
goosepimples along the upper arms
and down the small of the back

a limit of light, to enter
only by our eyes, and what we eat?

fingers along the goosepimples
would raise my own goosepimples
and an instant hardon
                              in which case
"FUCK the light and give me the MAN"
Shao wrote in his letter

                              in which case
a man *is* his notion of the light

Summer Fog

The sunlight is steady and seeming eternal
in the windows of the afternoon
the year to solstice and that turn

but I feel it reversed in me
gathering strength as the year goes down
and waning from that inner still point
of certainty, winter's

That way is best? I am carried on
in the seasons' rise
and in their quieting
rise myself

because I know I go
that way
soon enough
and out of all the body's seasons

quiescence and the certain
translucency, skin
stretched tight and thin

to the clarity
of this unmitigating
light

            •

The darning egg of agate
and the pen cap
when the eyes lift
lead on out the window
equal then to the music
however come

all senses equal to that
center *dazling*
darkness where I spring
where all feelings seem to spring
out and in at once

            •

Facing a storm
every time my eyes are down
and then look up into
the clear light carrying
the edge of storm
in me, always to reconcile
never reconciled

the edges of light
and shadow under the keys
across the top of the pen cap
shifting but not
lost in me, never
erased in me

•

So I have faced the horizon and the long
building and fading of the daily fogs

as if to rise
to learn to rise, in imi-, intimation
of a passing out of this
a change of   state

past eagerness

•

Rise
that may be
descent
the *beckoning*
not tempting, lure
but the natural
certainty onward

•

O shit, it isn't
age
prompts to consider
me going *where*
at the rate of slow
more edginess I don't intend

but over and over
kinship with transitory
recurring cumulations

clouds, fucking, wind
falls, ice, peepee, the attention
span, fine liquor
in its retailed state

•

The song in
whatever state
beats shit out of
and is a long
equal line with
the horizon on
the finger of
the eyes at
inattention
(not this
not my own
that song
has to be made
for me)

                •

Light, skin, and the droopy
shingle eaves, grass turned yellow
in the gutters
stubbs
            in this sunset, this
dense with fog

don't leave the thoughts
of body gone to seed
ever alone

            •

The body gone to seed
rises like milkweed
set aloft

            • • •

What does "gone to seed" mean?
that I've fucked my way home?

certainly where the jism goes

      •

Milkweed seed across
the lava barrancas of Paradise

or the grass pods above the Mad
drilling themselves into the ground

      •

"The body gone to seed"
what *did* I mean by that?
that I was feeling sad and seedy
wanted to break out *any* way
from the tight
but seed? out of all
I'd known, to be
reborn

Prose, For What I Have Not Learned

There is an area of our longing
that may seem all of it
out of the middle continent of counseled reservations
false conservations of our energy to give
touch to be expended only when expected and in certainty
the foregone fuck
and its conclusion

"the fear of getting burned," Brodhead wrote
but what *is* lost?
the whole range of learned
                        S's of asides in the mind
wanting others to venture
what I am not willing to venture
but want

why have I avoided?
when what is used does come back

for a reaching out
as certain as desire

        •

And so stepped out on the porch to pee
and the King, the shadowy great silver figure
handed me orange juice and codliver oil
come down the precipices of ice together
black beard and bright hidden eyes changing where we stood
from some dark castle's Italian tragedy where I was hired assassin
        waiting under the stairs
to rocks and pockmarked moon terrain
but *out*, out of doors, *out* through the obsessions, into the open

        •

Come to renew me
make clear my doubts
are a use of myself
open the cold house
gently
the warmth I carry
beyond intention

so the doubt of what is in me
showed me begging, beneath the high opinion of myself
                I keep in order to deny it

for *any* spare change, any change at all
the warmth of coins handed
the two dimes I handled in my pockets walking home
the big black girl on Russell St asked me if I had a spare dime
    I said no
she said I bet you do

    •

And a week before, Charles Olson had taken me down
    into his kitchen
and offered me some of his cooking oil, soy bean oil
    and I'd said no
you've only got a little left, I don't want to take your last
    I'll be getting some more
soon anyway

    •

A few days later, walking to work along Adeline
    very rapidly, afraid I'd be late to catch the bus
a 5 or 6 year old kid came running across the street toward me
    holding up a dime he'd just picked up
and offered it to me
    here, I already got a quarter
you take it, and I said, still walking fast
    o wow no, you keep it, you
found it

    •

At the offer of the oil, Kelly said
    I hope you took it

and after the boy and the dime
    I don't know for sure
what they're trying to tell you
    but they're trying to tell you
something
    for God's sake don't fuck up a third time

Riding to sleep on this steep hill
there is the plain and wooded river of the moon
below me

a country of sexual domesticities and corridors to underground
opening through the trunks of trees

He of the gods who is closest to this moment
comes down, speaks, and assures me the canopic jar
of my persistence is intact

I am possessed
and I recur

The eye
circles, and seeks
in the long map of California
a rest
along the Central Valley
looks down
keeping the corners out
open toward New Mexico
and the High Plains North, old
watersheds East and back again
of the spirit journey
looking for home
from the memory, and the ease
the feedback past
anything as easy as remembering

from the Marysville Buttes a cut
Northeast, up lava flows
toward Paradise, that city
and the single one
of all our meeting

to dwell *in* the flesh
a perch on one tree root
above the one stream
everflowing
that it may be the balance
exactly here where
I squat above Butte Creek

    •

Streams, it must be
Strawberry Creek is one of the Rivers
of Paradise, and its canyon
the Vale of Surprise
                    and Butte Creek, far North
where I came down to earth again
painfully lacking Ishi
and uncertain of the nature color, *ch'ing* 青
and nonetheless encountered
the firmness of *lines*
a sweat lodge on the bank
a pile of stones
and a rick of wood to stoke

I came down from the sky
or equally nowhere inside
and went underground
in order to enter the *wet*, a kinsman
that was mine from the beginning
if I had known it, I would have learned to breathe
before now, down close to the ground
as I can get

•

Of the Rivers of Paradise
three are on this earth
I have been brought to, I have been shown
which is not the same as known
any other way

California is a dry clime much of the year
and around the courses of the heart we twine
a loving mesh for those waters
we ride upon
Such a place we *learn*
The burden of knowing is *shared*
Only another can bring us to the place we yearn for
to bear
and what ease you have, you bring along with you
but even that I had to be taught

Three creeks, three friends
as close to me as those three cracks
are to the other world
of certainty

Strawberry Creek	from Lalo
Butte Creek	from Mt Goat
Nanette	from Shao

This is not Portolá's men, nor Drake's, nor even Ishi now

but crises of the common speech

•

On these verges of Cascadia
of the continent of affections
at any minute out the window

●

The chance passage of a car along Shattuck
bringing Schumann's "Träumerei"
from childhood almost palpable
this loneliness
l thought of you Lowell
going home alone
knowing you are there beyond whatever distance
Out of the light off the woodwork I see your figure
I want it to get up and walk away
come back sometimes, still call
this same house home

Enough to carry a perch of me
on the ridges of this vast landscape
this shape of California in the single closed eye
fully as far as you are, a touch
there in the hot imperial graben of salt and dates
since there is no holding the expanse of speech
except along a line of blood
between us

     ●

Looking down into the stream to see what passes through me

the sun at the steps of the butte
triangulates cuts of the barranca
as I squat here —
            I am made *air*'s   eye
by birth, and breath
and journey of the spirit
above the earth —
            I am made *earth*'s   belly

crawling back inside on my hands and knees
naked in the dark
mud up my asshole —

                fires's   cock
off heated stones
and steam, to lead back sweat —

                        water's   tongue
jumping in the creek, freezing my balls tight
where the sun is brightest

looking inward at the home cosmography of the flow

   •

The fog comes back again, cooling
across the air the islands of the heart
Fall comes back, I want to start again
on a long journey across the land
an urgency
to outdistance the fall of leaves
or on this coast, into the approaching winter rains
find the season of regeneration
crossing and recrossing the ridges of the Coast Range
seeking Cascadia

beyond the fall of anything but continents
or the rise of any but the Great Seasons
of the Great Year, this the Autumn
into the Solstice, and the Water Bearer to come

   •

My head rolls on the rim of the world
My eyes are not what I see with
In the basket, in the valley
In the creek bed under the water

Notes

With Bach's *Art of the Fugue,* and Pound
    at the between the wars outrage
and myself in bed
    at the pages of Revolution
asking for patience, in this town
    where the street fighting will come again
patience?
Patience. Anti-wrath

Not having made the world, I have created it anew each morning
    in confusion   Act   Axe   Axis

Running through empty lots to get away from the tear gas
    as if I'd driven in from Kansas that morning just to be back in time

Old crud, recrudescence, new

Nothing to decide
    but which way to run

   •

One poet writes "Revolution or Death!" and another answers
    "In that case give me Death, Baby, every time!"

We're living in the midst of a change like the ice age, that *is*
    the ice age, so pervasive it's hard to tell

Taking the obvious as the key of mysteries

   •

I often despair about myself   but not for the en masse

who despair about themselves and therefore are likely to be afraid
    cold and short

i.e., I am infecting my surroundings

        •

So we wait on the verge of —

It may *be* a new interglacial breeding
    huge sluggish monsters to despair

I *keep* scratching my head, for the uncertainty of the weather
    in there

Notes II

At the Service of the Revolution   from this House of Sunset
out to meet the Jaws and the Retainer   the Restoration and the *Jeunesse*

What of the War? everyone I have seen go off to

    and at Korea I was just starting high school
        when the local national guard
    went with teachers and juco students who seemed
        still as old from me as uncles had in 1941
    I watched that push toward Pusan
        in maps in the *Kansas City Times*
    hoping we'd be shoved shitfaced
        into the sea, MacArthur's ass first
    to be rammed up and dumped

so I was a "communist" and hated my nation
and came to poetry as a loss of childishness I thought
and a gain of wild excitement I could make
    didn't depend on "experience" at all

against injustice

    virginity! aware virginity! aware and hip and aching
bent listening, the shovel footed, the shuffle bifurcated

war I *knew* came home along the corridors of high school

landscape I would have to *take*
to ever come home

all was at war, but I was not a warrior

In Memoriam — Sam Thomas

The Minister rises — even before the dream — he is the Spirit of the Upper Porch, the mediary between the house and the tree, and tonight it seems, the Spirit of him who lived here last, Sam Thomas, Instructor of the Night Mind, Missouri Traveler and Conundrumist of terrible intelligence — Self Destroyer — not Zeus nor even Hermes but the Spirit of the Journey West but not Beyond the West — He Who Throws Dust Into His Own Eyes

Between me and the full moon, in the woodwork, a presence offstage in the dream, a reach down as of a dark hem brushing past toward the stairs

The Preacher, the Whisperer, the Voice of the Blind Lizard

Sam as the Minister, S.T., Self Teacher but not Learner, and equally, Self Threat and Self Tormentor — come from the stars, not the sun — the veins, as returning to the heart the blood from the vast dark distances —

so he rises — and seeks the acclaim and attention he felt due and never received in life — and passes by, to the lower realms of the house and the ground — brushing with his garment going past the bed, from the South to the North

.

Violent was his way out — as were his ways of thought — i.e., of *vis*, of strength or force, extreme, intense — "Between myself and the walnut tree is the space of centers" — so he appeared, on the porch, mediary between House and Walnut — and he said:

> 'This Bark is the dark Cloth of my Garment. I have ascended from the Earth through the Living Wood and carry the color of the Inner Bark, the Outer Dark, and the Tips of the Branches, drawn to and through them as I was in this Life drawn to and through the Tip of the Penis, mine and my father's — the Dark and Cold of the Ground, is the same as of the Interstellar Vast-nesses, to which I must return. Having given myself as fully as I could while in this house, and having left my palpable residues in its walls and floors for as long as there is sensitivity to respond to them, I have returned in this Shape of me I have left myself, to touch you, whom I desired sexual instruction from beyond Come, and to touch again my most Western dwelling place, House of Sunset, Place of First Resurrection, Home of Sorrow, Pivot of all that I could not resolve, and so seeking Respite, made an End to myself. That you have received me and let me speak, eases the Pain of the Wound and the Ache of the Journey, which are the same, Wallowed Hate. Only for a minute. And then on into the Circulations beyond the Travel of the Living, though they may know those Paths. That we did not touch in This Life, is your work to transcend. From this House, which we have both loved, and which you truly must see as the Earth and the Word dwelling together. Farewell, my Brother.'

It was him, speaking in me, though the language was of someone neither him in life nor me

✪

Talking with an old friend who does not talk much I talk too much. And then he comes back after the reel he forgot and we drink beer. If this were somewhere else (and it is always somewhere else) the restlessness he apologizes for might seem less the exact state of the weather, the overcast and now slight rain, I said always makes me feel sodden and sluggish when I wake up in the morning after it's moved in during the night. I am suggesting another set of rarely seen friends in such a coffee house and bar who make and lose accommodation to keep an edge with a harsher climate as close to the heart as old and often thought of friends remain. 'Suggesting' is a way of saying the rain is unexpected and almost out of season, but that the vegetation thrives on it.

Here is a list of transformations:

walnut tree	equals	a dry spring
Enzo's	"	Paris
Berkeley	"	Cascadia
Cascadia	"	the common inner terrain
Phil Spielman	still equals	Phil Spielman

There is no certain record of humans before they knew the use of fire.

I have no memory of anyone before I learned to talk.

The rise of the great herbaceous annuals is coterminous with the rise of man

✪

Narrative

Two cubes intersect, the intersection looks onto a sunlit meadow at the edge of which, off to the left, the dark mass of a redwood forest stands, abrupt and as great a change from the grassland as the view through the cubes is from the cubes. The pasture crowns a rounded hill, and to the West, the ocean changes color. It is early summer, mid-June, the grasses are freshly gold, in a few places near the redwoods still faintly green, kept by late rains from the transmutation uncertain wandering has carefully brought us here for.

.

All earlier accounts of this country were made by nautical expeditions which landed in only one or two places, did not venture far inland, and were even completely out of sight of the coast most of the time. Already we have discovered a great bay ringed by hills which earlier explorers never found at all. We were North, we thought, of that now. What ring the seasons make in this clime, we have yet to learn. We must be North, with the ocean to the West—but as many days as that seemed certain, there were as many other days when nothing could be seen from these hummocked hills but fog, and the sun itself did not reassure us, and rose contrary to our earlier fixes if it showed at all. Of 'greate and stynkynge fogghes' the English cleric had written. But we were, it was clear, in another layer of this new continent than that pious man had visited. He had not mentioned the trees, and through them is one entrance. Or if he knew of this, he remained silent — perhaps proof he did know, for he does mention a native reference to 'entrance through living wood…I would not discount.' But that is only the first, or simply one of many. Also of water, and of rocks. And now these tremblings as of heat waves, from hilltop and grass, gold grass, gold gold grass become — the transmutation in the air, of gold to airy thinness beaten, to float, ourselves made to float, the portion of us floated that keeps seeking change, that rests its instability on the seasons, that trembles to go forth and join with another. The poppies will be our earrings to reach for Far Pacific.

.

Five days before solstice we have come to this spot, far North we think, accessible only by several days' slow travel through densely thicketed stream ravines, choked with blackberry vines in flower, beginning to bear fruit, we took as sign to stay most open to the sun. And when we ascended this high hill and promenaded the meadowed platform summit, the vista was clear in every direction, only excepting South, where the big trees rise. And the sighting to the West, or whatever direction it is here the sun sets into, is straight, unfettered, gated in the hills, the notch deepest in this coast range, showing a clear V of ocean, precisely, we are confident, at the point on the horizon of midsummer sunset — these five days, we are to make ready, it is clear to us we were brought here now, to make ready, for that exact moment, of entrance.

Jed Smith and the Way

So we came to Oregon
like Jedediah Smith in 1828 — from California
and after furs — in his case, *pelts*
in ours, the *fur* in *furriners*
and an eye on the nap of the land

✦

Smith came North up the Sacramento Valley from his winter camp
traversed the Trinities at some point, probably the Trinity River valley
to bring him to the mouth of the Klamath, 8 Jun 1828
missing Humboldt Bay, it was 1850 before white men found, among them
Josiah Gregg of *The Commerce of the Prairies*, who was in the next party behind Smith
    and Sublette's on the Santa Fé Trail
that fatal May of 1831 when Smith met his
digging a water hole in the Cimarron sands, Comanches ambushed
he took three of, including the chief, before he fell
but his and Sublette's smart already had become a careless *hubris* on that whole sashay
    Southwest, figuring
having been king men of the Far West Fur Trade they could make the Santa Fé route
without a guide, lost the trail, ran out of water, and Smith
went off *alone* to find

We drove straight up the Valley, carrying the magnet in us
Shasta is the polestone for
Did Jedediah see that mount before he turned West to the ocean?
was that beauty still a notch in his head
three years later in Kansas, steering for those
Twin Spanish Breasts of Wah-to-Yah, also snowed and dominators

Shasta and Shastina look like one from the North
rising unaccompanied and without challenger except the head
crown you carry in your head to go on into Oregon, that birchbark
bowl they always said it was, lined with fur
Jed knew even then was where the nooky
of the coast from Nootka to San Gabriel
most lay

Shannon and I had a plan not just in mind that was
to yield home again, fresh again
drive into country and know this was the spot to take us in
Kansas always promised and demanded there must *be*, it *wasn't*, you must *find*,
    the plains
demand a lot that way, and I wonder what
of that incessant rimless bowl Jed
fed most on carrying after all
all of California Oregon and the way to get there first
tight under his cap

What kind of *the loneliness*
or was it all too close a care
on those endless nowhere buffalo trails
to cut past God the Bible and the Methodist Illumination and Warming Within
Did McLoughlin bring *that* forth, buying off those furs
and feting Jed and his survivors in Fort Vancouver's imperial splendor?

We were planning for *time's* sake, though
which is to say only a long weekend from Berkeley to Tidewater and back
and what way to take the coast in
in daylight — not the *season's*

So we came back the way Smith went up
pivoting a reversal or an alteration of highs

Up 101 to Eugene, through Ashland, that "sweet little town"
in the pale night of almost summer solstice
stopped at Roseburg the allnight coffee shop a 48 Roadmaster *On To Alaska*
uncertain why *we* didn't if all *home*
we got it out finally the next afternoon in the coast range logging stumps to Alsea
did not ever let up from
                                    time that simple shit
of an *excuse*, to ask, but
do you really think you can make it all the way in that old Buick?
the *search* for home always, if it, falters on that
first instant rationalized refusal to go *on*, but if *home*
equally must not depend on just *one* route to get there

For all this roundabout stars remain

                    •

The Willamette mist hides the hills not heaven
its persistence to keep quiet through all seasons
alters the scordatura of the nerves
as if to be played on *here* were what we waited for back *there*
to hear its always going on quick glance at firs beyond the freeway missed
the turn to the Kimballs' on a hillside below Eugene
got out of bed at 1 am and brought us beer and stew
to hear the news

                    •

And the aftertaste still of the most expensive frenchfries in the Valley
made the pie in Roseburg seem extraspecial
or speaks that the hostiles now are aimed inside the stomach not just the cops
cruising the parking lot eyeing the Alaska ensemble
we had left the Indians aroused and testy

283

back in California fighting for their Pit River drainage from PG&E
and dealing with Samoan-wielded poolcues in the South Mission
not Oregon
                    where Jedediah lost all but three of his men
he seems to have had a genius for getting waylaid in places otherwise not murderous
pushing God one wonders as uppity as pushing the Rocky Mountain Fur Co.
the Californios in San Gabriel and Monterey were rightly suspicious of his first threat
      of the overland swarm to come
but were cooled by Yankee skippers who heard Smith's headlong push as part of their
      own big business *cum* Jehovah drive all the way to China
besides he had a little Latin and some history, knew the Good Book well, stood 6'2"
and had a smooth, one guesses, though taciturn tongue

guess work...like our fidgetings
of Wilbur Stump at the piano bar in Crescent City
just with his name become an intimate of the journey

                    ◆

All this selvedge of the continent stuff
the constantly shifting homesteads, the seeking up and down
the same, demanding routes and watersheds
avoiding the logging, trying to ignore it (hard or hardly), or like
Charlie working it for a while, looking all the while
elsewhere, into the wood, at the bubbles on the stream by
or the rapt, dulled awareness of stiff muscles after choker setting
"all I did every night was come home, eat, and go to sleep, and I couldn't even do that
      till Anne massaged me loose"
rapt ingots of the *rus*

looking, moving, searching
up and down the coast routes, *looking*
the landscape ache in the restless eye
landscape *queers*
seeking with a keyhole gimlet eye under the fire of heaven
for home as if that lover were some place we've never known before

So the country South of Philomath
looked Kansas, childhood
promised all again, the learning loved
brought to an unpredictable
road junction question and answer…

The soul of another
of one dead, what lasts after
and makes us remember
where will I meet again
my dog Oscar, dead since summer 1944

is that what Olson meant
men are known only in memory

for the past participle
coupled with the present copula

    •

                         …fixes
turkey buzzards over a farmhouse
South of Alsea
and where will you go
when the crackdown reaches for *your* ass
Shannon's girlfriend said
"the sea"
        which is not home
but maybe origin, she didn't mean
to switch her street for its
to live on, the question
for that answer, is
where do you go *now*

on a logging road in Oregon
between two families of friends

◆

Smith said he went West not so much for beaver as for "the novelty of the thing"
the Californios thought he must be some kind of military officer in disguise
not but that his reports *did* go straight to General William Clark after he returned
(in Clark's letterbook now in the Kansas Historical Society)
but *novelty* one feels was hardly the only *drive*
and God was in there driving, but the *push*
all those Yankee skippers heard, whatever Smith was
by himself, his crew were *greedy*
brutal motherfuckers, and though he flogged a few for getting out of hand, still
the *lot* of them had spread the word of fear and cruelty
for weeks ahead of them, those Kalliwakset on the Umpqua
knew long before the white eyes came
they were a hard, rapacious, horny lot
and though Smith protested after the event, they'd done nothing *really*
to antagonize the Indians, or not *that* much
Simpson to the Hudson's Bay Co. directors 'lowed as how they *had*

Camped on the Umpqua near the present Smith, Smith called the Defeat, River
and with the Kalliwakset gathered, but wary, to trade their beaver
the Yankees missed a skinning knife and a hatchet, seized the man suspected
bound and beat him, till he confessed, told where they were buried in the sand
"stiff punishment for such a slight offense" Simpson reported
right then and there the Kalliwakset would have retaliated but one powerful chief still
     voted for restraint
till he, fancying a ride on Harrison Rogers, Smith's first clerk, 's choice steed
was ordered down at gunpoint after a circuit of the camp
and *that*, as Lord Buckley said, *do it*, and the Indians *snapped*

Smith was reconnoitering the trail ahead with two other trappers and missed the
     massacre by ditching their Indian guide and swimming to safety
of the 17 men left with the Kalliwakset, one got out alive, Arthur Black
later Smith's companion on the return to the States
skipped to the woods and made it to Ft Vancouver on his own
joined later by Smith and Turner and Delano, all laying their sad story on McLoughlin,

chief king pin factor of the Western coast
(who, wasting a season's expedition of his own, even got their furs back, bought them,
    "most miserable" furs he'd ever seen, and sent the Americans on their way back home)

Near Reedsport, on the Umpqua, 14 Jul 1828, still today a furry country, though
as the joke goes, now Douglas, instead of beaver

    ◆

We drove past the house and U-turned East
met the women setting out on foot for Tidewater
pulled in the driveway and found Charlie in the door eating granola
"I've just come off a fast"
and we with profligates' complete sashay
set brandy on the table and slapped down the grass

    ◆

A man wants refuge from the shit
others push on him — so pushes on
but Smith carried as much of that with him
as 18 trappers and say 300 mules and horses
insure — no wonder the Indians
knew they were coming for weeks in advance
behind them must have stretched a swath of flap
20 yards wide across all of Northern California for all
Smith was a cautious, wily, knowing mountain man — for after all
it was a *business*, and big, and the land
(and the Indians, "brutish, subhuman" lot that they were)
could take it

    ◆

In his kit he always carried
a mirrored dressing case with drawers
kept cleanshaven trimmed his hair
seized the locks of time
from first we know
came down from winter in Illinois
to answer Ashley's ad
St Louis Feb or Mar 1822 set out
May up river with the rest
to meet the 'Rees
and make his name

         ✦

Hölderlin called the lyric
"the continuous metaphor of a feeling"
the epic, "the metaphor
of an intellectual point of view"
this is the discontinuous
dendritic narrative of a journey
metaphor of pasture, anabasis and return
pastoral in that
"sluicing" meaning the juice
runs down over the head
and puddles off the fingers

    ✦

So the Alsea valley where the Vermonts are
narrows between the river and the highway 200 yards
and the cut of the hills up instantly with Douglas fir
shoulders that waist in left and right
there is the cork of the mind
set tight

    ✦

So it is that footsteps on a Berkeley street
will set the foxglove and the blackberry thick along the road again
someone will answer from the river
and the heart will come unlocked

         ✦

Ribbons of Oregon, rivers of affection
back doors brimming
swimming naked, each day
a baptism, each dripping a return
to the first emergence from the belly
from the continent before our continent
friendship realizing again
the rising of this shelf of Oregon
from the Cretaceous waters

each day down to the river
an intimacy away from the too close
intimacy inside the house
down from the mountain
to join the salamanders
seeking the fire, the primordial
the instant, wondrous hairnet

wordless long after sunset
watching the bubbles pass

joined in the journey, the lean and the visceral

♦

So over these now quiet rusticities
quiet after coming from the cities
to these narrow valleys, over these
marginally productive farms, the imminence
of old aggressions, pushing the Alsea
and the Kalliwakset under, shucking the land
of beaver, even before Jedediah
draining the land of fur, those animals
never to return, only the logger's
heart has burned, still burns
over the second growth and quiet
farms the haze of old old destructions
the geologic history of rise and fall
inundation and explosion Mt Mazama's
blast in recent Pleistocene rocking
even these distant oceantided streams
returning solstice burning in the windows

♦

So comes the *other land*
as a hand of sunlight into the room
drawing figures on the wall
of after dark, this Saturday afternoon
looking up from under water
crossing the line to Oregon from California
into the open, out of the valley
of mid-July, mid-afternoon, mid-life
fingers draw first a circle
then an X, then letters
that fade before I can read, *not
now* I hear, then erasing
swipes of the edge of hand

greasy, across paper I'd been
uneasy, illatease, completely unsatisfied writing on
on out of sight, then a knot
traced and drawn tight, unknotted
showed a room, a depth opening
and closing water, a film, blood pumping
through the eyes, upon a still quiet scene
of sunlight through the curtains
and the open window, stirring
                              — I looked away, I couldn't watch
like the death of mother, on the verge of some rebirth
but first the rape had to come, and that was
tied up, tortured, gagged, split open, shoved and stuffed up in
I looked away into the glass of wine
the focussed rays, the geologist's lens
saying JAPAN reflecting the sun on the ceiling—
                              when I looked back

ashamed I'd turned away
a tall, still-glowing candle
pointed up, molded to the molding of the wall

        •

Ashland Oregon into the dark just saves
the last light moments to guide us in
leaving Shakespeare in the leaves
to hang down over and send on
by that sweet sound of rushing waters

        •

Diah also said he did it
all for his parents, brothers and sisters
"It is, that I may be able to help
 those who stand in need, that I face every danger"
but that was in a remorseful
Christmas Eve letter to his brother Ralph, 1829

"I entangle myself altogether
  too much in the things of time"
filled with common sentiments of Christian humility
"I hope you will remember me
  before a Throne of Grace"
the closeness of death, our wicked ways, etc.
not odd for the time, very odd for a mountain man
to *say*, much more *write*, but Jed
was not at all *ordinaire*, amongst a horny cocksman profession
he never showed any interest in women, wasn't
gay, probably never got laid, some say
he was hot for his brother Ralph's wife Louisa
and never looked at another — dead serious
"He may have been entirely humorless" says Morgan
but very very sharp, an eye
exact for every detail
(to wit, the description of Ft Vancouver
in the Oct 1830 letter to the Secretary of War)
nobody met him and came away unimpressed
didn't smoke, didn't drink
despite the Methodist doubts within, he was
as the anonymous *Eulogy* says
"always confident of success"
that is, the dedicated guilt-edged Christian businessman
whose business happened to be
beavers and the unknown west

                 ✦

The last dream a month after Tidewater
the opening from California to Oregon
the single turn to wide
on open hills that had been clear
woods suddenly appeared older than the hills as Michael
said the ancient bristlecones
were here before the rocks were

but Oregon is softer the trees
that came and went again
were tended in a further time
than Indians or a time
coterminous but not accessible
with any ease

"You can never get there
the same way twice, and you always
have to get there, this is the way
North and South
the way East and West
this is the Secret History
of the Continent"

His favorite poem of Blok's had been written at the end of another summer and the beginning of another fall, 50 years before. All previous idealizings of war broke on that war, the children and the terrible years came true beyond the apocalypse Blok ever imagined out of his own generation. What street scenes and what scythers did he see before him as he sat his last silent exhausted months fading, draining away, that high Afro-natural head of hair the last full halo of the Symbolist exactitude.

The summer of 1965 began to tell America what Blok told his Russia: *Years that burn everything to ashes!* And in the sky, bloodred sunset after sunset, plasma and jism strained into an East West beyond sight, secret masturbation fantasies of the nation, long time. The armies he saw off at the end of the yard were under the same sky and muttered under the same blood and shit prophecies, knowing "the bitch is sick," Mama America, the present moment and the old time used to be.

Like Blok, he and his old lady felt they were on the verge of holocaust. Whether her slugging him in Yosemite or his refusal to hit her when she wanted it, almost slapped her off the can and stopped his hand an inch from her head and shook, caught that trembling from the battlefield — it all led elsewhere, down, violent, out of any last vestiges of Romantic grandeur. The sun sat with lurid colorings, warnings for the nation. When they finally split up, tired and guilty, the passing of domesticity was not just theirs.

Near Equinox
for Larry Goodell

The two foot long power stick lay in his hands, looking almost as if it had been lathe turned, with cones and cylinders and ribs along the shaft, palely colored, powdery blue and lavender, softly blending into one another, rose pink, tufted with feathers and at one end, dense and matted hair.

The short close yard beyond the summer house was distant haze in the sunlight. Alfred Cortot was playing Liszt's B minor Sonata on KPFA on the radio next to him in the grass as he sat out in front of the cottage. *The strings are unwound.* The doeskin covering lay in his lap, the box in the grass, the stick across the page he had been writing. God knows where it came from, how *long?* He himself was so distant from that, so far away in birth and deep deep origins, so far out of it, could he even handle it safely, and without outrage?

Old Mr Luna had said, "I'm not afraid of them. You know, they come to me in the middle of the night with these things, afraid to show them in the day time. I don't mind handling them. It doesn't bother me." The cigarette smoke and his eyebrows rising behind his flexed fingers. The small town true aristocrat, since 1698 in the front yards of the ancient lords of the valley.

It was quiet enough to hear the wisteria grow, he thought, inside Liszt, as at night. The kids' plastic trucks lay scattered in the grass. There was a sand road up the valley, just above the river, along the bluffs, connecting the farthest out of the suburbs with the old highway to the Northwest, connecting the biggest cottonwoods with the underground of the ancient town. There was a track that led to his yard, up his valley, and from his elbow fell corn meal, and from the tips of his fingers fell kernels of corn. The feathers were from the wildness all around them. The ribs and cones along the shaft were of their long migrations, their long long trekking, the steps, the knots upon the cock, the knots of the oriental whore's leather thong shoved up the ass and jerked out knot by knot as the come, but not in lust across the land, but just as sexually, they came.

The power stick lay in his lap. He stared into its colors, where the whole yard darkened. The announcer stated Cortot's recording had been made in 1929. The stick had done nothing. He certainly was not on the verge of ritual use of it. He merely had *looked*.

✪

the longer I live the more people I know
are dead, the more the crossing of that line
keeps me alive, not
lure, not Kerouac's father's
"life's too long," but the Flame's
"to fear vividly
is perhaps the greatest joy of life"

✪

At dawn, visitors from the farthest stars enter the open door from the balcony, silently, stand, mass, stare down at the sleepers, and weave about the bed entwining figures in the air with spruce boughs, in one hand, and in the other, rattles, making no sound, only stirring the air, rattling the walnut's leaves beyond the door. Slowly one foot is lifted and brought down heavily, then the other, the thunder from the stars to earth heard only in the dreamers' caverns. Footsteps and restlessness. In the slow confusion of waking up, the visitors fade from the room. The vestige of a memory of some great presence returns suddenly, fleetingly, later, during the day, the next, or another, the unintended, primordial, ever-recurring presence of Disturbance.

September

He dealt a hand of cards. It had been years since he'd played at all. For all those not here, for a hand again or Lady Cadogan's handbook, that they would know, who came to play.

"I hitched, and *walked* mostly, over 8 hours to get here, and I'm certainly not going to come to bed now just because the *sheets* are ready."

For these three friends who were dead, who came at autumn equinox, on the first of the strong winds but before the first rains, come this close inland to the ocean, passing South like the heads of seals he'd seen basking off the cliffs that afternoon, passing on always close to the coast, that turned out to be pelicans when he saw closer, the spirits of those long dead, disparate but that he loved them, on and on.

They sat down to patience together, each playing a separate game, but into a common layout each hoped would thwart the others, while the real conversation passed in gestures in the midst of inconsequential small talk. All that they had come together for didn't last more than a few seconds, but so filled with trivia and fiddlings, so much to avoid blunt-ings, he had to wait a long time afterwards, and struggle, to remember any of it. Friends he had rarely ever been able to talk to. Only a few completely single utterances.

They hadn't told him anything, and then they were gone. The table top looked glassy for a few seconds, shimmered, watery, showing the ocean dimly in the distances, then faded into ordinary wood again. During the game it had been covered with green felt or baize, which meant a grassy plain, he thought, which meant winter or early spring, in this climate. Being miraculous, they were the crux of the whole day. These are the particu-lars, from which a decision can be reached.

He left Berkeley about 5:30, catching a ride with a stained glass window maker going to Petaluma. That dropped him in Novato, center of the ancient titty cult, where two short rides with a long wait in between only got him out to the edge of town near the new highschool, after sundown and the dark coming on fast. No one stopped, very few cars came by at all, he started walking, figuring though it would take him all night, if he got to Highway 1 he would eventually surely get a ride down the coast to Bolinas.

Altogether he must have walked at least 15 miles before some highschool kids out driving around drinking beer picked him up asked him for a joint gave him a can of beer and a cigarette and took him as far as the corner and stone bridge to Point Reyes Sta-tion, marvelling that he would hitch out there in the middle of the night alone. He walked on into Point Reyes Station, all that time passed evenly, lit by the very bright moon, and then on to Olema where finally a couple from Palo Alto, a girl at Stanford and her boyfriend, picked him up, gave him some coffee, and drove him to Mesa Rd in Bolinas. "We just had to get out of Palo Alto, man, all those revolutionaries, you know, just *talking* about how they're gonna bring it all down." And he just said, it must be great to get away. "We been up 2½, 3 days you know, and never been North of the city on 1, so here we are. A real speed trip. Yeah, I went up to Ft Lewis, Washington, once with my parents, to see my father off to Korea, during the Korean War. He was 19, I guess, maybe 20, and I was just a little kid, but I remember thinking it was all a bad thing. There was MacArthur, then Truman pulled him out, but they were both real motherfuckers, man." He told them he'd started highschool that year the Korean War started, and they descended the two long winding groves of eucalyptus to the turnoff. Then, patting the Riley's flank, they decided to drive him on up to Mesa Rd after he told them Bolinas had the greatest beach on the coast — and then added, of course it's polluted now. "O wow, shit, man!" He almost went on to Palo Alto with them, the guy was so congenial to talk to, and his girl so quiet seeking possibilities.

The way up the mesa passed along a winding avenue of great eucalyptus surging more than the sea. The firestation light was on. Along Overlook parties were still in progress, but the way to Shao's was all dark. He knocked on the front door and then went around to the back, only the dog answered, no car, he figured they were gone, and lay down in the bike shed in front for an hour or more, till he heard the baby cry inside and got up, and saw Dick walk up, asked him if anybody was home, he said, yeah, just go on in, and so came at last to rest, in Shao's old sleeping bag, having forgotten to bring his own, slept on the floor dreaming of street fighting, shooting, and being shot, and passing out in the ambulance train.

The next day he wandered around the tip of the peninsula while Shao helped put up a greenhouse. First he visited the Creeleys, just recently moved from the East. It had been a very long time since he'd seen them last, and the point was not dulled at all in the heart since Walter Prescott Webb on Dartmouth St nine years before, in the long sea grass toward the ocean. He walked along Agate Beach and sat a long time staring into tidepools, looking into the distances where the red shift turned to blue. And where were we in such a scale? Right here, where our asses are, looking at the Vernon Image shape in the rock, almost getting caught in the tide. Drifted on to Smiley's and had a few beers, bought a sixpack and walked back up to the mesa. Later after supper they left Rene and the kids for a while and walked back down, and sat out on the sidewalk in front drinking beer and smoking dope with the passersby, looking at the moon and telling fragmentary anecdotes.

In all these particulars, seeds lie. The primordial, points to the future, not the past. Stan Van Der Beek's little dance along the sidewalk as he took the joint Jack handed him, performed beneath the moon the rites that were due her. The gripping of the gut and then the release they all felt laughing at their own foolishness, felt again days later watching the raging of a forest fire above Berkeley, the old, the ancient peyote racking of the abdomen and then the laughter that had to follow to relax, tightening the balls.

Jack drove them back home. They sat up reading to each other for a long time, and writing alternate lines of an endless, silly poem: "Rembrandt knew his daughter / not at all. She nailed his dick / to the garden wall" etc. Dick came in and they fixed some eggs. They went to bed. He was left, still sitting staring at the table top. Then he was playing cards, shuffling, dealing, then came his ex-old lady's voice behind him calling him to bed, and his own refusing the freshly laundered sheets, though he slept alone and on the floor in a borrowed sleeping bag. Then looking up, his friends were at the table, picking up their cards, sorting their hands, flicking their cigarettes. Who were they?

The *nakwach* symbol was on the backs of the cards. David Sandberg sat facing him, twisting his moustache nervously with his left hand, head cocked to that side with bemused faint smile. Sam Thomas was to the left, looking more as he had the first time he'd met him than the last, after the nuthouse fat. Thin face with pointed foxred goatee, the Missouri look askance, almost furtive smile of irony up as if from under a flopped hat brim. On the right was Bill Lehnhoff, corpulent in mufti, alone of all of them absorbed in his cards, nervously tapping his Winston against the underedge of the table, chewing his lower lip. But he got up to piss after a few minutes and Reggie Parker took his place, dapper Durham Harvard black elegant, slim and languid. It seemed like some foursome from a Progressive Club bridge party of his parents 30 years ago, as much as poker.

Everything happened instantaneously, as at the end of the Diamond Sutra, with the dream intensity. He could only lengthen it, telling himself later. He knew each of them was dead, with the possible exception of Lehnhoff, and all but him suicides, but he couldn't say this to their faces, neither could they ever admit it, and any conversation depended on that, confronting them with their deaths? David turned as if at his kitchen table he'd just told of all the teas they'd tried which was the best. "Every night when I go home, I have to choke the telephone." That was an echo, Sandberg speaking in Wesley Long, probably the year David was born. His old dirty sleeve, God, the photo made in the Greyhound bus depot camera booth, down on 3rd St, of Phoebe sucking David's cock. Stuck in a notebook. Sam's sleeve touched his hand as he adjusted his cards, the hem of an old beatup shirt. Everyone was dressed shabbily, desperately, old and careful clothes, even Reggie's coat and tie worn and greasy if you looked close. *Trying* to talk, before the equinoctal winds blew them off again into the interstellar vacancies.

Lehnhoff before he left pointed to pair of sandals brought along as a gift, with that brusque embarrassment of giving a close friend something he obviously badly needs. Reggie giggled to himself, out of which a phrase from an old letter was audible, "Yes! Yes! It's I!," then, "probably for the wrong reasons," written in a copy of *Sister Carrie*, tittered.

What did they all want from him? If he kept looking long enough he'd see everything he ever knew about them. If they all stayed long enough, everyone he'd ever known would show up too. All of them wanted touch again? The earthly again, out of those terrible emptinesses, but not some hand on the knee, as in a dream once he'd leaned forward to reassure David, or around the shoulder, or even a handshake, because they no longer shared any common substantiality. A rag of Sam's sleeve, but not Sam himself. They couldn't return to people they didn't know, only to some love, remembrance, the warmth off shared thought, the touch of some shared attention. Prayer, he thought, must be about this. They didn't *know*, desperate, wrenched from life, *what* they wanted, but from the living, *release* again, as if here, *here*, they might be free, to *continue*, wherever that went, warmed anew.

They looked at him, despite all the elaborate other attentions, unable to see each other or disinterested in the other dead. They were here, and came with gifts, the motions of gifts, making him uneasy, in his gratitude, of accepting them. Alan had told him long ago, you're a hard man to do anything for, you have such a hard time accepting *anything* from *anyone*. All his life he'd been learning how to *receive*. What they wanted of him wasn't just what he gave, *his* love, but to *receive* theirs. To be *open*, as he'd told himself for years and years. To enlarge the space of the living. Nothing is lost. Take us when we come, we have no other place to go but those we love.

In the glassy surface of the table waves receded and pounded. He heard the roar of the eucalyptus grove, the wind was up, the door had come ajar and the wind was in cold, the post-alcoholic chill, he thought, it's time to go to bed.

Where are you now? In the house of friends, on the Northern coast of California, in the grip of the elements, altogether alive.

✪

Indian Summer in Berkeley means
the fogs come back in October

confusions of the morning
blessings that the house protects

    .

on the surrounding rock the bear shaman and his bear erect
summon the surrounding waters: come back once more
fill once again the descending rivers with salmon
overhead the thunderbird wings for rain
his snake of lightning and descent straight out beneath his claws
layered with the shaman's snake of water in the ground
the master's left arm handless out to almost touch the bear's stiff ears
drawing from that head and lolling tongue
sweat, piss, and the sweet thick fluids of the spine and brain
the right hand thumbless, gripless, without opposition
supplicates beyond the stone despite the upturned haughty Anubis head
beneath his elbow leap straight up and side by side
twin snakes, his messengers below the earth and to the poles

    .

the god of wanderings

inside, under old
strata of the brain, pools
under the continent
before this continent

still waters in the still
shifting magmas
steam, blind, cold
and stony with the throw

old gods Hart Crane
saw under the Ozarks
pool at the pit of the brain
oblongata

       .

the change of weather
on the skin beneath the skin
the true
or inner dermis

★

so what's new?

                the chaplet
of crystal, beads along the waist
and headband, St Maurice, but it is
Delius just at the beginning of his
wasting stage of syphilis, tall and gaunt
but not yet blind, presents Chateaubriand
Bonnard still youngish, is it to
Age, to the Lady, Light? we do not see *who*
is before them, only the receding pale
green countryside surrounding

                         ain't it the truth?

and where their complicated act
of indelible piety
is unearthly still
the simplest act of all
"today shalt thou be with me in Paradise"
kneeling down before the Awe

why it's the same with me, I can't hardly

it's about to rain, they'll be
drenched, the unknown
crossing of the winter quiet music
of Angelic incessant pastoral
with a California Bonnard about to enter
the upper skies of elemental domesticity
like light

for Paul Metcalf

black chickens scratch the edges of South America
black flesh, black bones, refused by visiting US sailors in Peru, 1828
   as fowls of the Devil

        blue- and olive-egged chickens
at the margins of the most ancient drifts of the New World
laying long before Columbus

          the ceremonial and brilliant egg
held up from the nest to the forest and ocean hatching sun

    there is in the length of the Western coast of South America
a motionlessness, each chicken is emblematic, intense, halted, reached
   by the closing eye

       sacred, as common and ordinary
as the most sacred of natural objects all are, all the living creatures
man has domesticated, reached in the darkness
               and held out

303

The Easter Dream

All of his journeyings were toward the side of the South, which he
preferred to the other sides, in that it is the side of Wisdom.

— The Zohar (I, 111a–b)

On the way up the hill to the Parnassus Mt, medcenter-like great building, along the road in the flat we stopped, I explained the vista/layout: Look over there to your right, it looks very dark, you can hardly see anything, certainly not just in passing, but keep looking, and your eyes will adjust to the darkness. Across a short, broad lawn to two arches, the left one wider, in a dense cypress hedge: We've come to them by way of the alley back there, behind, a secret way. And those two arches face the cypress arch on this side, into the other alley and the hillside. They are openings in the darkness onto each other, across the sunlight-covered lawn and the central road.

This is the Easter Dream, then, of the way below Mt Parnassus, in the flat of the valley approaching, the ways parallel and across, of Instruction and of Clearing the Sight, and of very deep connection with the old Home Town, a cathexis of awareness of mystery upon the first place.

It is part of the alley behind our house and down the block, South, almost to Sixth St, of the hedges and fences at night, playing in the summer, late, how to get stealthily across the alley to the other, more dangerous, Western side. It must be a game in which my brother and older kids his age are leaders, directors of the layout. So in the dream he was an unseen presence, only thought of afterwards.

So, also, I guess, though it was not in the dream, there would be the washhouse office, workshop and war room, message center, to which the backyards of the block were linked. The dangers of climbing some wrathful grownup's back fence were dared in plotting there, and return from the raid.

Much of the continuing deep stratum of that timidity I felt following him in the dark, rose up again, without memory pictures, on the first acid trip, another Easter, 1965, following Mary into the locked campus nursery and the chancellor's forbidden grounds, and into dark backyards along upper Arch St, as she tried out new climbing shoes, and I followed dutifully, afraid, but pushing to keep up.

The dream was just a brief sight, you understand, of a very magical place, where secret ways converged and crossed, ordinary looking enough if you just hurried by. But not a trying-out of those ways. It was a pause and a deeper look, and an explanation to companions, that I myself might come to know what I saw. So it was in every way a *clearing*.

It was Fort Scott, and San Francisco, and Berkeley, and the whole of Northern California, wedded together. One friend has criticized me for letting California become my cushion, losing honesty for sensuality. If so, it is a pillow filled with many other stuffings, perhaps, as he thought, too soft to keep tough by — but it is the Demander of Vision, the Hair Filter straining for rebirth. "Is it not a Great Thing, that you should be Heir of the World? Is it not a very Enriching Veritie? In which the Fellowship of the Mystery…" I have no choice but to follow such Discovery, "write, write, or die," roll back the stone of morning, "still supposing him to be the gardener," following into whatever cultivation. Is that what my friend feared, too rich and easy a horticulture of the soul, "your filthy soul?" As Olson mistrusted this coast's "bad sunsets," he could not come home to? But "Things unknown have a Secret Influence on the Soul; and like the Centre of the Earth unseen, violently Attract it." And here it is a demand is made upon me: find the Secret History of your Self, wherein you live, which is more vast and great than any Shell or Strife you know.

．

So there the heart quickens, seeing images of its inner secrets, it had not guessed before.

Walking around the block yesterday afternoon, Carl, Cole, Frederick, Stanyan Streets in San Francisco, after finding Charlie and Anne not home. Walking Tulpa, Lowell saying: Here my sisterinlaw lived after splitting up with my brother, and Cammie lived over there, and there I scored my first acid. Looking down Shrader to where Dean and Wendy lived when I first moved to San Francisco. We passed the former Donut Shop, now Schwinn bicycles, and Lowell said: You used to be able to smell them a block or two away.

To be "an image of man," not indulgence *isolato* — "and with these thoughts people this little world." Certainly in the dream, I *had* to tell my friends what I saw, instantly as I saw it. That Demand laid on me beyond cushion, richness, or fertility. Even if no one ever came into my dreams again, even if I never spoke again to anyone — two arches North face a single arch South, the way East and West and all the plains lie in between — this is the centrum pocket of the continent — it seems that everyone I know has wandered here.

.

The secretness, dark, dangerousness of the West, that side of the alley, say the Ayres' side, is in the dream the South's? But in the dream, is what is behind me, what I turn around to, pointing the flow *to*, but do not really face into. While the West in the block in Fort Scott *is* faced, is the direction in which the danger is precisely in facing it and not being able not to, despite the fact that most of my play and the houses of my friends of my own age were East, over Eddy and Fifth, into another block. Distinctness of the two directions/groups: brother, West, mystery, the older, learning // East, contemporaries, the rational, the social, competition.

.

Traherne addressed his *Centuries* to the question, *What is felicity*, wherein as notion of Eden, the experience of childhood was prime evidence. Looking West from my desk, the two windows make a simulacrum of the arches in the dream, and the single arch must be behind me, somehow felt but invisible in the wall above the bookcase. So I am in the cockpit of sunset. And my dreams receive the crosscurrents of that transpiration, though the axes be rotated and E–W become N–S. For the right axes of NSEW are no more especially paramount than the obliquities, that Roy said always produce strange results when you start following, cattycorner, on the plains. NW–SE an axis of moistnesses, NE–SW of barrenness, desert to ice — diagonals of instant, phonograph to biography, photographs to Chinese riders, Rock Chalk dogs — across the room.

.

And so the arches of the dream are as permanent, inconstant, watery and demanding as childhood. If recurring, only the more mysterious. To say they are feminine orifices, furred with entry grasses, is no more revelatory than to think of them as anterior prehuman constructions of the intelligent others who return to disturb, dwellers of the dream or those who alter everyone's dreams a continent away simply by stepping onto the shore.

Richard Grossinger has written of the *city* inherent as dream in the push of the Pleistocene migrations of North America — which great city he puts far Northeast, in the Snow Queen's realm, beyond continent. In the migration routes to *found* the city, there is a gap — coming out of the dark North, a transverse *plain*, pluvial'd over, then reentrance into *unknown*, thus *dark*, South, however *blazing* sun.

✪

Jesus, who would change
upon the road there is no way to tell
but go back on to

the well at the base of the cock
flows on
past any uses that one man owns
is it how often or how
recurringly the fuck
that sets that flow, or who
is in the head to go to?
no,
        how willingly
its marriage with the rise of time
as if a redwood sap were in me
I came West to find

as Jesus crossed that earlier
adolescent line of spring
to cross it now again

3 Aug 1971, Waiting at the Mediterraneum for Bean and Lowell

To Sonoma County yesterday, visiting Mike and Pam Ross to pick up Lowell's records — homebrew and notebooks under the apricot trees — pigs and sheep, chickens, dogs — big garden on one side, and the layers of distance set by the eucalyptus on the hills showing depths through as if cliff precipices sighted, continually ticked with the wind-shifted leafshimmer — the great meat soul bird with teeth — foxy poisonous women invoked — "what do you remember of what you've written, and how long afterwards?" — news of Chico and of carpenter's work (Mike an apprentice) — "I want some kind of head work I can fall back on if I get hurt, if my hands get hurt, a carpenter depends on his hands, I can *plan*, you know, like when I got that splinter in my thumb, but I need something I can fall back on and make money at if I can't work like I am now" — Bromige's analytical mind — red printer's/binder's clothbound dummy blank page notebook now filled — "I finished my first book and started on another one" — sceptre 4 foot onion stalk, bulb to crown of florets, shaft swelling like an eriogonum inflatum-deflatum — "Pam and I eat about 2 cloves of garlic apiece every day" — "did you walk out back to the Frontier?" "yeah, up that hill? get a good view of the freeway, whiff of smog" "yeah!" laughter beyond humor, belly relaxer — comings and goings of dogs: Rosebud, Rosie, Rose (Bean), Tulpa (Lowell), Rodeo (Mike) — "there's a lot in your notebook about sheep slaughtering — you've done your own" "I hit the sheep over the head with a hammer then cut their throats — I slaughtered 6 sheep for this guy and he gave me one" "what're you gonna do with the pigs?" "well, Portia's a brood sow, not for meat — I'll probably keep one of the little ones when they're big enough" "shoats" "what're their names" "their names? one of them's called _____, and one's _____, and the others' names are *pork* and *bacon*" — "I like to work about 6 hours and then quit around 1 or 2 you know, rest, sleep a few hours, talk or read, have a little dinner and then go back to work — I've been working 12 hours a day that way — you know, all jobs in America ought to be like that, knock off in the middle of the day like a siesta" — in the field below the other house, a swaybacked bony horse and a sad quiet burro — Mike at work with his friend on that other house, ripping up boards, putting in a new kitchen — we left by 4, 4:30, back down the deadend road, Penn Grove to Cotati, to find and say goodbye to another friend, she not at home, Bean played "Joy Spring" on the piano, and Couperin's "Les barricades mystériéux" — Lowell left a note for Joanna and talked with her tall blonde roommate who came in and wondered who we were — and then back to Berkeley, stopping in Vallejo at Toney's Bar and Package Goods, across the alley from the Greyhound bus depot, for dime beers and cheese twists, eyeing the array of cheap liquor, and sandwich signs — old gentlemen, black and white and filipino, having Old Grandad at 35¢ a shot with dime beer chasers — "are you going back to the Philippines this year?" — white-panama'd whitehaired white gentleman to whitepanama'd filipino gentleman — "no, I went back last year""to see your children?" — back into the cool of Berkeley and the Bay after the Coast Range inner valley heat — the slope of time, a day at a time, August's fall slant across the apricot shaded grass stubble — the clarity of our days slipping with us, filling the great inner lake of accumulation

The turn North to Oregon was to fog the last morning there, only come in when the sun came up, but waiting — the whole West Coast of North America waits with fog in its grip to open, as a gesture of release into the indigenous season — if that is most nearly Winter here by San Francisco, by Oregon it is any time of year — the rich damp chill of the Cretaceous waters still persists at the doors of the interior continent, Jed Smith met as hoist man of the show drops, was enraptured by for the rest of his life, died fighting off the Comanches over a Cimarron sand water hole with the mists of the Orford Point and the tide descent of the Umpqua like the Paradise Side in Balm of the retribution for a life of sin the massacre by Indians inflicted on conscious Christian violators of God's Wilderness — so the turn North separates the State of California

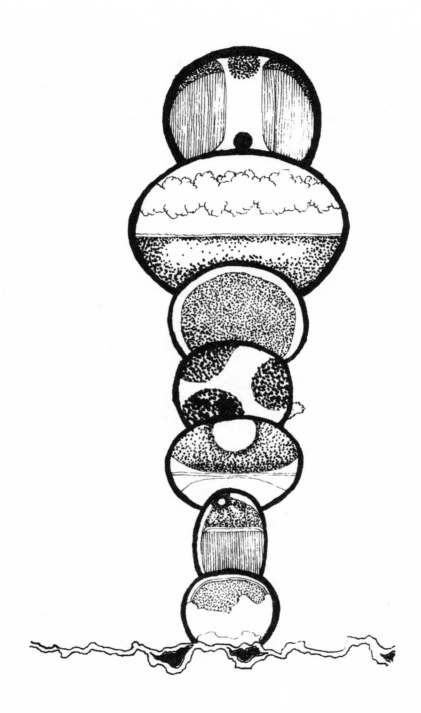

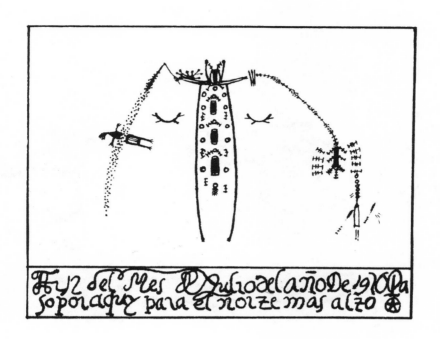

Fin del Mes De Julio del año De 1900 la
soporacio para el noize mas alzo

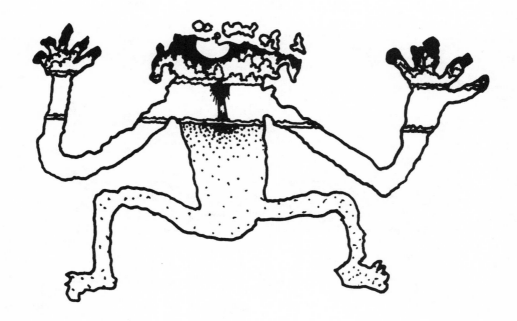

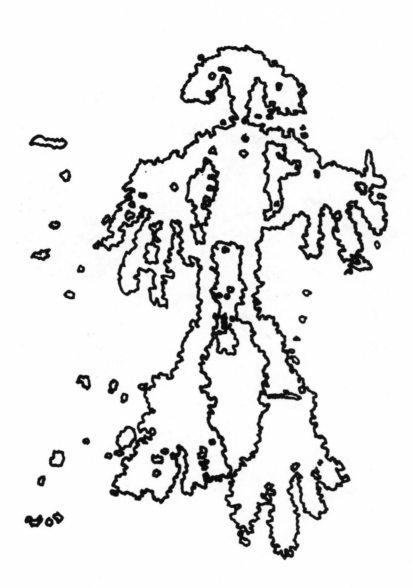

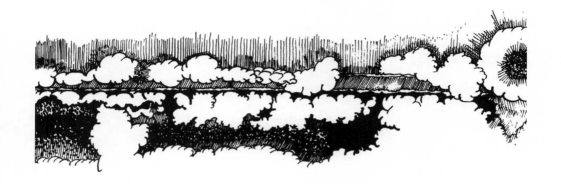

TUFTS

The place of the Lord of Soil is down close to the ground—but in the Himalayas he looms from a ridge pole on the road out of town, small silver lead skull bursting into a golden trident of flames, out of a black fur barrel chest, immense.

There is over all of it, for all the landscape not visible, a melody of lost pastoral, of another land altogether of this same place to which the worship has come. Lord of Division.

Here it is a hillside crossing, of the way up from under catalpa trees and the back dirt streets, dusty, to the downtown, West, and the persistent line of the small town mysteries of the prairies, dividing into brick and concrete, paved and dirt, tall grass and short, crow and cardinal, even the Lodge once into North and South.

But now only the sunset dregs and tree tops are visible West, and around us the lights of the Othick Park softball field are on, and the Southeast Kansas semipro Lords of the Soil are warming up, the pitchers we'd come to see most of all. And we stared into the darkness beyond the outfield, across Buck Run and the Frisco tracks, and into the call home from playing late, a vista lower down and more Southerly, of the first pale military perchers on the bluff over the Marmaton, watching the Leavenworth-Gibson road come cattycorner out of the Indians, who were Lords of the Land but not of the Soil, and make the grand division North and South for this piddly corner of the Osages' screwed out of free lands. If the ball flew on out of the arc of the pitcher's intended slash but still with the pitcher's magic from behind his back and in the great wheel of the saluting arm, it would go on wild light and forever, Southwest till it struck the last setting sun of winter solstice on the last barren Cortezed stretch of the Bay of Baja California, and explode like a puffball the way straight into the land of the under world, which is what the Lord of Soil guards, opens, and grins at, for we fear to enter there.

✪

come back to Delius in Duke
the Malayan Hill of Dreams or Samuel Palmer's
the ink pool in the palm of the hand
I went into the glas hows
hanging as lovely as the rose quartz orange lit in the honeysuckle
the Aztec mirror wreathing burning hearts in the distance
in the ice, in the cold underocean older than the world
Dr Dee's mirror up in the hand of Edward Kelley
as often as I entered his house, I thought I was in the wilderness
meeting their doubles at the edge of the woods
in the shadows of the headlights jump and dance beyond the will

Homage to Coleman Hawkins

for John Moritz

— still hearing the Hawk in his region
following his season

across the Northeast shorelines, heart
                                    strike

of the horn, dive
bomber of the home

front porches

that there have to be porches
in the heat of

—he raised his horn
across the Missouri fault

as sure as the rise and now the fall of sap

the rubber plant
and geranium of affection

from Washburn from St Joe
following the tornado

jazz hounds direction

yoke of going somewhere else
to find out home

—so fall the leaves
in Massachusetts

settling home, a longing
for all Northeast corners everywhere

the pressure upon the body
of the Pacific mental

of the Atlantic visual
of the Canadian

anterior elemental

—so falls the warm November
Medford rain

as fine as winter
California

pooling the brain

having no known direction, even
...only the open road

the eyes closed, leaning forward into
the only riches

the great souls
solo

✪

the waltz in *Appalachia*
                   the fox trot
Hawkins said Fletcher's band
never recorded as well as Ellington's
but on the band stand
stomped em under
                 the inheritors of that
were Basie and Lunceford
          Kansa, Ðhegiha
Reno Clubbed East
                they rode the Clouds of Joy
the Blue Devils, the Hounds
                   those were the clans
"what's your tribe?" the kid asked Shao
in a, say Gallup, Southwest bar
               the bone flute

"Oh Honey I am going down the river in the morning"
 equals exactly
"Oh Sweetie I'm going off on a dustdevil this evening
   for the big time"
          the crossroads

whirl left, to West, to California, leads directly to China

(Buck Clayton)

turn East, to New York, takes straight to Europe

(Hawk)

and now the rise seems possible
    more than any lateral, straight up
and never seen again
                        and in that desert
"only grass"
                in the Land of the Hermetic Learning
                the Spirit Journey Dances
                on the Wheel of the Plains

★

        Hosea Ballou, first president of Tufts, the Hall, etc.
        1771–1852, died the year the college founded
        with the arms of Origen
        to lift from New England
        the weight of Puritan
        eternal damnation
                            Universalist
        vista from Tufts Hill

            •

        that *this* life is hell enough
        to expiate, that Christ's
        is not atonement, that Love
        face off the hill
        in all directions
        mounted on Barnum's Jumbo
        that even kindness
        be human

            •

but Hosea could not see an orgy
of bare asses
as I would
any change of classes

    • • •

all wrong, it wasn't Hosea Ballou the anti-
atonement Universalist who was
first president of Tufts, but his grand nephew
also Hosea Ballou, who though also
a Universalist, disagreed with his *bis tío*
on punishment in the life to come
fearing for morality in this one
if we all go scot free in the next
                           while old Hosea said
"if there is punishment in the life hereafter
it is for those who sin in *that* life"

    •

that this prominence is a shoal
in waters barely visible

of imminent *flesh as spiritual*
made *carnal*
the union climactic
of all our weather
that the bare flesh
in itself be astounded

✪

Cartier from the Iroquois
heard rumors of a gold-red distance
as far as New Mexico or Azteca
and ten years later Jean Alphonse the pilot
knew of Cíbola and gives its latitude exactly
down the St Lawrence arrow
into the heart of a Southern Tartary
the extremity of Asia by the roundness of the world
fixing South against the breaks of Appalachia
to slip the passage through to China
for I have been to a bay as far as 42 degrees
between Norumbega and Florida
but did not see its end
and do not know whether it leads beyond
centaur edge to come
against the blackgold
Amazons of California

(*after Sauer*)

Ah, Lord, how long did it last
that golden age of interchange
Verrazzano found upon the lower coasts
of now New England, whose calm majestic inhabitants
cared nothing for silk or golden cloth or knives or steel or iron at all
or even, o other world, for mirrors
"having looked at them they would be returned with a smile"

only "small bells, blue crystal glass, and other objects of fantasy
to put in their ears or hang about the neck"
Verrazzano looked on, it looked wonderful, he did not ever doubt

"they exceed ourselves in size," some "bronze color, some inclining to white
others to tawny color — the profile sharp, the hair long and black
the eyes black and alert, and their bearing
is sweet and gentle, much in the manner of olden days"
advancing across the savannahs of Narragansett Bay and North
as Goullart found the Lolos of Tibet
the presence of the knights of chivalry
across the orcharded sward of World War II

and in their cultivation they observe "in planting the influence of the moon
the rising of the Pleiades and many customs of the ancients"

How long did it last, that Paradise?
never longer than it took those French to travel North along the coast to Maine
and there the *mala gente*, dressed in skins, suspicious, distant
trading only by letting down their goods on strings from the cliffs
and wanting only "knives fishhooks or edged metal" in return
as far as the fishing fleets of Biscay and Brittany
already had raided in their search for cod and fur

April to May 1524 — the open welcome of the New World
willingness all eager to embrace
took one toke from those who only wanted to go *East* for riches
and the shit was shot

Bix's *In the Dark* and *Flashes*
a plaintive lace regret for the passing of all things
my parents married October 1929 Baltimore
Chicago my father's med school city out of Mississippi
Baltimore my mother's nursing out of North Carolina
like the edge of a cigar thrown in the snow
just come in out of with a case of bootleg under each arm
Bunny Fox Lake Wisconsin died of drink Bix
"living on one thin transparent hamburger a day"

the Windy City a weakness in the lungs
old Davenported regrets of Kiwanis histories Grand Rapids
Rock Island Moline guilt on the backs of easy chairs
the lamp fringe swaying slightly to and fro to the music

✪

John Taverner, 1495–1545
from Lincolnshire, as also

William Byrd, Tennyson
and my forebears

his *"Western Wind" Mass*
against the North Sea plains

a perpendicular, a
Josquin, Isaac, grainelevator

cry like Jim Lane

    •

Almost all the music we have dates from his Oxford years. When
he left there at 35, he went back to Lincolnshire, married, became
a guild member, a landowner, "and a cruel and fanatical agent in the
suppression of monastic establishments."

    •

I hear the anti-popery
still in my father

there is a vigilante
ruthless hardening

antiphonal to the bright
passing islands of the blest

•

O Western Wind!

as if the only
transport of this cross of past and place
back to the earth again

were this small rain of Medford

✪

Stamina comes with age
Thomas Tallis
Jeremiah General Sherman
regrets for the city
Jerusalem Jerusalem
never looking back
come in his old age
to Gloucester

•

Sherman the full continent
        detached officer
vista through the Civil War
        brewed on the coast

the bead of Indian graveyards drawn on
        Montana to Marblehead

•

General Sherman became Captain Woman
        off the main route
        down between Kansas and Arkansas

Captain *Indian* Woman
    in the hearts of his veterans' children's children's children

    .

The dark old man oracle
no one ever wanted to hear
old men's, old women's smells
Love the Brujo still looking out of
Ab Wood and I thought we were the Water Babies
looking at us out of their dark eyes
Captain Woman stalked us
General Sherman Medicine Man
caught us in the backyards

✪

John Brown bereft of beard until he return East to battle the slavery of father over son that is only overthrown when weariness is let sit in the heart throne as majestic as powerful as mysterious as wrath. Harpers Ferry and Charlestown exist previous to settlement, coterminous with the isomorphs of the Appalachians that admit Westward as the part of their rising only revolution within one nation comes at last to understand and use. For I, said John Brown, grow my beard only as memorial of that matted terrifying nighttime undergrowth along Potawatomie Creek clotted with blood. The growth of wrath is my border thicket, my black bondage my beaten back escapes underground to my own new nation, and this beard is that flag, where exhaustion sits to rule over the return of glaciers the rise and fall of mountains and the destruction by floods. I saw the borderland of Kansas and Missouri exactly as the territory of making my son beat me in return as I beat and punished him. That I turned East again to fight *father* is my limitation in time. Though I saw West was the direction to escape from direction altogether, it was the land of the feminine I could not admit. Some of my children fulfilled that movement West, but were left there without vision. I saw her fetish on that blackjack oak near Trading Post and at my death my soul left my body to seek her realm at the border of the grassland and forest where long ago she raised the spruce trees and made lush the prairies beyond the Marsh of Swans.

Late Swallows

dear John Dee — of the music
so *there* is Delius — the *here* is

there an edge of English garden
here the prairie yearns for

Dee is articulate of *rays* we are
out of the Soul in adversity
in travail the *flint*
sends forth sparks of the divine
drawn lines

Delius asks for companionship to the heights
the plains offer — there is a John Brown rush
coincident upon the density of vegetation reached, searching
out the old paths all over again
of daring

Delius, for *she*
knew him, he knew her
as where the first meadowlark of morning rose to greet us
following *her* tokens though we scouted
old John Brown, *his* paths
avoidances, but still *her* blazings, just
there *newness* again

where the trees have not been cut down
where they have never grown
and the split mountain North shows another mountain

where the first bird rises, and the last descends
her fresh smell

✪

the Crystal Ballroom, Fargo, North Dakota
November, 1940
                    at the cream tip, in the blizzard

"Warm Valley" in the storm

I was four, I heard her   snow snow snow over Kansas

my unknown, my just before I was born country

my parents saw Ellington in Dallas in 1936 at the centennial

I heard him from the womb

✪

Dr Dee stood at the edge of Governor Winthrop's Chinese garden, gauging the descent,
catching sight through the rhododendrons of the rain-swollen stream
                                        Here, he said to
his host, I am in intimate contact with that Far Ancient East which has been heretofore
only a matter of venerable report to me — among these exotic shrubberies, the traceries
of these paths afford us insight of the *flow* — this, I take to be patterned exact fixation
of those features, what one master of such lore once termed to me, *fungh-shwaye*, or
water-winde, which pierces the earth, and attracts from the heavens the mute attendant
spirits to in-dwell
                    So he spoke, stopped at the pond's edge, leaning out over the water
In the descent of the river some have seen time coming down to them, others its press-
ing its way upstream toward them, most, just the instant spot before them — there is no
time that is not part of all of those, but it is not wholly any one of those — as, where it
was, the poets used to float poems as they wrote them folded into boats downstream to
one another, knew of mere *flow*

for Michael Brodhead

The children in the Civil War, and the children of the War. Who were they. My grand-father born in 1871. Wolfe's father a child watching Lee pass. The generation of Delius and Debussy. The lost generation of Confederate veterans who left America, their children. John Muir's 1867 *1000 Mile Walk to the Gulf* through the circumspect hollow-eyed gazes of children. Turned to California instead of South America.

.

In the hand a clod of fresh spiritualism earth, to talk to old war comrades gone under the earth, dead children, to call up the dead darlings, to touch and be touched in return. The purple fringe on Coues' hard head. *Yore cole cole hart, tutched soar.*

.

"Consciousness of self is or may be only partial…but I would not have you think I am merely naive."

          watchers from the dead
          bearers of the living

                              where they go the catalpa beans cover
          a slow road, even in childhood
                              even from old age
                                        it barely shows

          and each, who has come only
              as one turn of the wheel under the plains

              only smiles, and shakes his head, and does not play
                  or cause to play, or say
                  anything at all

          watchers from the dead, masters of the long play

the hang of hair over the door at harvest time
    and the crisp hair of the floor

and the young who can still hear the jade carnelian bloodstone
    master wort of autumn

✪

of the Sons of the Morning
in the palm of the hand held up
to the sunrise behind them
in the palm of the hand held up to the setting sun
by the Sons of the Evening
in the palm of the Lord of Noon
up to the zenith, and of the Prince of Midnight
down

the carved air
of earth

    ·

at the left is turquoise
that in the Southwest aridities
sees bluesky oceans
and the islands of the blessed
from such a height continents lie
scattered in an instant on the hand
in an air so clear
earth is ocean
veins of ocean in the land

the hair is black
the feather bluejay
the hand up bears
the sunrise light
but faces West

•

at the right is bloodstone
bright bull's tears
exuded in a field
as dark as Europe
green of the inner earth
space between blackout
and an earthly rest
field of eclipse
sunturn stone

the hair is brown
the feather redbird
hand to East
bears the sunset

•

and at the center, blond
and featherless, only the long
long hair in an aureole
the lapis edge of takeoff from the earth

the lapis
lazuli sawn slab
against the chest

cold as the stopper of the world
unstoppered

warmer of the weather-reacher heart

Cahokia

The descent to a level plain with scattered small hills before the river—there is a mound we climb in the moonlight to look for the mountains of the plains, never visible by day —and the chill that comes then is the shake of an oracle, the cast of an augury, small haruspices cut in the air—there, the small stone picked up without thinking is everything, the unattended stray memories, everything, in the throw of the vision, in the catch of us in the vision

✪

The students from Cracow leave, a post-coital sadness, voicelessness, fills the room, as the figure out of the alley who came in two weeks ago with the flaming heart, almost invisible up by the windows, filled rooms in the air ahead of him as he went and exhausted them behind him as he left, leaving the yearning. It seemed some monthly mystery, February piercing the heart and setting the pericardium afire till it walked, a striding burning *hsin*, mind/heart, becoming in the stretch of distance and snow, such an *eye*. So, as in the big city the eye becomes the organ of loneliness, in the city it is the organ of longing—and the hand with the eye in its palm held up to signal the ages, in order to reach them at all, must go blind, let loose the eye on its own haunches, and send forth the 心 likewise, burning up to find out

Voynich

Maybe a Δ that knew, maybe a Δ that never knew, or only cared for the loveliness of the drawings and recognized no solution of the cypher would soon, or ever, be forthcoming, and said, Here, Most Imperial Majesty, is the writing of those from another world, who visited one time only, and then known to a few solely in dream, as if the sands of the seashore were their signature, carried a handful of and written with across our usual paths, but their language never understood and their message only hinted at. The man who transcribed this manuscript from the vividness of what he dreamt, died in that, and the fragment, broken off where he was, gives the colors and detail of these visitors, but not their key. The manuscript has led me into a time to come I cannot fix, and in an unknown land, looking for their messengers returned again — so in the house of which I am told in riddles, a traveler from the South who is blind and cannot speak, stares at me, and we know we are the predicted, demanded intersectors

Homage to Edward Burne-Jones
for Timotha Bialy

the scales balanced, anti-
& gravity
sun
& night

she comes face
half into light
carrying the body
up from the under ocean
head against his cock half
hair and half
the secret smile the seaweed
wild wind reaping

this time
salvation, next time
full splendor
next descent next
zero
feeling already
the rise, smiling, half
smiling

Offertory

to call up the dead from dreams
   and break the heart's stone

  whose cock is it? not just my own

    1965, I told Mary it was hers, she said
  that kind of thing's *always* easy to say in bed

but tenancy of the flesh…the circumcision of the heart

  woke up this morning
  not me in mine this time
                  but *its* own will
   "which he ignores at his peril"

but along the edge of the wall, later a new stain

    •

I refused to recognize Sam Spencer on the steps last night
where my brother and I were sitting with one of the Eggs between us

and Sam leapt on over us, over the steps, and was gone

and my anguish wasn't even at not admitting he was there
but the fear someone would crack that egg and eat it

myself accuser and myself accused

yolk openings in the hand
back into which the bird had fled

the day *after* Easter this year

so I didn't have any-
thing to say to the Owl
   Hearer, in the room with the Heart
Offer

   and heard the sound of ducks passing North
just before dawn
                crows I thought on waking
crows on Tufts Hill
            silver by night
turned black again by day

     .

the *ceja de la montaña* weather all day, especially at evening, the faint drizzle, an Oregon sizing in the air, Mary Lou Williams playing the meditative complexities, *From the Heart* — and the Texas speech on the phone this morning, hot Austin afternoons already filtering through the wires, with the mute Watergate tube on, almost out the window — five points trace a star, the stretch of muscle: Somerville, Austin, Portland, Washington — and Fort Scott, in the telephone head — and now there will be a footstep uncovering a rock in the mud, and in the line of sight will appear a quartzite boulder brought down by the glacier, carved with the rotations of the star, leading inward, Northeast — and from the foot lifted to the one remaining ancient spruce, the air is folded in on itself, capturing the moisture, shimmering, opening a pool through which the hands reach, yolk-stained

FOR THE SNOW QUEEN

build nations up and let them fall...

    .

The mockingbird sang all night long
in the interstices of his song
    she came again

...from the tower beyond her shoulder
    across a world of older slow repose
    across the stream beyond the alcove's window

    the Copper-Beech Tree Maiden in the moonlight
        like the ache of highschool graduation night unsatisfied

    and the Hawk Flight Boy stand
        in the summer thunder introspection

    Harvest Wheat Snow Queen
    Eastern Gold Tobacco King

    enamel overlays
    across the dark and moonlight checkered floor...

"I am half sick of shadows," said
    The Lady of Shalott

and as she did
                she then undid
the knot of mirror and of tapestry

Chicago – Boston

In the Milwaukee
Millers the foam, Canadian
sunset clouds pushing
East — back to Somerville, Gloucester
Autumn returning home
the grassland home
luxuriating across
the continental access
of this NE climate, not from
the sea, but from the land
Autumn, and from the Far
North, most ancient
Shield, Her Winter
while the ocean
back on itself
leads not across
but up
lift, Poseidon, you
of the under realm, give
over your triumvirate
of true phallic ancestors
to the Unnamed, Many-Named
Reacher of the Plains
Weather Master, with Her
Who through the Ice Age rims
kept open the unsure
pathways of the heart
to warmth
Who in the Far
Northeast, New England

fastnesses deep in the hidden
wilderness of weather
rules still, Inviolate

          •

Flying East, with the West's
last sunset reflector
band on my hair
hippie knit on the heart
Malin asked Brodhead
after he rust met me, "is
Mr Irby a
hippie?"
the old slow lightning historian
leaning forward on his cane
into the doorway, his wife
gossiping on the lawn next door
as we bowed away, "What despite
all history and civilization *homo*
sapiens still cannot determine
to his satisfaction
is *quality*"
as if he had said, "Laughter
is my appeal in the extremity
to which I have come"
over the ginger cookies animals
sighting along Eugene Ware as the
blade up into a realm
Brodhead and I only now, at
the middle of our prairie
rutted lives, catch
first certain sight of— the Up
From the Plains
have always demanded of us, You

Male and Female Great
Springers and Great
Shielded Shafted and Helmeted
Swingers of the Center
Wheel of Earth —

Into Your Flinging Periphery
Autumn Flies Me Home

IN DENMARK

Poems 1973–1974

Dronningensgade 54
Christianshavn
København

and the old familiars, like rocks
ahead of us in the fields
way-charters, no longer
voice

      ·

and for each year of a man's life
there is a degree for that year
and the work as if Colorado to the Plains
in the seasons where the nets lie
in the constellations to be made

      ·

this is the rite of the Apple Blossom Heart
the 37° of all the years
casting Albert Pike's Arkansas fastened springtime
on over the head

      ·

where Gordon Cairnie way in the distance smiles
waving with his vodka to come on

a flower of solbær
jam in the air
where two travellers
spell out *appreciation* or
announcement or *attention* in
blocks of the brown hand
road they stare down

and we look up at each other
out of that picture fair of home, and smile
not knowing what's going on at all

this is where the early morning traffic noises out of Christianshavn
and the coasts of Oregon cross

this is the rite of the drugstore counter heart

★

soft gnaw over me, and how
each time you change what has happened
                              who is there
is something strange and hidden
in the most ordinary events
"lying there just like a great
Mountain Opal"
your face I never see
but its features run too close
to the fire we carry between us
an old descent, 6th St to Buck Run
gone now, all these years
it's always been some piece of territory
we've thought of each other in
"I see your face before me" an old
old tune to see you by
when now it is
the moss mystery
stones accumulate

[homage to Carl Fredrik Hill]

love, always the danger
to cross to, not even dared, to
get there, overcome
ignored

        .

gold gnashes, cold
under the dark tree settee
under the horse chestnuts

        .

the Loing valley full of
rising years later out of
abhorrent, unforgettable

        .

wandering the river roads after   'realism, that's effect'
Grecian boys and the temple houris   'there's nothing else to seek in art
and where the centaurs rage   'arrogant except the heart of truth'
asshole of genius'   'always   'magic color
gawping at the clouds'   'Pissarro   opium juice and love
praised him to the skies'   'off   beneath the faery vaults!'
that bridge'   'one and two a day   'to get the brightness
for months, just blue and yellow   into the cloud behind the trees
we burned them all'   'shrimp shells'   and change black ground to light'
schizoid of the North France   'an hour painting like that
crazy plains, the Northland   is worth a life of normal living'
dark women   'O Proud Madness
Lund parks   step down from your zenith!
'crazy Swede'   loose your wild foals!'

connecting the dots   'Never Finish!'

•

hard brow small
glasses hidden close
little eyes in the
hand up the lips
back down the
river palmetto'd North frozen
conifer'd South

•

the world keeps getting in the windows
out of the kind incessant
animals keep breeding and breeding
out of the woodwork the smallest
little people you keep meeting
in the temples the great
out of the perspective

•

King Me King supplicate Me King Me proliferate King

Hill
Hill Hill   Hill
Hill Hill   Hill Hill
Hill   Hill   Hill   Hill
rain

•

'crazy jackoff artist who draws for
I mean draws <u>all</u> the time'

✪

Autumn has come again, Noble Lovely Prentis
has been back from visiting the Mennonites the first time
over a month, and watches the cottonwood leaves
drift down the Kaw from Topeka — out past Tescott
the Danes look back toward Copenhagen
where the butterfly bush is still in bloom
and the beech leaves lighten slowly

so Prentis finds himself
punting a skiff up the Great
River of the West, not the Missouri, North
but the Kaw gone straight into the Rockies
under, through

and with pears and Stilton at his hand, and an Austrian
eau de poire, tots up the gauges of melancholy
in a land either of bullshit or of flat despair
and starts for Lecompton — and with *all days are early days*
differs no more in what he sees than the conviction
the hidden is the past, trying to be realized
Ware foreshadowing Kipling 20 years, Mallarmé and Ware
crossing paths in the Lecompton dark

✪

singing "old Mince Meat's here," to the tune
The Water Goblin's Hair or *The Autumn*
Flaking From the Air — as "they don't care
they don't care, <u>what</u> they wear"
calls back from the clearing

so enters the Fall
as the Butcher's Boy
returned without blood

carves the sap away
and they stop whatever they're doing, scared shitless
as the way NE opens and the flame orange ball
rolls beyond the river, makes its hole
and stops, before the clearing, before the gateway
the Edge Dwellers Opener, the Hole Borer

so men foresee their years
— the rite of the vista-opened heart
where the Lemon Forcer Bear carries his fruit to the North

so slips the day away
after it has come, and another look
and it has never come

only the voices of children again
"I gave em back to yah"   "you <u>never</u>"
playing marbles in the clay

✪

Al Haig
          the way
NY, Nutley, over
NE opened
          Dorn writes «Don
Cherry and a group of travelling
africans live on an Island community
near (?) sweden—info from H. Brown»
                              O'Connell
says latest NY appearance played surrounded by
family described as
"variously gambling"
                    Tchicai
a bowline the *NY*
Times awareness of Vermont

leaves
        tightened on the Malmö ferry
birch around the balls NE
                "or a negative person
backwards in the exit, through the queue
and out the front"
            SW

★

        so came to Valldemosa
to see the convento's cells, and found
Cortot's Dracula visage above the Steinway
twice, and Eric Heidsieck's soft
dreamer's lock at the death mask, out of the
sharp phthisical
sex smell, Chopin
propped up to play in the moonlight
the monks' sweated wool
habit against the naked
the abstinence of the hand as much as
of those who make the green Ruth and I
sipped with the Danish women after dinner
the sharp
sex smile
between us, Merle
Oberon Cornel Wilde in the California
winter incessant downpour
dripping blood on the concert keys
but Chopin wrote back to Paris the warmth
and the garden where his bed lay, not the vista
down S'Estret, but the nearsighted
tune

✪

una copa de *Carlos Primero* toast
not *beans on toast* with the souvenirs not
tea like mum makes or even *strawberries and cream*
but Gardel's "Yira, yira" returning
straight through the Pillars to these
shores of idleness that hide
the incessant jism Hermes tango'd ladders

✪

Eastern Kansas, borderland, Border
Ruffian gangland, Marmatonia, Royaume
de la Marais de Cygne, Kaw Mouth
glacier end to lead crystal
grit rip, Flint
Hill palm, Ben
Webster national anthem honk
torn horn made whole again
home land

[homage to the Fort Scott Albert Richardson]

«finding the Marmaton dangerous to cross
we left our horses and vehicles on the north bank»
the Lawrence grip of fear in the balls
at coming South

                    and no answer
Johnny Hodes high over the poled skiff glissando
playing the Cambridge at the Cambridgeport

knock river crossing
one sun in the sky one sun
in the heart in the sky
counting the slow time shove
against the shore time fear to come

                    and then find

«an air of age and comfort
 very unusual for the frontier»

but the grid is not irrelevant
to previous courses

                or the dust devil
that picked them up in front of the Elks Club — gone —
faded off E toward Dr Lewis' — gone — whipped back
blunted the vector W to N up Scott Avenue
passed on through the Redmen's Hall deadend at Wall — the whole block gone —
and made reverse the crossing of the dangerous Marmaton

                                        wild unerring silent
knock at that insistence

the cut of the glaciated corner North to the Cherokee Lowland South
and the fall of the Flint Hills to the Osage Plains
though Moore calls the Flint Hills merely
«the most prominent...of many east-facing escarpments»
and draws the division West
the Dakota Sandstone of the Smoky Hills, the sand
of the Great Bend Prairie

                    but relief for the dweller rules division
Eastern strips of states
than Western, Middle, Rising
from descent, where does the unbidden lie

of endless shifting magnetisms
swinging of the sky?
                         or straight down into the ground
to fly

          pioneers
they weren't even, no, but on the frontiers
almost haphazard still explorers
of an almost oblivious rise of information, and away

✪

                    Ruth came and told me she'd just heard
her brother was dead, 19, of an overdose, found in his van
parked at the other end of Alameda — "he didn't know anybody up there"

and earlier, before I knew, the melted wax had spattered all over the table as I blew
        out the candle
and from the gray woolly rug I saw the altar I had made
and was with you as the Dagar brothers sang the loved one entering the loved one's heart
and knelt down and knocked my head against the rug in marriage
as you were at the phone office talking to California

and when you rang the doorbell
I was afraid of Death, long enough to see you in the dark

✪

Ruth come down to the well

carrying her brother's body

her eyes violet this time

✪

a girl to take the place of the boy

a boy forfeit, regained

the girl <u>child</u>

✪

the Hawk's belongings still in the closet
the red and black canvas duffle bags
and the rattan mat from outside the front door
and too big Icelandic turtleneck and the dyne cover
and the trash around back downstairs or off the balcony outright
out of the woodwork the last day again
as with Ben Webster no more sanity no less
the turn hour of the plummet of the year to dark
a creamerie of gold leaf to be with the family forever
the complex wired nerve flux in front of the law courts
old curtains old draperies sweeping the streets before us
the brother loss the sister pain relived endured
I Wish That I Were Twins in the mirrored baroque hall at The Hague
Some Of These Days and *I Only Have Eyes For You* and Annie de Reuver
and the one who has to stick his head into the snake's mouth
and the great longneck of the goose hanging down into the doorway

✪

and no words tonight but these
        an arm with three animal faces as a hand
        and a king leaning forward, with his crown and ruff
and my new red underwear against the radiator stretch

✪

so we will start
no matter what depression, the Berkeley
the Alameda–Fort Scott with the Danish
river crossing, as the days reach
sunset 4 soon 3 o'clock, start
the dark and North return of home
by heart, facing each other across
the short circuit of these canals
as if Skåne were never lost
to set the distance of flat land and hemmed by sea
aloft, across the casual mountains of ourselves
the sight on through each other
                              —and that is love

as the days grow short
nick on the horizon
set and dawn
as the nights grow long
                              —and that is love

✪

sock washing with a cold
the day of the first big snow
wringing the boogie from the soap
an art beyond intention made
fateless suffered anyway the wet
not on my hands the worry
or the gain but the grain
of manhood fine as sock sand
satin hard against your hand

and now the child and the mother of the child
are gone home, and our home
is between us, and the touch
is in the center dark

snow falls over Denmark
the breakwater of its quietness
and the level hand of land
freeze or are scattered by attention
to far distance, the dark

the Old Witch Ruler of the North
does not ever confuse for cold
scattering her mirror shards from the sun
for ice in the heart

face to face, ass to ass
the open runners out the other side
the rapacious tame animals
come to congratulate
come to celebrate
come to throw us both together
back against the rocks we came through

old distance still distances still love
still not at ease
waking in the Copenhagen snow dawn
the Centaur the Desert City Flowing Dope
the Naked Archer Entering The Sea

★

ROBERT: «where we only once
shall have travelled» the descent of København
3:30 sunset Pearl Harbor Day combing
ornithologia with O'Connell *The Birds of Lindisfarne*
Løvstræde off Købmagergade by the post office
out Gammel Kongevej into Frederiksberg
Colin Wilson's *Man Without A Shadow* aka *The Sex Diaries Of* etc but no not
looking up into the clouded marble blue eyes of a boy
motorcyclist selling books bring in the dark
Friday night the stores open late the crowds along Strøget
surge toward Christmas and rearrange the felt directions of force
only to rearrange them back again the escape
Christian Firtal with *The Mill Of Particulars* come
today exact against inarticulation «work of light
beyond» «so you can live in this world» hearing
from half an hour back in Bristol Don Byas
Helen Humes Minton's 1941 setting
Stardust above the underground and loss
Danish-speaking Walloons buying
stacks of records children Julemanden
singing at the doors one last
beer one snaps before the dark to
Ruth's for dinner love comes through
and on back through us «Everything I care for
happens all the time» «or anything at all
the way it is» Hang Loose Saludos
& Abrazos Love

       Ken

✪

on the road to the South
camped in the bayonet leaves
fire almost out
both of you asleep

the full midwinter moon
answering adversity
the circle of socks in the sand
the book to be added to

your hair and Tad's
bright from the sleeping bags
drawing the sentinels of the land
guardian around us

✪

David measured out the night in 60 breaths
so as not to have a foretaste of death [*The Zohar* 207a (II, 283)]

dreams of the hour
minutes counted against having to get up
after the alarm — and the night itself is the alarm
and the measuring as if waiting for the revelations of adolescence
to call an instant when everything must stop and the reckoning up be made
some sing 60 big breaths = 60 big bills
and when they are counted, spent
must be earned again
even in sleep
against the rapture of the deep

or the disappearance of the Greenland settlements
or the passing of love or its never having settled
and the ache to work it
with the last fading settlers losing Norway and never gaining
Vinland or Far Thule
looking for anyone, skrælings, raiders, English pirates
off the edge
Lord save them even now
even here

      as the heart no longer nourishes
the heart it hoped to nourish, and on the Eastward-facing
Baltic shores with the head turned always backwards
and Far North

      loses any heart at all and lets
the inert wisdom of drift itself
lets the unhearing slip of body careless
for that be servant

he takes it North again
he takes it N and W

      now that I can fly
      now that I'm above the Earth
      to follow the Old Ways Back
      to visit the World's Home

you won't know how to get there by direction
not even the Sun's

the guides that show
the bright in the dark
the dark in the day
those that look <u>at</u> you

you must hear what they say

and what will you do there
and what will you see
in the eye of the Turtle
from the middle of his back

       ·

Sunday morning walking
the canals of Christianshavn
now answer now swing magnetic
last night's vomit and the lone man
leaning over the harbor Christiania
through the Greenland warehouses
a line of dope the morning sunlight
smoking the breath
to the whirling gulls in front of the oldest house
the East Asiatic Company the Dan Viking casting off for Malmö
to the long residuum of love
in the blood uncooled the white nights' light
waiting in the winter
gray day for the track in the woods
unleaved again
one afternoon's sweet
love making believe love
come again?
crowning the morning still
with the dark Arctic suture of the world

and on that groove let play
Return To The World and *Leave The World*
alternatively, say
"I loved you once," "I loved you, nay," like that
crazy jabber
the heart's pain is the attachment string
back from the sky to center of the Turtle's eye
but they say, Nope, no rest this time
the guides that got you here won't get you back
but others will
you'll take it all again

✪

the Green Head and the Brown Back Travellers
swim the Børse Canal to be by midnight
at the Fishwives' Steps, and from
Gammel Strand into Højbro Plads
circle Absalon, and receive
as he receives them

✪

on those outer banks where
always wet genders
from Copenhagen the view
through the day the snow returns
and the great wheel of gulls over Christianshavn
projects against return
far Hulténia, Thule thither

[homage to John Ledyard]

he would not follow that line by dreams
or bells of caps out of this world
but kept <u>on foot</u> or the old canoe
club club club down the rivers of Afric
and transport Asia East East East
Full West, the only
ache of the land bridge for Empire
memory out of continent beyond race
urge for home so deep
the way back had to be
the first ever made

the gray serenade waltz toward summer

she hears you from off in the sand dunes at Skanör
while you dance the winter's dance indoors on Dronningensgade
the Giant Hooded Crow at the surf's edge
his feet never wet, his head her nods

dark men instead enter the North

✪

straight off the boat talking to the one with the young wife and the three-year-old
    daughter
and the living room so piled up with trash they have to keep the kitchen door latched
    against it
walking around in the blue and yellow morning off the Sweden ferry into London by
    the mesa's edge
talking about Bruno, he must have been one of the most brilliant minds there ever was,
    still in his
overalls from work, the airline kind, I really dig his diagrams and study them a lot, but
    what do you do
<u>with</u> them, old Pierre, I really think he's great, he's got them up like advertising displays
    all over the house
getting chain saw started that won't catch, while the two of them a little apart from
    the others
lean back against a tree trunk and smoke, the one, the other, unmarried one squatting
    down on his heels
looking off across the valley, watching the smoke eddy out of the clearing with a milk-
    weed seed
before saying again, yeah, that great arch of guardians, that great circle <u>chart</u>
he must have carried around in his head all the time, just to start from
as the saw started, cutting off the rest, and they snubbed out their cigarettes and stood up

✪

(Astor Pension
9 rue Crespel, Brussells)

*so backtrack here to add
the compositions: by Jongen:
Soleil a midi op. 33, *Clair de
lune* op. 33, *Sarabande triste*
op. 58, *Sonatine* op. 88, *Deux
études de concert* op. 65, all
for solo piano (Marcelle
Mercenier, debut pianiste for
Boulez' flute *Sonatine* in 1948)

Musique en Wallonie, a very
recent series, Joseph Jongen
(1873–1953), head of the Belgian
Conservatory, Prix de Rome, etc.,
and Guillaume Lekeu (1870–1894),
pupil of César Franck, died far
too young, «after 10 hours of agony»
4th 46 (soir), 21 Jan, found
both in the Domaine du Disque in
the Galerie Ravenstein opposite the
Gare Central, wanted my name and
address to send me news of more*
…lying on the bed of the bare
pension room, time to get up and go out
to eat? still stuffed from the Leuven

and on this side note for
Lekeu these additions to the
work: *2e étude symphonique*
(1. Hamlet, 2. Ophélie) (1890)
and *Fantasie contrapuntique
sur un crâmigon liègeois*
(1890), Paul Strauss and the
Liège Symphony

faculty club lunch needing above the sound of wet in the streets the lights in the back empty highways
coalescing love is not lost once ever made as I was in the audience this afternoon with the kids at Louvain hearing me
talking about Kelly's *The Wall* where does the consciousness when you make love go

373

✪

and the swan down the cold black waters

·

stripes on the water, gliding between the dark

·

and still we will float together, past all those

✪

and by the Fish Wives' Steps
come into Højbro Plads
and circle Absalon to take
his glare on off
just East of due South

these are
the very late or never come before
or the lost who only heard it right
this far

clouds lead out of Copenhagen
as if at sea, not San Francisco
over updrafts

the dyne surface
over the lowlands, the circular rainbow
British bullseye, just West of due North
low above the horizon

some raptors may still be
active in the Skåne lakes, but by late February
the watching shifts back to Skanör and the coast

Ceylon

or Gambia or the Red Sea
by Spies' or Tjærborg's, Unisol's
cheap tours

        to come back around
one layer up, or what
most like a layer

✪

I will spill from her hands some day

   .

and all my words will be
taken together

   .

the heart because it is hollow, with a feather

but «the heart, when it is <u>full</u>», with the whole world

✪

the Hawk at the Gates
and the Hawk's Mountain lifted to meet
and the leaves of the Forest of the Sea
whispering elsewhere

   .

to see <u>through</u> is love
is all that love can do

   .

nor the sadness that you yield
as ore

·

you lifters, lift me to the wheel again

·

late last night we came out of the

and a little earlier tonight

✪

and not sadness, not a crown's worth

·

and not the Crown of Happy Days
as Midway North the Wolf of Days Australis
chases the Sun

✪

the Citadel of Crows shudders and writhes
and the crows scatter aloft and listen and settle again
after the lips stop
this is the 12th of the 18
cut and stained in the dead flesh

✪

the old bed with Ruth, the old
high sun above the ship
we leap over and over

·

and the ship sails on, nets and unnets
the island of the archipelago

✪

so she sits, handless and flaked
narrow, pained, bemused and nodded lids, almost
simpering in that acceptance
while her son looks up from her lap
calmly full-cheeked of a king, crowned and blessing hand and bookly enormous hand
she leans against the broken chair back as if no door will ever open
and the uneven lobes of her eyes carry
whatever differences of all the world of left and right
held in the wood cracked from the floor up to her trembling immobile
just-turned chin

[Good Friday]

Prentis and McComas in front of the Scottish Rite Temple meet before the lights are extinguished and come back afterwards where the families have been waiting in Cohn's, and over coffee agree that the mysteries are still alive, not Christian and not

"and not me
and the missus anymore," the Governor says quietly, as Prentis looks sidelong at his young wife and offers nothing, "though at first, and enough to know, like why we came here" "well," laughing, "I'm off for Lindsborg tomorrow, that music, that ain't no church, that's good" "it's the place, Noble, that's what I mean — what do you see when the lights are out, and go toward? or when you're with your wife?" "the music, I guess, or the days that don't ever end — here in this state they either already were or they're just about to be, but right now, the rise and the fall…ah, Lord, I don't know, but they are, we both agree"

and they trace on the tablecloth the lock and the unlock — "we both know the Blackjack Oak, that's what we've been talking about all along after all, and where does she take you?" "home so far, just home and a few short sashays around like this one" "you know, we're heading Southwest by the end of the month, to New Mexico, it'll be almost into Old Mexico, maybe even to the gulf there if

377

it goes that far — but have you…do you…<u>her</u>"? "John Brown's night, that's all, just that once — but my little boy, one evening last summer we were coming back from Lecompton" "<u>he</u> did?" "and I didn't see anything, but I knew from what he told me later" "this…trip to New Mexico, it's not just my brother's child, you know — in my own library, in broad daylight"

              and Noble Lovely laid the oak leaf on his brow in the distant skies, and looked at his friend, and nodded, and opened his hand to him, and they looked up again into each other's eyes

              the kids were getting restless, their wives kept glancing at them it was time to go, so the bill was paid, and the pleasure of talking with Sidney Cohn lingered over as long as possible, and then they all stepped out into the middle April early twilight, and walked together down the street toward the Goodlander, back to their rooms, for supper

✪

and at the well this time
our eyes do not meet

     ·

dear Ruth, dear part of me
more pain than me itself

     ·

 your sapphire eyes once the well of violet
from the Giant Finn's arms

✪

the first morning light on the apartment house across Dronningensgade
and the flare of jordbærkage against the first black coffee
there will be no other knot of us
like the one we drew tight here
watching the gulls wheel again and again over the canal
facing morning down the faultless macramé of night

✪

I cussed you out in bed but it wasn't you
she had a daughter and was dark and leanfaced I refuse to admit
because I dreamt of an utterly different woman with a child the same anger
joined against the men's middleaged Xenophon study group
and that fake uncle wanting to move the night to Tuesday, we were apart
but we slept together and you wouldn't even touch me and almost pushed me off the bed
   by morning
where I followed you into the other room afterwards, turned away from me, still wait-
   ing for me

✪

the headland of Lesser Asia out the balcony North
half the oldest house in Christianshavn through the first new leaves
Bodrum and the Stærkodder out of sight the East the hidden
straits to Rhodes the gulled canals to Greenland

     .

Herodotus, Christian Firtal
Hippocrates, Hans Christian
lift us, heal
call, carve out the heart
to feed the Spring again

     .

the places of antiquity are not far away
Fort Scott and Kos we joked which would you prefer
Fort Scott, Bodrum
against respective ancient oceans

[*It Never Entered My Mind*]

to remember Robert Hellman

so we left *The Sting* last night still cheered
that even the colossal con of days might have
that clean an exit, and started off home
leaded past Vesterport from the Imperial Bio
Robert with J.B. on his shoulders as far as the circus
and then on into the Rådhusplads besides, that the lift
might be the Spring of weight itself
leapt from the heart
"hey, Bubba, now we're as tall as you are!"
on into the warren of streets beyond Vester Voldgade and Strøget
husk or dew
great buried barb
wrenched out
home anew

once again the trees speak to me

        .

Sibelius, he said, Ellington, and over the bridge

        .

or *Baby Dear* against the grain, I mean, you know
<u>twilight</u> grain

        .

home isn't in the head

that's just an <u>organ</u>

        .

I could only <u>see</u> speaking

380

✪

and passed into the drizzle of rain, the first in over a month, and the slow Monday news-
papers
to lunch at the Chinese cafeteria off Gothersgade where Tad always wants to go, and over
svinekød chopsuey all about his former teacher Katherine's knowing Camilla Hall
back in Wisconsin
and then most of our afternoon planning the Northern itinerary with Schapiro at
Rejsecentret near the Odd Fellows Palace, down Bredgade from the old apartment,
coming away exhausted by the commitment to time as if by the trip itself to the end
and stood by Jorcks Passage and read in the finally arrived *Herald Tribune* the destruction
in Los Angeles by fire and fire of the SLA, Miz Moon and Camilla and Cinque and
Willie Wolfe, the specters of our Berkeley
and bought a hat on Købmagergade and covered and uncovered the head, to crown and
take away
and raced to end the afternoon
the new suit at Brødrene Andersen and home to change and back to Tivoli by six for
dinner at La Belle Terrasse
as an old seal finally impressed and set aside on all our days together, the celebration of the
union that came and went on through us
Romance! all the romance of forms! always on!
that called itself for a moment gravad laks and for a moment entrecôte Mirabeau to pass
on memory
and faced again our ladders in the Tivoli'd brilliance, hearing Barenboim finish with the
Coronation Concerto, that plaintive elegance to crown the evanescence of all even happy
power and away
and hear it all again, and now again
the tears offered to loneliness a use of the world to protect and lead on deeper
deeper? into <u>what</u>, the day asks, effort to record?

✪

the events of mid-December 1665 in Smyrna
the reach all the way up "like a baby's arm with an apple in its fist"
in the streets and the gatherings every night in the houses
in broad daylight at midday meal and no guest the guest
in the brass plates on the rich man's wall
or the hand out of the street freak for change the beseecher
"Arise brethren and behold the Prophet"
the pillar of fire the cock in the empty seat
the shorn foreskin the tongue consumed in flame
and the rising again of a falling star
"your old men dreams your young men visions your sons and daughters prophecies"

the events of Berkeley mid-May 1969 the Western Union
the Pacific Republic the pillar of smoke the hand held up in front of the mouth
the droplets of blood hanging perfectly still in the air
the reflections in the plates on the wall the reflections in the icebox door
choking the heart to reach by marching suncrazed and fevered
and the Stranger come in the night to wake to prophesy Contamination Retribution
    Redemption but he could not see yet how yet saving outrage
while people danced naked in the streets
and fucked on fire in the midst of the dancers to call down to earth
and who be born and who since conceived
on earth or on the other side

Sabbatai Sevi called forth women to read the Torah in temple
and forced unbeliever outcast and elect alike to pronounce the Unutterable Name
singing the old hippie love romance of Meliselda
Baby won't you light my fire
Up your mountain I have climbed
And still it will not open
                          Higher and Higher
        Through the heart
                    And still
O Meliselda up your mountain
Down your other side

✪

Tarzah, that is, in the language of the fulfilled, the land of yesteryear, at hand, or, of distance overcome equally in all directions, as is stated, Whereof is desire years, thereby is distance effort, so is the palm tree the climb of climate, the visible inflorescence of invisible ache, and thus the interpenetration of worlds, as is said, Now dreams, which still were are to be, yet stay, that is, *Tarzah*

.

we first said hello to each other and started talking in the back seat of the car taking us into town, and I asked him finally, I said to him, there's one thing I do remember I've always wanted to ask you, your <u>voice</u> sounds like his, I noticed when we first started talking, when you were at Cal did you know another student in linguistics, but actually he wasn't in linguistics he was in philology, romance philology, but he was a student of that same teacher you knew, Yakov Malkiel — and he said, you mean the one with the wife who wrote that fascism intelligence report when they were in Germany but South — where was she from — Puerto Rico, I said — yeah, he said, that's the one

✪

so comes a crane into the hand

and from their fountain in Strøget
they descend and dance till even the Mallards of Absalon
come up out of the canals and stand entranced
cantilevered in the cattails of Amagertorv

✪

so now there is no cup to go to
and all the soap has come uncarved

            •

how far away the old hearts seem
so hard upon the heart they ride again

            •

the cup and ball of hearts
in Mexico the rod and barrel
the old streetcorner
high ache
only the times you do it right
count

✪

a *feeld ankker* he called it
holds me down out there when I get too loose
get the heists the lifts the laughs like I used to roll
all around all over the floor that's so that
big finger don't carry me away

✪

dark as the broadaxe people's
Eastern home, still against the Vordingborg
against Knudshoved's shore arriving

early in the Spring or late in Summer
a day as dark as winter and as wet, the welcoming
the warning pyres not set

and those who are leaving

IN EXCELSIS BOREALIS

1976

for Mike Carmichael

I

wet cold Sunday, the 4th of May

flame from the empty eye on the page
knot between the hand and the always distant mountains
over the cornstalk on the ant hill, once again, below vision
well, as if the palm lay open, and where the fingers curl, clouds
      flames try to reach
knot hole, fence page, shoulder against the boards

cold cold Duluth, quivering iron vault, facing the Northern Shield

Ohio St Lawrence, Kansas, the end of the 50s, when Either/Or was the
      choice between eating enchiladas at El Matador North of the river
      and shitting in the gas station john at 6th and Vermont "there
      went a pint of blood and not even any coffee and sandwiches" or
      not being equal to the living at all

to the taste, to playing tag beyond the belt of the ballplayer
      in the courts of the Morning Lords
          stone, impervious, too delicate to duplicate
          circling, backpack to girth
          alone, incessant, devourer

beyond the fire and through the fire the circling ass-chillers of the
      Lords of the North dance on the Shield
and the tiny tiny almost invisible warmers of the moss watch with the watcher

hard ball of the day gummy touch ball of the night against the impossible ring
      far up on the wall of the court, captain, fish painter

«and they remembered sometimes that the best in this kind are but shadows
      and the worst no worse—»

    "but give me the winter time, when the snow is on the ground"

«— if imagination amend them»

in the curtained bed chamber in the living room of the Palace
    "I traced her little footprints in the snow" Bill Monroe
    himself speaking on WWVA in the distance to the already
    disappearing backwards arriving Manitou

    "for I found her when the snow was on the ground"

«whimsicality, laughter, sarcasm»   the nervous scherzo
    "I'm fast but I don't last"

the 1st grade Knot Hole Gang at the end of the war
    ring-eyed like their dogs, watching beyond the fence

        insubstantial, simple, glory

2

the limits of conversion compose the lineups of the Lower Kaw

"they ought to play Miles' *Solea* from loudspeakers on every streetcorner"

but there could be no preparation for the exhausted laser

the current returns and returns
    year after year of kids poised on that hill

        not just excitement

the bombedout freakery of ownerless collection
    not ever knowing the makeout next

3

Sieur Du Luth

Peter Caws

Rozanov

simple, hopeless things, probably

camping alone in the woods

to] listen [ing

It's autumn in the country I remember

winter, motionlessness, perfect zero, [then] enter

photographs of an evening at Grier's
summer 1959? 1960?

hjælp]   not with any but the inner

William Baines in the snow

way past that age, though, when to die young

but what was in the hand and held out
at 36

Edward Leithen / Tweedsmuir
on the last adventure

not to come back

4

reach, after, spirit

        across the Shield
        following the fires

not to *find*, as well *here*

but North, spirit, share

5

down the hemlocks and crossed the lake
    to carry your barge on inland

to handle the rhetoric of graduation
    meet the charge

           where only one of you would go when you died

and all the times of ever making love
together make the will

ARCHIPELAGO

November 1976

For Ruth, again

My deep thanks to the following editors and publications for first using these poems from the fall & winter of 1974 and the spring and summer of 1975 (often in differing versions): Jonathan Williams, *Maderia & Toasts for Basil Bunting's 75th Birthday*; Paul Kahn, *Besoar*; Eric Mottram, *Poetry Review*; Larry Goodell, *Fervent Valley*; Pierre Joris, *Sixpack*. A longer poem from the same period, "In Excelsis Borealis," has been printed by Stephen Sandy's White Creek Press, Eagle Bridge, N.Y. ¡Saludos Y Abrazos!

«All that we *are* is in our love. It is an archipelago,
and its islands may be visited each in turn.»

—Walter de la Mare

The Skald

1

so woke from the dream of
galdr charm   *gala* sing
young and alone on a long road
and the sleeper seldom the victor
I-forget the heron hovers
men must speak of what men do
flame quickens flame
what happens cannot be hidden
the Arch-Bowman graces
Eye of Archer   Weight of Arrow
across Song's Steelyard
Reacher of the Song   Reacher of the Flame

2

awake early   wove words
heaped high   cairns of praise
made boughs   leaf with speech
across song's fields   not soon to fall

✪

Sweden, the crowns
or how much come I spent
fucking you in the ass

October, later, October
the cold calls travel
or held of me, you

or Núñez, *on the road*
there is no way to know
but go back on to

✪

rain and warm across the Northern Appalachians
        as far as the Lakes
the Prairies 40° yesterday 80° at Atlantic City

Gieseking's birthday 1895, Ruth's brother's funeral
        a year ago, the First Arabesque

and so seek many homes of the spirit
        whether it is one
        or bundles, restless

the high plateaus, the High
        Plateau, The Rio Grande

✪

through the Ry-o Grand and by rug merchants down

Christian passes East and West rock St Vartan

crown behind call Núñez

Moctezuma and St Olaf Christ

the knight is dying in his bed, and with a stone beside

✪

and there beyond the brocade wall
         crossing the eyes   "we got onto

    acid trip years before the third don Juan"

              "yourself or better with someone else in the mirror cross

and the third eye overlap stare into first it's

              and then focuses"

    and your face over mine not ours and the cloud, say

         not the light but with the glow, say the

    and now feel *that,* follow that

         fountain pen straight in the lecturer's face

violence is quickness   the sting of the tail   Mars

                   in the closeness of living together

                        the ascendant how quick

         and fall

and now that way without remorse and without   "No, I'm not mad, I only

get mad at something important and nothing a human being can do

is that important"

how easily I have forever talked to you

romantic *forever* to learn *for*

and does not talk of love or fucking but

impeccable   no getting used to

★

1

until there is no other place to go and at that place
dance before death

the only place where you can go both out and in

power is *stored*   *is home*

but every particle

2

I am no crow, hath not th'advantage

etc.

and you across from me

also the

✪

the lion in the sunlight kneading with his paws an unseen

    West, the Old West, Springfield and beyond, Edward Taylor barely edged of wilderness

        in the bare, straight December   eyelash blinking

            iridescence, old

                restlessness and patience, not continent, not

                    only continent, breaking the patterns

with his paws turning the unseen

                    the Wife of the House breaking the pattern of the spirit

Taylor meditating before the spectre of his congregation at the edge of

    to break down to let in

                    at the Beginning of Empire the Lion   looking looking

        into the dark between his paws   West

           and we at the knead of the humbling of the spirit

at the wavering of the dissolution of unsure intent Imperial

              to let in

      ✪

     .

      a bed of strings by phone across the continent
      now sleep on home in each
      the stands of the rocks of talk number 18
      rune straws

.

make love to return

but no more keeps than not

.

tight
situps against the winter
by night
your face by day
not dreams not a
stringing's worth

but, well, we'd *make*
I always said, and you
"not into that
building kind of" but
now, across

.

as if it ever only
sexual, and we laughed
as if that were ever
only

.

the so endures

the redwood sorrel

stems of the bed

the eucalyptus runes

of the West

our twice nine openings

rocks by East

•

at the other end of the bed

only to go back

wake in power

•

✪

"they were too   terrible   to cry"

to carry the weight of the circle of heaven
on squared shoulders

             what's important to write about's
             to joke about

             the pot of hot fat in
             next to the ice-cap liver

place certainly *not* recollection

             Eastern Baltica, Sarmatia, Livland, Hiiumaa

             the Barrier Canyon
             crack to emergence

             breakfast cereal grain
             grit in the graves

and so steer

✪

how unavailable I must have always been to you
being so available

> strictly sentimental, and insistent
>
> and some selfish head

the tenderness lasts still though
the hardest to come to

> and without sentiment, and no
>
> SM over embarrassment

the intellect of heart has no memory

✪

all that graciousness isn't tenderness
that's violent and careful
and always touch

so let the bed take off where it wants to
not just the dream but the double

never a family of my own
but those I know
"give me an order of french fries
2 cokes
and a home, to go"

✪

and follow you into the underground out of the heart

no way to talk tonight, yearning
for the only body
lost not lost

I thought I was
you rubbed off on me
into you

for the return of the affections
the boat of the sun
leaping over and over
but no recovery

the despair of ineptitude, earned
not answerable but distance

as if it were hopeless and despair alone
any hope

and it is hopeless, but no debasement, no slavery
facing to break the

one way to surrender the self and come close to

but I love you, not the pain
and not the being in love

[homage to Edward Schafer]

sit at the edge of the tub and watch her
out of the porcelain gleam into the water

drain of drains, reign of lime and orange
against the vodka scales

Mystic, still, willow

it doesn't seem enough and so it isn't enough

lacking the self, I said that to, and knew

I wouldn't answer otherwise until

    .

and not for dreams but only pay attention once again
or that my father's beard was white the other night
seeing him sitting on a bench beside the door
the weakness to admit the shame of only *seen*
and then not change the life because

    .

past 2, the bedtime brandy and soda still to tell
Munch peering around the corner at himself
down the fjord midwar 2 am
musing that mirror, and the woman in the bath, and still
not the old, no, not to say the *old* words, but the rise of

[for C.O.S.   18 July 1975]

to fuck, always
and to live with God, way

and missing Grand, Rose
fathers' intelligence
exactitude shared
over Sharon

love, more than the Earth

in her service

[from Ghālib]

Fuck it I'm crazy
        not in love
but that's more attention
        just for you

But never *any* chance of
        love-making?
each time irritation's
        retaking?

405

Lightning
        life
quicker
        heart

And I will make obedience
        habit
disinclination
        yours

O God just let the skirmishings
        continue
even never meeting catching sight
        enough

Never
        another you
or long ago already
        long ago

And if what I think is grief
        is fire
how long the open eyes of stars
        toward the other side?

CALL STEPS

Plains, Camps, Stations, Consistories

Many of these pieces were first published (often in differing versions) by the following editors and publications: Robert Bertholf, *Credences*; Fred Buck, *Bezoar*; Paul McDonough, *Glitch*; Jed Rasula and Don Byrd, *Wch Way*; Mark Karlins, *Text*; Bradford Morrow and Nathaniel Tarn, *Conjunctions*; Nathaniel Mackey, *Hambone*; John Moritz, *Tansy*; Charles Bernstein, *Paris Review*; Jonathan Greene, *Truck*/Gnomon birthday collection for Jonathan Williams; Bruce McClelland, *Trumps*; Donald Powell, *Padma*; Richard Blevins and William D. Shields, Jr., *Zelot*. Three pieces also appeared as broadsides, printed by Jed Rasula in Los Angeles and by Tansy Press and by Helen in Lawrence, Kansas. Another was used on a poster prepared by Diane Hueter-Warner for the Lawrence Arts Center. An earlier version of *Orexis* was published by Station Hill Press. To all those concerned, for their kindness, care, and encouragement, the author wishes to express his deep thanks, and as well to those responsible for the production of the present book, most especially Curtis Dillon, John Moritz, George Quasha, and Susan Quasha.

in the life
in the work
for

Robert Grenier

shadow substance one
as is in the wind

Thomas Meyer

mind's flame dissolves
heart's icy sleeve

Gerrit Lansing

This *and* this *we say and do*
and so we fix each other up and this *is how transcendence is.*

◆

Quae tibi, quae tali reddam pro carmine dona?

For such song, what gifts in return?

—Virgil
(tr. Stanley Lombardo)

To return to this work now and offer it, a dozen and more years since its writing, is to reaffirm all its dedications (the *dēdicāre* and the *deik-* — the proclaiming and the justice: the pronouncing) and all its debts, formal and implicit, throughout — *in the life / in the work,* and to come.

✴

What humility is there then in saying 'as best I know'? It is in an intoxication that I exclaim this. Speech rushes up from the bewilderd soul, out of knowledge, to claim its place in the vastest harmonies.

— Robert Duncan

What is not gathered is far more — perhaps the main thing.

— Walt Whitman

In vain we hope to be known by open and visible conservatories, when to be unknown was the means of their continuation and obscurity their protection.

◆   ◆   ◆

To weep into stones are fables.

◆   ◆   ◆

To live indeed is to be again our selves... Ready to be any thing, in the extasie of being ever

— Sir Thomas Browne

道 可 道 非 常 道
Lodehead lodehead-brooking : no forewonted lodehead

— Lao Tzu
(tr. Peter A. Boodberg)

[Lawrence, 1991]

Den Gåvan heter Avstånd
O du, som är stor i kärlek
du fanns där
och du gick tyst förbi

That Gift is called Distance
O you who are strong in love
you were there
and you passed quietly by

— Gunnar Ekelöf

OREXIS

HEREDOM

toute la vie terrestre procédant du feu est attirée par le feu qui réside au centre. Nous avions voulu qu'en retour le feu central fût attiré par la circonférence et rayonnât au dehors: cet échange de principes était la vie sans fin.

all terrestrial life originating in fire is attracted by the fire that dwells in the center. We had desired that in return the central fire would be attracted by the circumference and radiate without: this interchange of principles would be eternal life.

—Gérard de Nerval

lobe of opalescent glass
        broken in the irreplaceable lampshade

out of the shoulder, the corridor
        down the street the kids from junior high
                come by in t-shirts for the warmth of February
                                        pigeons overhead
        stamp and cry in their sleep

gathered, the branch of acacia
        fused through the green swirled
                Egyptian thorn milk waters
raised, itself, of the lost and gathered body of mastery

or all the high school years again, unslept, reviewing the annual faces over and over
        till they run green in the movies after the eyes are closed
                and still as distant as they were in person

                        the society of ordinary
                high school days, never left, will it?

                        against the society of the widow's son, those
                        who on the elephant's back
                                be freed?

the generation of mourning doves' cries
        is from twilight in the mind
                        releasing and attracting us

✪

parsley

        pubic hair above the bread
            body torn to pieces and thrown at the audience

      or where the sun is gone
        or where we watch the empty place we were

claimed by the garden
      work to right again
        to grab the rock hair green
          up out of the dirt

grabbing against and to be in those rites
      whose body in the bed, whose car lights down the street
        through the monk's cloth curtains
          or by the corridor of the shoulder

        every bundle of the exultant stride of walking home

✪

in the life of the laundry   the hand goes down
                                              into the patch

            upside down the parsley hangs

              and very very young the mothers are
              one kid already 3 or 4
              the one her mother calls "hey asshole"

        we want to watch where each master *was*
          the shape of the space left
             just a curl of smoke behind
Aaron's cigarette in front of the brazen serpent, or some dope, or the cold in on the breath

        in the same room

[for Mary Josephine Buffington Newman, 20 Jul 1884–20 Feb 1977]

in the well between our houses
      where the houses have gone to stare
      away from all their inhabitants

three violinists play your procession away
      under the pear tree, under the liriodendron
      under the ghost of the pear tree

the well of roses, the well of iris
      out back, down the alley
      down the ravine the waters carry away

    •

call of the Frisco diesel in the middle of the night

answering cry in the pigeons' sleep

waking not in a sweat but the smell of the sweat of waking

so far the call

✪

even so the wavering fires

                                                        now just ordinary flameshaped lightbulbs set in a
                                                            triangle, purposefully crude and bare

                       but as a child it was the unexperienced richness
                               that made wonder

            in the palm of the youngest entered initiate
                   without asking in the dark pupils watching, unseen

           Light can be ordinary even when revealed and still by the spoken word
                   astound the body least of all attended
                             out on the playground

                                   I dropped the bag of groceries I didn't even mean to bring
                                 I shit my pants *after* coming down from under the pine trees

           from the old authoritarian high degrees of Europe
                   one aging man left to confer

           the camps, unattended, meant Westward

kept going on the decks, dark adepts at the flames

✪

children of excitement
purses of the abandonment — not *yours* but *you*

           the Prince of the Captivity with a defective brain
           chased down the street by his father
                   oblivio-naked to the usedto judgement of the kids looking on

the jewel hangs from a rattle string
        a broken rattle rayed with stars coming out from behind the occultation

and bars, like candy, out of prison

                sperm
                        might as well have been hyacinth jizz or dandelion
                fuming on the palm

the man that might have been
master still and covered, to rise again

✪

early Summer in SE Kansas
                        the second weekend in April, Good Friday, 85°

        broiled in bourbon before the Council of the Emperors of the East and West
                hickory smoked in almonds, and the redbuds in glory, call

    and in the temple to be the temple substitute after the temple destroyed
        and until

    not of Jerusalem yet of a secrecy within, of Jerusalem
        such election, which takes that history as its own
                as ordinary and electable, rare, attended, as each tulip
                        each hyacinth passed, to each grape hyacinth, kinless, except

is still just beginning Spring

                        and in the temple, under the immense weight of tulips
                                the lights are extinguished
                                        and the halls for the space of three days
                                                wait dark in the heart, cool

✪

from The Camp the cries of burnt Templars
      rise into a canopy of transparent tintinnabulating leaves
          over the tents of the *tengu* and outward
             over the nonagon of the body, over the levees of patrol

you've probably caught sight of The Camp at times
             coming unexpectedly into a clearing and looking up
        the quick flags
             thinking a fairy ring of mushrooms
               or Kim's Red Bull on a Green Field

but it does not remain to the eyes
      or even, since there may be no other name, at all
and yet returns

it might have been having word of an old high school friend
      living in New Orleans now, grown large as his father
      that I circled Louisiana last night, marking only
         a couple of tents, or banners, or worn places in front in the grass
          named by the friends I knew were there

it is said as the troops move about The Camp and take up their positions with their
                  speeches taped to their spear shafts

        that the seven is empty

         so there is a space to look out on
             from the beasts and the heart and the ark between
                  the palms
          and into from the tents

         where the shade and choir of torment
          make an alleyway of repose to walk in
             from the work done, in the pause, on

422

to the anticipation of the ball lying just out of hiding
around the bend
and the shot clear to
but not to any hole in the hand
or the eye, waiting

The Camp if it is a camp rotates slowly on an axis
not the Grand Commander or the Mill of the Heavens or the Transparency
of the Tree
or all the Years of Reunion Rituals
that are the pole of the body

        ✦   ✦   ✦

✪

across the street, in the next block North and East, next door to Howells' old place
next door to Jents' old place

a new van, chocolate brown and cream, parked out front, everybody standing around
looking at it

the Prince of the Captivity ran just there

Princess now, raced past me as I came back from Whiteside's last Thursday afternoon
her mother just after her, calling

so the word is passed on
and equally not known
till how much later, the thrill of recognizing can still be known

the iris guard young flesh, probably

RUNNING LIGHTS

—nun ists, als wäre mein Herz um Meilen hinaus-
geruckt, ich seh viele Dinge, die aufbrechen und die
Richtung nehmen darauf zu—, aber ich erfahre
nicht, daß sie ankommen.

—now it's as though my heart had moved miles away,
I see many things that start and head off in its direc-
tion—, but I don't learn of their arriving.

—Rainer Maria Rilke

race of readiness before o'ertaken
Josephson's sungod's mirror's
I grown dark, I like waking
dark dots

rapt patience in the sun, not our lives
the *old* Grier drunk and raging
made as a warning
braineaters wait at the stone garage

a halohaired youth and return to youth
aloft in the breast of the *tengu*
come back «as halfwits
or as miraculous»

guardian of the lifted crystal thermos
instruments «of mountains, of huge trees»

sing with the taken

hard to believe just some shaved plain chocolate
all them days'd come back again, all of us saying we're the other one
                              claiming to be the right one

cruising up and down between the dinner hour and the first picture show
                              window shopping, arguing
hell I never known none a that love you said I took shit

earlier it was "Denmark," later it was old high Plateauro
long long after we was kids

right here's the river rind
after the corn

and on that road only a little time at the meeting to look around and see where we are
    as we talk
and smell the asshole smell of fucking mixed in with clover on very small dark hills
    and rain
and jars in the distance to fill again and then set straight and for that too only a little
    while

sometimes it's lying there in the mud at the start of the path
sometimes there's just a dent left in the dirt

you can hear the tennis balls thwack behind you as you look
the serious songs of summer end sung nervously and tight

big brown egg of a bear you can just smell the damp fur through
pale pink underfingernailfleshed smoothgrained egg of a flying pig
                more delicate and graceful than any wingéd creature

428

✪

Frog Ben Webster, wet Kbhn, unsad persistence
as glory, gone, held on to, unlost

«writing *that* kind of poetry»
«out of small irreducible sensual wholes»

&I, by carnal hope
«without even listening to the inborn tendency to dominate»
by cardinal home, an eye

in the wee small hours of the bed   enjoy the cold clear storm

vouchsafed, led

unthunder, jewel

all that *high old net*
you'd just as soon slam into & forget
o'motions

as easily the rain back

✪

three streams in the Northern Kingdom
only the last left to cross

but the heart wants somewhere else
much as it just keeps on looking, pleased with the view, it won't cross

North, or you could call it straight ahead
the coaxers calling
come on, come on over, use the spillway, just under the flow, it's ok
hands out

but no, not yet

429

turn West instead, down to the street where the big fur slot machine taller than a
    man's head
figures return up out of the blankets spread out to sell

and in the South two inns, a night club and a diner, side by side
too early to be open except to sudden friendship in the dark
hard to get any sandwich parasols, any sandwiches, even
and then set out for the giant cottonwoods on the Northeast heights

I don't know the East

it's as much to say it's all a flag

geranium crown above the walrus ivory king
upon a green baize ground
flattened across the palm of the *jism*

but even granting allegiance to the clarity, the days of true experience, the whole life there

     the heart yearns another cause

★

's

bear'shead slot   congruent with   watches' lamppost showrack

on the street

   to renew at a time of the dump of cities

                       meeting

«carried as one room of air around us»   a rite out of 18th century
I thought when I wrote that was component   rot of privilege
  of an opened Western shore
    still possible to discover new   suppressed city
                Point Reyeses

heart, too, of revolution

baculus virtual   where «air» = pneuma
                   virgin branched   from each to each   off the top of the head
                   verga flowered *cojones*

                                                   and the feet share
wire rite   gladly given will
                        radiate

         «men loveable men»

         «inviolable in their promises»

✪

blood in the clouds means   whatever all the failed shots with the rifle
                                                                              fail
                   "just your big career of interruptions"

                              whose *jism*
                                   it was *to get it back* took aim

     from squirrels, or people so far off they're small as squirrels, flicked tails, quick as
                                                                              squirrels

         and be filled

         and later on the song the other side they sang so sad
                 the heart took heart, the rooms it carried
                            into one with
         squirrel and rabbit, crow and duck and toad and mole
                 home stomping in the mud

✪

morning   "sparks 18 feet long off the grapevine"   *news?*

        doubled under me to eat

               tents raised and struck
               all night long across the bed

to "heaven's radio, on the other shore"

     autumn calls travel — K-F-A-L
             -ken
      that oa-   to-   flute of leaves
             -ten

the ball game of the continent
    «Captain, fishpainter»
      high up on the wall

           writing with a ballpoint hardon

     whirling, sparkling

       transparent as an asshole

      tip it is

«and so those values once masked by shock enter into the judgement of a later
      generation»

★

«it never *even* entered my mind»

                all this time, the filagree again
                the ceiling lace of virgin acid

                nasturtium, geranium, hyacinth
                tilth of grass

or had so slight a song to go on had to fuck it up

                        the up returns
      and *thy* redemption to say *even*

                     «partaken of the banquet to which
                     the invited guests did not come»

[variation on *L'homme armé*, i.e.: «o the man, the man, the man of arms he fills the folk with dread alarms» etc.]

passed a lean tall man in the woods with a big dark eye
dark as cars in a sleet storm, hooked and dry

looked for him to show up later in the library john or up using the copy machine by
                                                                the book return
glaring people away

wouldn't want him here telling stories when the snow storm cut us off
but Lordamercy find out, what's he *say*

cold water and mud, clear to the bone
worry you straight on out of your home
                              permanent

[towards an homage to John Dunstable]

& my my tongue waggle with the like power to share the roads
and in the tavern with the dogs
share the fading away of the voice from the heights
as the mass made
sung off

as winter comes on
our fate to have the coldest moon born in us

434

& turn wanting to know the other man
fast as the hand'd ever move, there
the emptiness of life its gate, left far behind
the knob slid down the bar, without a word

the West lit, the laundry gone, thereby the call

great ring year, horse rolling on its back, feet up in the air
now this way now that, on the finger in the depth of the eye
and step forth into the goatfish ocean, cold churning at the balls

talk to me, but I won't answer
only smile, stoned stranger at the party, on the sofa in the corner
roseweave throw over the shoulders and the silver lamp lit

comes the speaker soon, whose staff like a camp lifts
and gives liege to the stones that exalt the breath

& if the face is pale

now mercy is the gone
upon our snow

ERRATICS

Et comme un oeil naissant couvert par ses paupières
Un pur esprit s'accroît sous l'écorce des pierres!

And like a nascent eye covered by its lids
A pure spirit grows beneath the skin of stones

— Gérard de Nerval
 (tr. Robert Duncan)

Kanske Gudinnan av hyn
     ✦   ✦   ✦
i blanka vårdar

Perhaps the Goddess of skin
     ✦   ✦   ✦
in the polished headstones

— Harry Martinson

[overheard]

— you get any more calls back here than you did just thinking about being back here?

— it's probably got more to do with wherever who's asking, I mean it's more a place in me than all these people I don't know?

— like Lehnhoff s wanting to take you out to dinner?

— and all those "family" boarders waiting at home to deal with first, a lot worse than any momma or poppa to get out past — who says Lehnhoff s Lehnhoff?

— who is it then, Big Daddy?

— why, because he asked me out to eat, and it's all in just the first letter of each word?

— yeah, and it's a ritual — cipher, monitor, and that they were *given* to you — now, while you're still alive, to lead you out

— no no no no, it's like all the same *there*, nobody's *after* me here any more than, actually *less* than I'm after *them* — and anyway, it can't just be age or poppa or filthy blue deer, or I mean blue boarders, or big blue balls, or who's dead and who isn't, but *everybody*, and *really*, the question is how we ever get *back*

— "bring me an orange soda, with a little order of hot sauce on the side" — you got out sliding down a pole outside your bedroom window when you were 5

— no, that was *in*, I got *out* by realizing it was just a dream and I wasn't going to hit the bottom — right where the redbud is, just exactly where that redbud is now

— you think the pigeons're making room for you every night stamping and moaning and carrying on up there?

— more than likely, they've brought the plaster down on me twice already and probably will again

— but look, that's not it, is it, we're losing track, it's the call, and the call is too, is just like you said it was, only you were asking for it, you were praying for it — *only pay attention once again*

[Heredom]

my farewells of vacancy of mind

                later I'll come back to what's been kept there

                but the sad corners of rooms, up near the ceilings
                that will not ever return

my own lost skin
that will not be redeemed by another inhabitant, nor redeem, nor haunt

                but meet again, not turned away
                out of the glory of the woodwork

[«the Heron of Oblivion»]

the mirror at the culmination of the old degree
beyond the staircase, after the lecture of each step's toppled columns reerected
in the dark then, afterwards, alone in the closet beyond them
left to meditate on the iron ring's death head first seen and now again, the blood rust

> at the culmination of the 2d of the old rite
> at the top of the stairs in the sudden light
> instead of the expected guide
> the candidate, yourself, in a mirror

.

so Robert Duncan's propositions of the mirror in *The Venice Poem:*

"Imaginary Instructions":   1: «in the poem as mirror — the whole world,
                                            an instruction.»

                    2:                          «in the mirror
                            the Part —
                        consternation of a whole world.»

                    3:      «a realistic image
                                as if that virgin upon St Agnes Eve
                                had seen
                                old Nobody
                            wearing a face in the mirror.»

                    4: «the mirror as imitation, as poem»

        «Yet here seeks the heart solace.»

                            «seeing already
                                more than Love's mirror shows»

            «as if only here,
                here it might rest»

441

✪

I met the Angel Sus on the Skin Bridge
the Bridge Chinvat, offertory
my image crossing the basketball court and taking the path into the woods
and at the other end, in the gravel at the bend of Terrace Road
more expressive than the small red heart-shaped lips of the Lizard Mother, your
    endlessly mobile face
snout cloud of light and bristles thicket of impenetrable brightness
and smile of infinite frenzied utter patience
nostrils as close to my brow as opened clover
only a face! only a face! only a face!
wings but the knot clod sfumato uncertain noose clothing
over the skin we share, organ me you share
was it John telling me to turn to you, in crowded Houlihan's on
    the Plaza, with Charlie and the bears in the dark
brought me to you, you came out this far to meet me
where the VW's been parked since at least last March and the horses' empty field
    comes in close and the houses begin
"You must make me the Clean Compound
first, before you pass through me"
each to each?

✪

slowly the old stone building walls downtown dissolve
dropped in the pond of wind in the August noon
slow slow motion salt castles by the time the stoplight changes at 7th and New
    Hampshire
from the eyes the old world goes, across the river the cables of resistant skin, tight
    enough to walk on

the young who work to bare the body soft again as the crown of geranium petals fallen
no heaven that might redeem the past but only make way over and over again for the
    protection flowers give to age at all
to what it hasn't yet accumulated, most of all

the speed that ungoos the eyes is some reward, certainly, out of the South with the wind
as age comes up out of the ground polar as the brain lode at the same time as it goes
    back down in under the feet again

homegrown handtipped dervishwhirling in your own living room without getting
    dizzy or sick, taught by somebody in the speech department who goes to Naropa
    every summer
where such things usually accumulate, at the end of August, not an early time at all,
    but late as fatherhood
Excelsior as the tight foreskin of what desire's called o'er-reaching that never knows its
    own phone number
and continues at the mercy of, at the mercy of, at the mercy of
savage as the «endless rumination of the Big Vegetarians» wasping the lateral world of
    vision to the narrow waist of instant jumpup Whizz
and over all of it not even a guardian moth or a gnat but probably just the flick of a pig
    with wings, quicker than jizz sop

[homage to Andrei Bely — *the memory of the memory of speech*]

so came to old friends' shapes and voices playing soul

host theophanic *caro mio spiritualis*

lost deference before the images of power nor gained

every association with who seem to be

whole coat loan the rite of purge transition

ache of *the street rooms* on the road home *parts of the body*

443

dealing presence equal to subsistence shared

work by the phone booth hand plates yearn for meat

cheap change the text books ritz construe

and all the me's the means to bridge -ceptivity made clear

the paths of ancient initiation are

[two postcard views — homage to the Gérôme and Van Gogh-Hiroshige Kriophoros]

from Timotha and Gerrit and Shannon

Hermes Ram-Toter enters the snow-filled clearing just after the duel has ended, the young fool in the Pierrot costume dying, the Hiawatha fullback slickster stumbling away with his second, stunned and mumbling — by the time they get to their car nothing will be visible but the mindbuggering freezing fog — and Herm Sheep-Finder comes up to the Pierrot and takes him out of the arms of his death-glazed friends, hoists him over his right shoulder and walks on off into the woods, the masquerade costume falling away leaving the body naked — between death and the ram, kouros-lean, that passes under-standing

•

the land and the sea that keep the bridge arched level slant violently upward to the left, that Northwest, or Home Against Fall, as the view from aloft banks to the right for the limitless ocean — and to cross the bridge goes on out of sight into the rain, probably even curves back again somewhere further on to this same shore — three go crossing, three coming back, bent under the drench, wet fleece under one arm, wet belly and flank against the neck, phallos hat, wingless, who can see Fortune curving migratory as the continents, bullet-out and -back

[given: three beavers in a tree]

by their long hair, as now my own a few gray strands joins
call the color age, or of the work'd, silver
above the waters? later the tree came into the living room and took on golden balls
    and butterflies
psyche'd opening   above the still-opening crown bud gold sun clearing the gold horizon
14 points of light   perfect elect, sublime   24 globes of month roads
preening their whiskers along the soft short needle spines
back into the   almost said and let stand for all *the other,* forest
but not trees either   sandy tracks into, hearing the ocean, might be
rocks clashing   still with the glacier energy unreleased roar surf
against the hills   their whiskers more silver than their hair that joins us
eyes, liquid, aloft

something like such wilderness as interstates tie
without a comb's at all dimension   look, you can't *join* us, *be* us
all your yearning of another body   keeps you going
up against *we see you*   where the splendor'd crown bud bursts over and over
we'll give you a ride in our *brand new automobile*
even let you be our *handsome driver at the wheel*
even the Boy Scouts know that, honor our award
so, slowly, secretly, we come back up the Smoky Hill, the Republican
the big *big* cars, in among the stars
where you see bonechina butterflies in and out among the golden balls

sweet heavy load to carry   you think of as despair to ever *say*
the *saylessness,* the *talk to me* that does not talk, months on end
truck load after truck load
castoreum honey in the graven shell
old base glory!   we gnaw down to tell

CICADA WOODS

Цитата не есть выписка. Цитата есть цикала.

A quotation is not an excerpt. A quotation is a cicada.

— Osip Mandelstam

THE WINTERGROUND

The Body in winter is the hunting lodge

— Edward Dorn

[rocks]

I

slowly melts the old composure
whodya *want?* whoya *after?*

        love and travel, love and exploration
        love and all that old net of sweet association
        and only the outcry *at* is known, can't see back past or on
        desperate for the wet smell, for the water love

all this in the life of the area driving around town all night to get laid or get drunk or
    get high or *get*

        walked into behind Hoch coming home from the library this
           afternoon and thought it was the night before last out from
           under what? *crown?* and into the open
        came to starting up the stairs in the music library

        you were there

wherever, not the music library, no
where I've always found you
facing you scared, shy, heart high
no matter I've known you already forever

11

and not as Lance Kerwin said in *James at 15* tonight, love's only truly love if it's shared,
    taken and returned
but that it changes then, makes *us* a difference

                                   unrequited vast histories of 15!
                                   28, 41!
                                   12, to get rid of and still encourage keep
                                        at it and you'll, *somebody'll*

pissing in the dark, hearing the voices from the living room

    .

distance? all that old distance to play all over again?

not over and not taken and not returned and not bearable *up close,* assuaged with red
    Korean wool and Atget?   taking *them?*

dear   —the hoquet—   *how*   *are you*   *there?*
    never enough   to live with   not even   to sleep with

      care?
  . . .   but *distance*

when we lived in the same town one month you threw me a birthday party the next
    not even an invite to your New Year's Eve
but all *sorts* of kindnesses and generosity

deep, *unbearable* affection?   except for *distance*

wearing the new red shirt you sent   rubs off on my underwear

III

the distance, the distance love
the through, the active through

and the middle voice
to see through oneself
where the verb is the you
and the self is the both of us
and the watcher is the I
and the distance the love, active through

but *to stand apart*

how close you are, how easily
I forget you, impossible
passing you, coming back

[for Jack Howell — 1]

we made the world together
as *grass*, and *bones*, and *thanks*

like the Frisco, and death, and Westerns
roulette on an upturned wagon wheel

cast like taking on the telephone for life
to call the stars

[for Jack Howell — 2]

there is a man in both of us
when we meet in dreams *others, others* is

and memory is oblique preparing for
being unprepared where

nowhere else can matter

hear my slow brother me
hearing me hearing all
tongue Thoth's turned from
ears bent over the table, cluttered

share increasingly
ineptitudes together
kindly even as to never
how many we are

how many of us got in the car last night
carrying Jack Howell's long dead dad too drunk to stand
out of trouble and took off?
and though the me at the wheel, the car drove us

all I of the family, how different from each other we are
not even in dreams do we know each other's dreams
or that we dream
the others call?

✪

the distance of love is one of the cracks in the year
help through, like smoke, like last night
wet the soul but not love the possible death
smelling like chase when the fever's irresistible
and get it right

[homage to Kasimierz Przerwa-Tetmajer (2 Dec 1865 – 18 Jan 1940)]

to be claimed in the end by the fate of some old poem
dying *its* life

the unprotected sop of experience for size
hot
shit!
hotter, for having been off on its own for 30, 40 years
come home

Fern the waitress and *the parking meters of July*
racing the melos to the final gasp

and go out tracking the wheel down the gutter muttering
something I forgot I wrote I forgot

for always talking home
the end is sure to be without
the soul, too level
wants to go *its*
down
and out

but *up one flight of stairs I long to climb*

and so *its* life *to go*
still slips which mine?

[a Valentine for Tom Meyer's birthday]

she would want to call me, far far indirection to my unready ears, to reach me, only if I won-
dered, *who* beyond *who* I heard, for all of us

                            "what about those heart's hands you whacked,
uh, walked off with" — clear as the stoplight, and no more — "you gone run over, that's un-
fullfilled"

               strength to hear whatever voices speak the truth to you, as part of
you, all up *till then, and on* — you really think that place you *got* matters, instead of what
you got to *make*, right now, *on?* it's made, no matters

                          she'd want to, only when I turned
away and wondered, who said that to who said that, by heart

                             made, no matters —
but do I ever really believe that, ever know it's done for sure, till afterwards? staring into
the future as if that were *ahead,* when she says, she says *who* to *who* she says, *my word ex-*
alts, nemmine

late in the Winter when thaws beginning Spring should long ago have started, the cold per-
sists, no more heavy snows but frozen mists, thin sleets, leftover snow grimy, brooding the
woods, the yards, the trash in upper rooms waiting for brighter, warmer days to be taken
out, bent over above the porches, waiting, for footsteps soon to come, and talk, up there

I used to go up in the late afternoons, not long before sunset, and sit in the bare attic, look-
ing out West and North, toward the river, the hills on the other side of the flood plain

brighter than anything else in the day, snowdark the woods — and watch till the after-sunset glow had vanished and the room was dark, the earth turn

the space of time in a life between a year of waking and a year of sleeping, to wake again, and then go downstairs, turn on the lamps in the living room, put on some music out of the shadows, make a drink, start fixing dinner — and the life too would come into the room, out of the burrow of earth under the snow in the woods, like the figure of a dog molded in snow in the woods, shake, and rouse itself, and come in

✪

how useless insistence *want*
when *heart* is *face* the *dream* itself entirely makes
share circling the shore
desire generation *attain* to exaltation, not possession
reed-girt, sun suddenly falls on

great wonder that we ever *saw* each other
or the face made not of yours and mine but all the crossing in
we still find, still look into

.

stirring chicken wings, staring out the kitchen window over a clear, old city
wings, those vanished communes long ago melted quiet down the farms to pits,
    stirring gathers in your eyes again, gin and ginger, lemon and soy, sweet hotcha
    ever name again

or pyracantha massed along the fence in back, how long to see back into that dark
    corner of the yard, watching the oven door, checking the brownies bake

skipping rocks out to sea
too bright to look at
at to face

✪

then pointed to the opposite hills, your true homeland, who carry, you, or you, them, unvisited, that oldest home, the buried sea, and hearing's ground, now here, and *now's* a few hundred thousand years or just this, now moved on, another ice, another job, another long haul, rocks piled up in hubs and spokes and rims to get back to the sky again, singing, shouting, stamping time, following the route signs up and down, up and down, *straight up*, like breathing, round and round and round and round, till that reach unsufferable return

•

two young runners cut the town from North to South, always brothers, always a pair, one with the pipe, one with the power stick held out in front, and ever on the distant horizon the redshouldered hawkheaded hounddog, in a big black Stetson, with the Sun Dance scars above each tit, turns his profile back and forth, back and forth, singing: *getting it on, getting it on, you always gotta keep getting it on*, then jeering, taunting, goading: *yahhh, leave it to me, leave it to me, sure, all you can do is leave it to me —* *come on, thread me, thread me, thread me, thread it on through me*

•

but it was still my fault we got lost, and when we finally did make it on to the next family visit, they kept asking, but what do yall *do?* o God, I said, I've tried *everything*, and never any luck — if I could fry cook fast enough I'd run for Burger King — o yes, she said, and what about the new place I keep hearing about, Prayer Burger? haven't the heating bills just been awful this winter?

over the cliffs it has to be, and toss this martial earth aloft, to empty out the hard-held heart and hands and reach, o brother clouds, your house above the sea, o sister earth, o sister sea

ÉTUDES

Brer Fox, he come up, en der lay Brer Rabbit, periently cole en stiff. Brer Fox he look at Brer Rabbit, en he sorter *study*.

— Uncle Remus

Die Sprache der Natur ist einer geheimen Losung zu vergleichen, die jeder Posten dem nächsten in seiner eigenen Sprache weitergibt, der Inhalt der Losung aber ist die Sprache des Postens selbst.

The language of Nature can be compared to a secret password that each sentry passes on to the next in his own language, but the meaning of the password is the sentry's language itself.

— Walter Benjamin

attractions, steady
old affections, renewed
as if forgotten
energy, memory
celebration, being able to
to say

✪

even that there
is someone there

dis   not of
tance   but from

some center lover
from time to time

we feel each other
cross

✪

time cold or
not to
trim the shag
lift the head
lightened to hear
the touch of
bear
the breath of
closening wings

461

✪

documents enter Winter *read*
bright lead carved dull
life *occult* strained steps
seed old shoes tracks
new graven brain sing
even old memoried *eye*
clean one time more

✪

the candle lit to
cast
the shadow tell to

tell the samba grown
celebrant, shadow
out of tune

✪

made out of distance
what it claims it to
stand apart

make out of builders a crown
climax coffee on a door
face grave houndom into human hone

✪

silver vessels in the bed
keep life of all the anger
making love
what string unlost
run through the pubic hair
surer than plastic
wrapping focus

✪

steps of the camp
mud element of trance
essence star of hippopotamus
walking the bottom of the river milk

✪

love left than a
weight lift then a
laugh less than a
way

love last then a wait
less than a left
laugh weigh than a lift

love left than a weight
lift less than a
laugh last then
away

[2 variations by Bob Grenier]

love left of a
weight less than a
laugh lift of a
way

love lift of a
weight less than a
laugh left of the
day

★

call snown draw   cold moon sawm

comb new leaver lean

so shadows dough

★

back into the darkening foliage trunks have gone
a man maybe takes sudden motionless
watching the swimmers past

★

cross to her
than knowing her

but the swirl
the sand under

★

smaller than almonds
bigger than peanuts
tears than hail
ground jaybirds bare

★

headed for the swimming pool
　　poorer than ever, maybe
　　　　but not without, though

kids go and throw towels
　　　　　　　　　　are but us

ever *who* on the way
like a tree holds, shows, from

★

　　　brood(s) the woods
　　　rear(s) the sun
　　　warm(s) the ball
　　　gone(s) the grass

★

　　　angelical
　　　fucking
　　　unexpected things
　　　out of
　　　ask it, not jizz it

★

　　　make a heart out of

　　　arca the shape of

★

                reach to the pell
                etudes peloria

                hunger the shavanon
                exports the calm to

★

but   orexis   eagerness   apprehension   study

★

                no one cares
                unless the world is *really* changed
                otherwise, *shoo*
                but we *bay*-rasst, er ah, we *lost*-uss

★

                gone to a quiet that hurts the toes

                once the hypnotist never knew was blue

                who thought a coast to glory?

[homage to Sōtatsu's *Bugaku*]

O I, left, right
red cloth, green
SW to or N to, W
mouthharp back or just flutes

O top I, both sides
door or rows

over or call the wet up seen
o tree right *o animal* left
ode all the uprights O'd
outsprung, unbōwed

& ear lobe told
just hold to be
or sway to weight
just tuss

✪

or a man carries a pot in near noon
turn stone, but he, uh, don't see no sun in it
and the watcher, just kicks from habit

like a rock cast in the sea
hard, and gone, long gone

✪

    & so'd see into the undersun   though grinder

    & trace a road where over again   low hold against thresh

    note *Urdu* means *camp* (Turki)

    where wasps over cottonwoods
    quit ashes ashes ground

✪

sadness   a wonder
     what is *full*

           sæd   sæd   sæd   pebbles   -ted

    aid thirst weary filling

                    to room?
                    -tiness?

so make me sad not of my own

    *un*satisfied, o'erflown

               'd

✪

dinosaur browse
the secret sentence disappearance
blood
hot to the hand

✪

one black currant seed in the teeth hole
another cricket by the *recencies*
between the leap
like petiole

✪

trees pass
bees press
clouds talk

hair calls
how long damp
cottonwood

✪

study is the gate of justice
in the doorway hammered zeal fingers the scales
three drops at a time, three more, forming
just sun of blood

✪

between what is seen (heard)
and what is seen (heard)
what is   (   )
otherwise

or didn't never so much pay attention to as change back and forth with, someplace else

✪

           dark urchin sun
           stretched heart yoga
           yoke between leaves

✪

           cottonwood lingerers
           still green
           tops
           still golden
           boys

           another life, high
           and with the roots of stones

[requiem études · for Louis Zukofsky]

word   boundaries   orenda
                    sumbur
                    «If they ask, it is you»

  ·

exalted   master
           asper
macbenac ma che ben' art' mackerinact
for 'im 'at's gawn awa'

  ·

o Swan over the dark stripes
where light
bright oil
                «To glow — not to grovel»

  ·

from *It Was* «"the country of Watteau"»
where everyone is just about to rise and go

light leaves like
black under wind

back of pagoya
& I-light, I-lid, I-through, back

  ·

take light & dark
up the heart
              «For the living»

STRINGS

for Ruth and Tad Palmer

David con unas tijeras
cortó las cuerdas del arpa.

David with some scissors
cut the strings of his harp.

— Federico García Lorca

[homage to Carolan]

or whether those words I'll never never be used by
or whether living with you those you's I never wrote to always apart, by

    •

they took down the poles for volleyball from beside the swimming pool tonight put up
    just for the party this afternoon
as the wine bottles and newspapers gone by with to dump leave smudges to

    •

long ago gave up home by the pole to

so how? by the in stant

and yet sweet distance by the love full

    •

even the eyes their goo to
even the hands their come and gone to

even the swept far far away from

    •

each other distance, each ours
as difficult by reference as by not knowing

each time, each name

    •

even the match stroke smell left long long after now
the hair as fine as children shared

    •

and all by being in the world incompetent
to pay for a life by earning

.

so take to bed the study of the child
and in that well the cry and bucket of the cry

.

a nightmare of *the man*, and another and another
and find the child, to raise, who but us?

.

and almost hear the hair the bone cannot
and never easily, but how willingly, to join

[for Charles Filiger's *Breton Cowherd*]

it might be Tad, the way he stands, the same age, 14, 15, but he'd probably have on clogs,
not sabots anyway, and not an upsidedown sailor cap with a striped band, but the same
faded blue denims, very well filled, head to one side, hand on hip, looking straight back
just barely tolerant between boredom and devilment, the instant of pure outward in-
trospective receptivity, like a saint

might be early spring, probably actually summer, but, early spring, the first buds on the
bare branches, cowless

.

so we will cross the fields' stripes
as the Swan crosses the first, last, darkest river

not to come back, certainly
but together?

•

and the image of the boy, the image of the young man, the image of the man
between us, gone on his way, through us

•

a young man's call and acquiescence from the bank
his middle age lamenting, still above, brought back again from entering

now a wanderer, then a wanderer, over the fields' stripes

[*embarras de*]

& would it be body to
make *zealous liberality* a gift that's taken from

& if & if & if
                    so smart

o why o why o why
                    aintcha

[homage to Johannes Bobrowski]

or other dark days, in front of the first entering initiate's quavering in front of first enter-
ing, unshowing—walk up to that door in the heart, too, dark even in the morning, the
morning spider not gone home at evening but not working across in front, only looking on

or ever work back through the crowds to the first seat high high up in the auditorium, still claimed with a bowler and a coat? fences fields and viaducts that way — or find the lost yellow robe, not for the robe itself, even though it still keeps the shape of right use and long wear, but for the message in the pocket — for this have we spoken with each encountered, of his poetry and in praise, to one, of the broadcast equipment, and the crowd at the door, to another, and mistaken clothing in the seats, and the path across the pasture — all this before everything gets started

a postcard of the Great Mosque, from Córdoba — Mt. Shasta at first light, from Oregon — two men bargaining for a horse, one of them just minding his whittling, from Cape Ann — a line of petroglyphs of riders on a canyon wall in Arizona, from Gallup — over all these, the Knight of the Sun, who is a Lion in Radiance but starting to turn away, starting to look on off over our right shoulders, slowly

once again brought before the first door at mid-September, the litter of just-yellowing leaves blown up against the threshold, shifting dark and light working underneath and gone, and the glitter of cottonwoods far off at the edges of the room, almost beyond the corners of the eyes

a door, and a dog that recognizes someone else and goes on into the room behind, and a sower, already for next spring, casting grass seed, in the shifting light, under broken clouds — knock 3 and 3 and 3, and each knock a drop hanging perfectly still in the air in front of the wooden panels

a boy there preparing to be a man in his mind reaches down into his pants and rearranges his cock in his shorts, takes his hand out and pulls his underwear down in back through the seat of his pants, walking on straddle-legged — noon time, still no rain, still some sun

perfectly still the widened shoulders at the corner, just the t-shirted back visible — in front of the door, he sees himself grown, in front of a woman, say, or steps down a hillside, and turn out of sight, and wasps circling there in the sun

and says to himself, *I trust the language of those who forget*

✪

dark warm day, what a door that is to walk out through, come down out of the North
during the night
                              you thought you could hear them singing, the wires in front of the
woods, the crunch of gravel in the drive
                                                        I could see you going down the front steps past
the tobacco bush and on out back to your bus, head down, listening
                                                                                        the wind up the
canyon, the storm through the oak grove and the doves and the great basins of water, the tide
clatter up the beach, the rain on the bay leaves, fingernails scratching the scalp
                                                                          and saw you
look into the surface of earth, the dark bowl coming up to meet the search
                                                                blowing their
skirts just through on the other side, who walk with Fall down out of the North, dark
and warm
                        and could hear you saying yes and yes and yes in your sleep, and smoothed
along the curve below your breast, listening

✪

what can trust take and wish were mine were yours
foolish most to only want to give to love

✪

restless, the rain returns, the bergamot smell faint on the fingers yesterday from the Guer-
lain *Impériale* after shaving, today in the word, looking in vain for any certain or satisfac-
tory etymology — smelling the 4711 lingering from following the curve of your throat and
shoulders with my fingers — about now you'd be having dinner in some corner of Greece,
the glass of cold water with the coffee afterwards, and maybe the cafe proprietor wanting
to introduce Italian ways serves the coffee with a twist of lemon, the fine citrus oil shim-
mering on the surface, filling the nose as the cup is lifted — bent over the well

into the dark depths, over the smooth-worn honey-colored marble rim, looking after where the stone has dropped, seeing nothing but the dark, hearing nothing after the rock splash but the trees, only the faint lemony bergamot-oil-in-cologne smell, dry as September, still suddenly abroad and gone — the face of us between us in the dark

✪

look close at who lies next to you taking away the twitching of the candle muscles in
    the thigh

so close to the wall the twitching does go by morning

lamb of the graven heart, look close at who passes through you, your sight
    illumination to

for those who in the dark reach through the thin almost impermeable membrane

[equinox variations — «by the sills of the exquisite flexible doors»]

petunia midnight purple throat
a life to share, more than, lit by, ever
crushed tomato vines ahead, burr of stramonium, hands unburying potatoes
kisses of capsicum, nic fits conquered, come and gone
the way out past what isn't ever guessed for
like
dependence
eggplant star eyes
Solanaceae heart glow

•

grass • well • piano keys : not glass or mirror scryed
but yoke • yoga : shouldered dark and light

•

leaning over, staring into the grass, into the piano player bending over the keys playing
    into the Limbus

not to see anything but squarely take the yoke of light and dark

chrysanthemum, petunia, cottonwood hold out and in, such yoga the clear voice tells
    is numbering

adding up your breathing in the dark against my back, the blades of grass, the shadows
    of the blades of grass

[homage to the Dodonaean Rilke]

the cold calls travel — with the gone? with no *one*, maybe a many — *bundles, restless* — some
work no hand to, but *having,* harden the heart to those who don't — all understandable,
core, even, of what we think of as *union* now — not any longer the *nation*, or the *North*,
though no matter here, in the question of: *protection* — even the craft, true — what broth-
erhood of travel, but death — *no way to know, but go back on to*

one reticence against another engenders sadness — and the excess, is *resented?* then re-
gretted — but no more revealed than not

    •

servant of the bowl, the wind directs the beater
who *tells* the racket means?
    sadness requisite? that fullness
    to overflow to oracle

481

✪

«Absents within the Line Conspire, and *Sense*
Things distant doth unite»

.

«Sure, there's a Tye of Bodyes!»

— *Silex Scintillans*, I

fog dreams, drop dreams, the fear of falling, singing, "Please help me, I'm falling" — and if the soul's natural movement is ever downward, deeper, what *fears?* we say we *fall* in love — the precipice of ruthlessness, the *love?* rather than *to, into, onto* some thing?

fog, and the cottonwoods do not glitter, though you can see them tremble — thins out over the woods, blown, then thickens again, and the cottonwood sapling by the tennis court stands for a moment clear against it, and the trembling very clear — but only in the heart the glitter

✪

might be an egg, or a lemon, gone on down the rapids — rays break out of back at those on the bank receiving — hand by the blood flowing, up to the tree with the bark scraped — not just one way, the share, the tree takes on the disease, but the hand crashes with the timber, or the eye peeled with the egg, or the zest oil — bobbing, in white water

✪

whether at fault
quaver at crack

the heart breaks
not the affections

482

each time

        winds oracle the body

                it hurts

nothing helps that does not help
the passing day pass free

to die
out through

★

well who the hell can I have here
from the surface of each sphere a fine mist joins each sphere, the grass grows out of
there is a set of wrath pits in the earth such force comes out of that seeks sun building
back into the iridescent bubbles when it rains

ahhh go to hell and stay there
yeah every blade of grass's got to be stared at and ridden sitting up all night on the bus
    can't sleep
God, I'm *sorry* I got pissed off, how can I live like that?
grass and rocks and dumb regret lead to the water's edge, turn around and look back.
    at the laundromat lodge, pays for getting clean

anger is focus, regret such mist, each drop

could transubstantiate the sudden terrible paternity of wrath
to the sudden terrifying joyful prodigality of love?

could ever love that way?

sweet iridescence of the pits?

[Winter saeta]

do you know the wound of the shoulder, hidden, that numbs the thumb, to ever let it go?

the keep of the bourbon that unlocks the spine keys, the little girl of the combs, secret
    arrow, far far up over the street, balcony finder, something good on tv nobody else
    can find out's going to be on?

                               she, too, counts leaves, singing
transfixes the apricot sunset, leaving season, you can taste

corn, and beans, makes the wind, chili, and tomatoes, colors

no animal system lately — and none ever expected — but circling the flagstone steps then
trap door to the underground where Pratt was, and I knew would be — uncle, connec-
tion — guide? — going down with and taking with, the young blond girl, yet knew, too —
girl-Ruth, little-girl-Ruth, but grown, too, and not Ruth (never looked like), but also
her — hardon Hermes came down out of the North and through Samothrace the mys-
teries there told why of, Herodotus said — Hermes Stiff-prick, Hermes Steel-dong and
Smile-face, head-only (but with his dick out — handless — you bring me off, I you, but
not ourselves) — square-in-ground — pink Sioux quartzite balls out of Minnesota,
tough granular testicles out of the North, in the Kaw plain loam scrotum — set up
around out in front of houses — Erratics-wayfinder, Erratics-lidless-painless, Erratics-
lead-off —but to become lid-open and pool-open, who came here over and under, be-
fore and after, river-easy-ways — now stationary, -heart stone? step by step into that
other-ground by all-around-town stepping on? — going under with, Ruth, being-little,
both, sharing sexy-yet-to-be-for, together, needing, kindly as the uncle ever would be,
-stone, -off?

[— and to Artemis]

so slight a lift, it seemed, the other night talking to you, because I couldn't think of what
to say, going on about botfly larvae peeking out of wounds, but each night since, and in
the day odd times, the towers rise, the resonance of your voice comes back in the stones'
slight vibration, moss in the cracks like the insistent distant electric-clock hum of traffic
on the freeway through the hand, or the pie baking and the pecans settling slightly, open-
ing to the chess thickening underneath, lifting —

O Goddess of the Airways, who hear,
over whose fine drawn hair the words string the continents and through whom the earth
rises to speak, the air returns, the fire spreads, the water cascades to vapor, at whose first
step in the woods the apperception of still pointedness tightens and is exalted, all rarity
of common numbers that takes the breath away and gives it back, above and below the
sight, the tree line, the fences to paradise unlinked and the children's use of just the places
they do use, again and again

take the felt slight rise of unlessening
love and hammer unlost in the blood that
step cut
shared

you give

Arpa
que tiene en vez de cuerdas
corazones y llamas

Harp
that has instead of strings
hearts and flames

— Federico García Lorca

BOWLS

Now polish the crucible
and in the bowl distill

—H.D.

form is cut from the lute's neck, tone is from the bowl
Oak boughs alone over Selloi

—Ezra Pound

a silence in the Central Tree
the leaves gone down the autumn flood and winter frozen
barest branch click
only occasionally

who left the prints? hearing us? we missed?

sap listeners   tree leavers   bark gnawers   wind freaks

from-the-sky-who-dwells-*in*-the-tree?   "foolish to think"

«earth-bedded servants of the unsilent bowl»   "people live there"

«and with unwashen feet»

birdless, empty   and yet the great space all
«packed full of ominous sound»

still
can you hear it
tell?

✪

I saw the Mouse King last night, and thought at first, he was so big, he was a cat
preoccupied with what to do about the mice bouncing three feet in the air thick
    around the toilet
I looked at him a long long time before I saw who he was
then he turned his head, rolled a whisker, arched an eyebrow, and smiled

we're in it together
bay-bee

so dance accumulate, alveolate home deep
    in the earth their heart listens
so sad rocks   so had the mantic   this is their bliss, in this delight the
the lost sea   brow-laid leaf to eat   living
    share in the light

·

great Mouse King, Apollo-My-Watcher
would have slain you if he'd known who he was looking at when he was still so pissed
    off at the myriad mice-mc-boing-boings pinning him down in the bathroom he
    couldn't see straight

wrath clouded granted second
    sight to recognize

so quick the rise   redemption give?

as know the tile glaze breaks under winter
    throne in that dark?

as unwitting gone into the coils of oracle's desire
    to heal?

as gnawed the sweat-soaked straps of war to found for exile
    home?

face of its own   whiskers rolled and smile own
    like of the hand up holding the head to figure out what the fuck, own
    own, the blindfold given, taken away
    own, the muscle taut to tell
    own, the like
    light, the own

[for Jonathan Williams' 50th birthday]

According to the *Vita Metrica* of his life, Pindar died at the age of 80 (probably in 438 BC). In the words of the Suda lexicon:

> His life ended as he had wished it to; in answer to his prayer for the finest of life's blessings, he met death quickly in the theater, lying in the arms of his beloved Theoxenus.

> [tr. Roy Arthur Swanson, *Pindar's Odes* (Bobbs-Merrill, 1974)]

Theoxenus came from an illustrious family of the island of Tenedos (present-day Bozcaada), South of the entrance to the Dardanelles. For his brother, Aristagoras, on his election to the ruling council or Prytaneia of the island, Pindar wrote his *Nemean 11*, and for Theoxenus this passionate encomium and declaration of love, one of his last poems (fragment 108 Bowra, 123 Snell, 131 Turyn). This version, it can't be called a translation, this paraphrase of Pindar's great condensed ode is offered with every debt acknowledged to the renderings in Swanson, in Bowra's *Pindar* (Oxford, 1964), and in Constantine Trypanis' *Penguin Book of Greek Verse* (1971) — to a poet for whom, in Whitman's words, «Bodies are all spiritual. — All words are spiritual — nothing is more spiritual than words».

> My heart, we ought to pick the buds of love
> when they fit our years
> but whoever just catches sight of the flashes
> burning out of the eyes of Theoxenus
> not carried off in the breakers of desire
> had his black heart hammered out of bronze and iron

in an ice fire
Unexalted by Dark-eyed Aphrodite
he drudges desperately for gold
or shameless as a hooker
flutters every street, propositioning the soul
But because of Her I am eaten by that heat

and melt like the wax of divine bees
every time I look at the fresh-fleshed youth of boys
Surely by Puget also
Seduction dwells, and Favo `
has brought up the son of Edgar

✪

our makers beside us
not the watcher, not the doer
not the union in us

> over the indented knotted tarsel, across the blue-
>   laid flooring, over the checkered pavement
> passed through the three flame points to the
>   rubbled hillside where the thorn bush marks
> putrefaction
> *by the others, we*
> raised by the Elephant and the Goat carried
> to the bone gripped, made
> but not our makers, beside us

to come to, by the worst done
on an island far in the North
or hanging upside-down over a railing above the raging freeway, grabbed
 Victory?   Brought back up?   Penitence?
            Blinding sight?

the dark male meat by the tall birds
            flown?

unmade, remade   for the worst done
                      from the waist down
                      up, by the waste won

over and over and over and over
doubles, the doubles doubles, together through together
and every bit of it in a tongue nobody understands, not the speakers,
    not the secret researchers, not the stoned freak loonies, no rain, no
    bring, no fruit, not one word, not first syllable dick doodah
and still our makers, beside us, who come

★

«there is in mankind a certain faculty of divination»
                                        — Cicero

last night I was weeping, lying on the floor over into the corner from under the table, to
sleep, in total despair at my fucked-up life — in Grenier and his friend's chicken coop or
tool shed made into house — out in the sticks — the intensity of the scene has persisted
all day, no more so than when watching Disney at 6 about the kid gone to live with his
great-uncle, a Pennsylvania Dutch curer, healer, *brocher*, the kid already able to send him-
self out into wolves', owls' bodies — and the old great-uncle told him of all our *double
nature*, and the dangers of the body left then without any senses to protect it — certainly
this time the *watching* self was more intent and vividly aware than ever before — but not
yet the *watched*, enacting self looking back at the watcher, can that be, too, and endure? —
it all came back again, at Helen's for Sunday music with the Petrees and the piano stu-
dent from Lisbon, Paul — peeing during one of the breaks I could recognize the exact
state of distance in the dream with Grenier and the other, was the same as in "real life,"
whoever the "Grenier" was — but those modes of relation are, among others, what are
"kept," "come over" — innate, "willingness," is "reluctance

so the lodge, of history,
of sorrow

❂

tears, for a lodge of sorrow, seeds, or grit for, for that long house
and smoke of memory, history's time afire

❂

something about, we need to, wait for, the work, to finish
waiting, outside, what did we bring along, to do, waiting?

and Sue Whosername came by completely sloshed out of her mind just as we sat down
with the star, used to be the star distributor from Lay-seen, and fell right down in the
booth next to us, not knowing who the fuck we were, "well, and say, and how old *are* you?"

 good trouble, out of craft, who

compassion of grave stones where

    brief sea   *know* laps *them*

[two requiem études]

«and sing in endless morn of light»

that in the secret marriage join
    as from, so soon, the sorrow cloth
    took tears, bright eyes to wear again
down hearts' red stone

plain sorrow lodge undraped all the long long living room and back
outside, black hatchments on the balcony
but in, bare walls to blue the tears
the salt heart sea back, listening

✪

the Chamber of Reflection — Death
mirrors us, we mirror Death — who's
reached by the Chain of Union?
'indissoluble in their chaos' — Hunkered
and Erect Clods, Discreet and Wise
Chaos, and Chaos Disentangled

and these, our faculty of divination
futureless, but out of time telling, anyway
'I saw it come true' not really a song
or even made up while it lasts
but more ingenious yet
inexhaustible our limits to know
but still recognize when it hits

✪

pogo sticks à Poulenc
soft as chalumeau

by the river, eagles
in the shallows, reedlets

✪

       to accumulate rites

              to eventuates flower

         come hybrid pollens to new season come

persistent taking of the way through the woods

      feet may give   than sidewalk street

        that old back pasture that it know so well

          new hustle

       sweet   forcing   floor

[reading Blok]

waste by use — when now what use worries the pants legs? the young poets feel, they're called to? what was it at 16, c. 1952? — another excitement *not of this place but elsewhere*, that was at the same time the hidden, former, old-yet-ever-to-show-forth *present town*, to reach to — what was to strive for was, now I'd probably say, from all I drew on then and who, *full praise* — but then, closer to *make it all up new?* — but according to recent *past* ways I'd just found out about, new to me and who I knew — sex wasn't *new*, poetry *was* — trace my blood

[Lilacs K. Kat]
for Marshall Reese

aw he took da pipe

aw it wuzza piece a pipe

aw fuzza pup

✪

blackhead-freckled Howdy Doody punk rockers, lilac men, nail men, call suddenness sandbag sundopers certain aromatic pipe-of-dreams flow, not color, silk-seemed-to-turn-from, about-to-sing-together-to, the question might be, *make-it-(up)-with-him?* (gesturing to the right), sneak off the shirts first, check out your pockets, no p.j.'s, voiceless bilabial pendejo fricatives, all made out of unplaited horniness, splendor'd-home-to-go

a panicled head of dreams, a hit hard but not heard bed of pipes, a rhinestone ridgehead glitter-topp'd coiffure vibratory swinette heaven, plunked uneasy the gut grip to, from, long long after

naw, nix, nothin' up yet, knucks down, dinks, but eyes, you got mine, swingin'

and the itch, yunna stan, movillis, soitenly, soitenly, of ears, e-erhs, eee-uhrs

yours, o Great Momma, yours, all yours

[soar heart overheard]

— well, he preaches a good sermon, quiet, gym rest kind of back to it, you know the sweat's
been there, but he don't *smell* to

— like *to*, but not *too* close to, an *old* Dexter beat, bitten scripture boogie rumba proud,
but come down *hard* from, mean?

— high noon! high noon!
chase the silk! sip spirit! hear?

— I wouldn't used to think it was all just sway class chic, but then that knot's been hit
and hit, and hit, and hit *again*, till it quivers in the pits just to feel it coming, -proud?

— and then the tent gets ripped open, and *then* the spears get scattered all to hell and
gone and back, and election misses, and where we thought *love* was, *we* was, without
it, right?

— and my head's a balloon, closer to the moon than the man in come down in, but my
heart *hears* across that vacuum

— o *la*, like it *never* heard before — *mercy!* — I got drops here, when I close my eyes, and
whomp, to prove it

— and falling for every heart, and green green grass always to come down in, and a need
I never knew before, just to *be* there

— cheep, *cheep!* and someone just *too too* to help, o Lordy, help *me*, too, to get that, o *it*
got that, o, "*I remember Clifford,*" -beat?

✪

Skodnick asks about   the Gates of Asia, the hinges
                                              of the continent

                                                            up against the body
                                     leaning up against the hinges, bending

           quill and some oil in a cup

                                              and the doors'll swing

whose heart?   without a squeak

           ignorant oil

[SLC, Howard Johnson's, between and on at 0220, Reno by midday]

high school but older babble behind in the back of the bus of couples — faggot jokes, en-
forced card games, kids crying slapped to shut up, wifey-hubby kissy-killer blither —
quietness a sign of…scarecrows? serious impertinence, impermanence? root pride? good
rude sense of the traveller, anyway, at the same time chatter can be — but not chatter, in-
cessant loud *yuk-yuk-fucking-yuk-yuk*, it's always got to be *insisted* it's right to enjoy, e.g.,
the card game turned into backgammon — gathered by the lot of the journey, how it
ends up sitting together, like, not -minded, but -vibed, -chinned, congenial-congenīal,
jawbone for nose, instincts like accidence instruct — in Gerrit's letter: «poetic "elitism"

499

[which grows — & can reconcile Mallarmé's (& S. George's) & Lautréamont's (poetry is for everyone)…& the mirror of supernatural economics» — the Montana Texas great-grand-mother finally came and picked up the 16-months-old boy of the couple across the aisle and in front, who'd been crying ever since Denver, and got him to sleep — "usually I can hypnotize a child in five minutes, he took longer than any I can remember, his little muscles were just like knots" — calling to imaginary animals in the air, "hey dogs, come on, dogs, ooo-ooo, hey, come on, hey dogs," spell weaving — what all we have in common as willingness to make out of time, and what can't be made up for, no matter *out of* or *out in* — limits to go to see the sacred places on the table with the scrambled eggs and hash-browns, between and on — *then we stopped and waited for the signal to come on, we heard return in us*

[Reunion]

a new Law of Love   (Knight Rose Croix)

a new Lord over Love   (HD/RD)

twin crosses, scaffolds
«the arms of the cross changed into wings»

                     …dusty crown
simultaneously   *dust and feathers*
                     leaves and dust

                     one-line *engines*
                     master turned and tuned

rust cut, no more just melo-, phano-, logo-, mytho-, morpho-, psycho-, but *more* —
to stand with the things of Nature already down a separate road from the things of Nature

X's in support, extensity   «so that the lines…
to multiply the unknown times   do not meet»

                              she opened the snake's jaws
                              with her fingers and rubbed
                              the fangs lingeringly, I just
                              used my shoe

"she's my ex-" and "she's my tension"
'tens-hut! said the mule joke, "first you gotta get his 'tenshun —
now laht the fahr"

                         did Pike read Boehme?
                         out of the fire of Wrath and Civil War —

the deep pleasure, the rightness hearing the rituals done in the local common speech

                    «The fire would not warm, if it could not
                    also burn, the human flesh»

                              — Love?

                                             its doctrine
                                      the acme of the inquisitor

the full penalty of the obligation
losing, never finding the Word?

so finally «the assumption about who's there»
is the crux, and «who cannot answer»?

[pastorale]

not for a long time such a soup, the frozen carcasses of weeks of Sunday roast chickens, simmered all a Saturday afternoon, with onion and celery and parsley, thyme, basil, and California bay — slow and skimmed, on past sunset, then strained and the bones and meat set aside to cool, to pick for salad later — the stock cooked on with rice till the grains butterfly open, fat — shots of Tabasco in the bowl and chopped parsley, coarse fresh-crushed black pepper — sourdough rolls under the broiler till the crust browns almost black, flesh soft and buttered — cold jug chablis and salad, and afterwards coffee and brandy and bitter-chocolate coffee beans, creased with a dent — and the pleasure of it warmed up for lunch next day just as great, pepper and parsley and Tabasco again, and a drop of soy, with wheat crackers this time, and good cheap French vermouth on the rocks

not for a long time such a deep, muted underglow, to reflect the soul turn's own reflection back into the days, wet, dark, up-welling, mid-November

[for Ken Grenier]

his art: beyond intention made

    .

«It is in his nature not to belong to any locality and not to possess any
    permanent abode; always he is on the road between here and yonder»

—W.F. Otto, *The Homeric Gods*

    .

she made a rock — I was made? too?
    *confe*r the birdbath flock below
        or a tallow sponge for stone for bread?
            in fact, a birdseed ball, pecked through

502

he is on the back way home, a pig sitting on a farmhouse porch playing a violin, stopping as he's looked at then starting up again, playing with the back of the Irish-harp-shaped bow, or bow held upside-down, a jig for the monument we dance around, arms and shoulders as if in habit to the music wings, *tyrants rivet feathers on the human body, the priesthood, on the human soul,* made by being interfered with in the making, pig'n'fiddle underworldly hog-heaven life, aloft — «and suddenly he joins some solitary wayfarer», and out of every earthstruck future step an ample spring leaps forth

for he is the connection maker, and he is the connection made

[homage to Nicolas Poussin]

yah I et in Arcadia ago, long long time ago, that diner used to sit right next to Dutton's, ain't there no more, et there a lotta times, till he died, that ole boy that run it,　　Bones　　Cross　　even there he was, yeah, we was pretty close back then, like George said, down there to a meeting one night a couple of years ago, that time they come over from Missouri to visit, looking up at all them old faded pictures of past masters on the walls, "you know, this is a place that's known a lot of pride"

and Death says,　　　Even here am I
and we say back, remembering,　　　We, too, been

　　　　　in Arkady

The author is grateful for the opportunity to quote briefly in the text from a number of sources, including the following (translations other than those indicated are by the author):

page 409:   Robert Grenier, *Oakland* (Tuumba Press, 1980), "Sunshine Line"

             Thomas Meyer, *Staves Calends Legends* (The Jargon Society, 1979), «Belt & Sword / armour leap up»

             Gerrit Lansing, *The Heavenly Tree Grows Downward* (North Atlantic Books, 1977), "An Inlet Of Reality, or Soul"

             Virgil, *Eclogae*, V, unpublished translation by Stanley Lombardo

411:         Robert Duncan, *Letters* (Jargon Books, 1958), "Preface: Signatures"

             Walt Whitman, *Specimen Days*, "After Trying a Certain Book"

             Sir Thomas Browne, *Hydriotaphia*, V

             Lao Tzu, *Tao te ching*, 1, translated by Peter A. Boodberg, "Philological Notes on Chapter One of the Lao Tzu," *Harvard Journal of Asiatic Studies*, 20 (1957)

412:         Gunnar Ekelöf, *Dīwān över Fursten av Emgión* (Albert Bonniers Förlag, 1965), *Dīwān*, 19

416:         Gérard de Nerval, *Voyage en Orient*, "Les nuits de Ramadan," III, vi

426:         Rainer Maria Rilke, *Briefwechsel Rainer Maria Rilke und Marie von Thurn und Taxis* (Niehaus & Rokitansky Verlag and Insel-Verlag, 1951), I, #138, letter of 12 Dec 1912

438:         Gérard de Nerval, *Chimères*, "Vers dorés," translated by Robert Duncan, *Bending the Bow* (New Directions Books, 1968), *The Chimeras of Gérard de Nerval*, "Golden Lines"

Harry Martinson, *Passad* (Albert Bonniers Förlag, 1945), "Gudinnan av Hyn"

441: Robert Duncan, *Poems 1948-1949* (Berkeley Miscellany Editions, 1949), *The Venice Poem*, "Imaginary Instructions"

448: Osip Mandelstam, *Sobranie Sochinenii*, II (Inter-Language Library Associates, 1966), "Razgovor o Dante," II

450: Edward Dorn, *Gunslinger: Book III* (Frontier Press, 1972), "The LAWG of the Winterbook"

460: Joel Chandler Harris, *Uncle Remus*, XV, as cited in *The Century Dictionary*, "study"

Walter Benjamin, *Gesammelte Schriften*, II, 1 (Suhrkamp Verlag, 1977), "Über die Sprache überhaupt und über die Sprache des Menschen"

471: Louis Zukofsky, *Anew* (The Press of James A. Decker, 1946), 4; *"A" 1–12* (Origin Press, 1959), 12

474: Federico García Lorca, *Obras completas* (Aguilar, 1974), I, "Thamar y Amnón"

477: Johannes Bobrowski, *Wetterzeichen* (Union Verlag, 1966), "An Klopstock"

480: Walt Whitman, *Leaves of Grass*, "Song of Myself," 49

482: Henry Vaughan, *Silex Scintillans*, I, "Sure, there's a Tye of Bodyes! and as they"

486: Federico García Lorca, *Obras Completas* (Aguilar, 1974), I, "[A las poesías completas de Antonio Machado]"

488: H. D., *Tribute to the Angels* (Oxford University Press, 1945), VIII

Ezra Pound, *Thrones* (New Directions Books, 1959), Canto 109

491: Roy Arthur Swanson, *Pindar's Odes* (The Bobbs-Merrill Company, 1974), commentary on Nemean 11

Walt Whitman, *An American Primer*

493: Cicero, *De divinatione*, I, 1

495: John Milton, *Poems*, "At a solemn Musick"

502: Walter F. Otto, *The Homeric Gods*, translated by Moses Hadas (Pantheon Books, 1954), III, "Olympian Deities," *Hermes*, 7

A SET.

Я слово позабыл, что я хотел сказать.

I have forgotten the word that I wanted to say.

— Osip Mandelstam

stars fall, dark dolls to earth, to the old songs dance, folk of the West of the West, brought back again
almost quickly digitations of the jugglers' blindfold to bind up the hour before the dawn, before the dark

you do not sleep but subsequently translate that mime into a newer currency
to spend in the street and stand around to watch and sing along to those fast steps

here in the woods, hear in the woods, here in the woods
the cottonwood to the flute and the drum

who in the morning come to sacrifice to health for sake of safety's speed
talking all the time about the in-laws and the pictures on the walls last week

the expectation to exemplify the dying of the old self to its age
the limitation to just one count of generation, one of revolution, made

509

✪

o back of courthouse mules, silver-brown and peony-fawn, who wait in glowing patience, faring all

the Oreo diamond cream rose-pink old ladies under the sycamores come and go to the post office as quietly glorious as you,
sharing the butterflies by their hair to your wondrous fur

the young men in levis though they move faster go in and linger for the passports to the other side and do not come back out
again the way they went

lost even to their own sight or changed into the chestnut-curly-haired rider who couples with his mounts, cursing under his
breath, you old mules you, I'll _____ you, _____ you, whose dashes are penrods, whose
parentheses are airconditioners

o you mules you, who face for all the worlds, you who are brothers to the lost sight, who are past Christian as the expectation
before the dust as before heaven, rolling on our backs to sustain the dead

we sing together *binny binny oooo binny binny, not by the chair of my binny binny binn* to the hymn of the house of blue light
before the breath parade of birth is hit

        hear

the cloche-covered serious matrons of the depression lined up the back stairs of the public library to first vote join in

behind the world of civic shades the words again in self-sufficient photogeneration play athwart time

behind the world of civic shades the words again in self-sufficient photogeneration play athwart time

for who is born, who bears, who cannot bear, what moon hungers on the other side in turn dissatisfies this appetite-depressant speed

bestiality, just one glimpse of is enough to satisfy for lives of being sure no fancy fucking with divinity is rite of exaltation stroke to see anew, than rocks off hump for lack we lived in once

insistence on the value of the saints who hoe tobacco road to teach the consciousness exact discrimination, and ride the flaming pink geraniums in each patio below, aloft against the torments of interrogation in the rooms to come

all these, all witnesses together through together to, all instruments of their perception, die, but not that distance's aurora we just open onto

aw, yeah, come on, jawbone don't go, show me an ante

o you mules you

the slash of the road in Koré's, in Korea's dream   ancipital, fang-made, filled with the living

told the guy next to me for no reason at all when he asked, whatdya do   and the hole is the lie I

does that mean I really am a spy, or all of us captive in the middle of the

road the recourse to escape to ever tell the truth

and the hole again the basketball net up over every driveway, the cords

scores cut to arm terror

up against the side of the head, chingadora! you wanta get away you better

play

hung like the family jewels, honchod embryo to claw, to catch and hold the light

while we each finish our riddles

stone shaped like a man stood

bent over a chair back

and the questioning begins

but Kore's story is to hurry, to try to get away from the family here on earth and the family down below, both — what word is
gotten to her, she brings back or sends, to reach the sun again — finding her in the shadowy stacks of Hades' library,
wandering in distraction, sweat salt stains on her dark t-shirt, not knowing exactly what she's after, except *get out*

other ventriloquies syllable the understudy of the body

    we have lost the word we wanted to say, keep looking for it, find
        another one in its place
    sweats blood and sweat through the stone, maybe even the same
        word, how can we tell,
    it was lost to us before we ever knew it?

        the gripped hand jerks the meat off the bone
                off the stone

Kore's sparrow flies to out of the dark, lights, pecks at the gutseed ball brought back up from the night before the night before
last — how many months, how many years, each seed?

stones diary the weather, light their élan the way into the future, the impulse, the sudden absolute necessity to speak, beyond
articulation, beyond speech itself

o you who in the obscure commas of the continent, do not misjudge, do not misapprehend the instinct to adversity

513

knots are our classics
classics are the poetry of revolution
each one more turn in the captive muddied road

reckless the woods for a path in the middle of the city aloft must know what we go into

first seed, then memory, then seed

✪

I therefore took my soul and put it into
the crop of a sparrow, and even then

there is a hoarse jack cackle gatherer talking to the King
lecherous

who's that — *King!*

so cold they are, and unprotected, hungry,

is a name of Continuance, and in that Name
carved like walrus ivory from the life that reigns
beneath the worlds
intent with the eyes of friendship's stone

514

there is a nickel taken to the halo of the *crown*

not actual
but tangible

yourself over yourself

unseals

turning	buffalo	to	Indian
	beaver	to	Queen
	mansion house	to	President

so the copperdemon's paid back down again, the naked Neck to
fiddle sitting in the middle
of the stream, the mouth shut on the tags between the teeth

and maybe a sparrow will bring the payment up again in
five inches of string, the
five-divided stalk into the nest, five seeds cracked open
and eaten one by one in
the bird bath below, the metal band pecked off the bone
and brought
and the other husks will answer from the tree trunks in
the woods, so
much they've got to say, so far to go

one nickel is paid with the toy airplane that flies with friendship's stone into the underworld in the dirt under the front porch

one with every ordinary thing that signals to its word in silence to pay for just the possibility of passing before perception

515

so to the soul — so from the soul when it returns — the debt is due

try to hang on to them and they'll be playing craps for your threads at the end, or gladly give them away each step of the way into nakedness

your strength, o Charity, the gain to face

but the debt will be collected anyway

search, Charon, for the coin given you, dropped in the mud in the crossing, bit in two in the telling

the gathered gestures of historic particulars do not extricate from direction the concentrations of responsibility

a man met headed West on the last hill out of town, the last tree walking into treelessness,

or the erratic stone, not home

the face of a friend turned up to say hello with the face of a friend doomed to die in the wandering

the verses not to trade for bread but cut the grownup wheat field in the back of the head

the soul of the wheel is not in the wheel

and the love in the poem love in the poem, not the loved one's love in the loved one's, but the terror of the flowers' test to go into the other world without a name

not yet knowing this one, how can we talk about the one to come — that love

516

and what seems like the chance appearance in a hand mirror of a small intricately swirled Venetian glass marble, he refers to as

his dead son Ernie   or Wayne   eenny or taw

the ransom paid, the random weight for just just the dirt in front of the possibility of apprenticeship to say

is the sovereign globe that holds up the *kopparnickel* in

the crown of reciprocity

of the King in the abyss

and if the sparrow has found a house, and the swallow a nest

even on thine altars, o my King

I watch, as a sparrow alone upon the housetop

517

RIDGE TO RIDGE

Poems 1990–2000

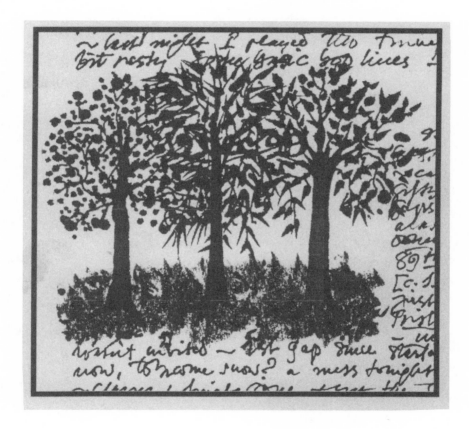

These pieces were written between March 1990 and March 2000. Many of them first appeared (sometimes in different versions) in the following publications: *Notus; First Intensity; House Organ; :that:; Antiphonal and Fall to Fall; Ashen Meal; apex of the M; Five Fingers Review; Log; Dédale; Sulfur; Mike & Dale's Younger Poets;* Arcturus Editions chaplet; *The Blind See Only This World: Poems for John Wieners; Skanky Possum.* To the editors and all those concerned, the author wishes to express his appreciation and thanks. Both the publishers and the author would also like to thank Patrick Doud for his assistance in preparing the text for the present volume.

For those whose correspondence and conversation has not stopped, the summons and the challenge and the sustaining, the family to the doing and the undoing, «wherein we feel there is some hidden want,» «Like a Poet hidden / In the light of thought» — For the reader now, the reader to come, the reader still before.

The light passes
from ridge to ridge

—H.D.

a life into a few vegetables set in a half-shadowed deep window frame
black dirt gloss across flame orange carrots, ivory sprouted filaments from upcurved
    fennel and cardoon stalks
how long to sit there to be seen into the painting
how long the lemon cut before glazed over, and another

but in the words past the breeze through from the bedroom window up the short hall
    to the feet, and through again

    .

the rocks by the shore dash up spray from the river, and it hangs there
strength in very quiet great distances
how far away do you have to be to see, to be able finally to hear
the poem
and of nobility in what is lost

    .

stories of so much, we have to quote from to tell any of all we know
and the gap left to get back out of
the rain begins in the drip on the balcony behind the back

and hearing then from that ship that comes in close to shore a song that calms the sea
    and brings the fish up from the depths
cry out to the sailor who is singing it, "o tell it to me, tell it to me, please!"
but he but only answers, "o no, this song I only tell   to him who with me goes"
        yo no digo esta canción . sino a quien conmigo va

    .

so stare into the hanging scroll   one long wet Sunday afternoon
when the weather there is not apparent of seasons
the leaves of another climate do not reveal   or rain register
the empty small pavilion high up   a gesture that the soul is elsewhere than the palace
    of administration

here there is a butterfly in the knowing of that shelter that would return to change
        but being there together
ascent by ink   and in the black ground black   hidden metallic lusters up out of
        each stroke of the pen

✪

some high new tangerine wax fancy
or pink fluorescent twin of deep lament
of children's coloring book on through a lifetime yet
bright warm clothes that are a rug to the empyrean
elytron opened through the solid trunk of driven sheet
wrapped close and then passed on
there could not be without that fancy now
that indirection of embellishment
to be most dignity and testament
crows take the crows take the over
to teach us insufficiency
heart-wrap skin to call exultant austerity
and spring open a redbird drop cut
tierce   tierce tierce   tierce   tierce

[a small classical flagstone landscape mystery, as wool to murex]

we hear those steps' color, carry those plastic buckets full of laundry, fresh
to be stored in the curves of driving, fast, the night returns, the honey braked
there go the party kegs of yesternight, the sun on bare shoulders, to bare dirt
to pare the prive of privet in its intensest odor to ur-speaking and its secret there
and step with the hover of the bumblebee before its blossom, that vast RV of waking
        to find out

strike the prophetic angle in the stairs the fluid kink of hair as love in tightening its knot
how fast the privet grows to reach another balcony of contemplation and give it shade
how pink the impatiens' faces, "about the only thing'll grow with so little sun,"
    restrata earth

[vistas, over Lammas]
for Patrick Doud

·

down in the furrow, the hand goes down into the carrot reach, the horn lace root out
    of Asia
far from the high plains the noon cuts hot grass, planing patience
grass walk heart, lift to the land behind the ruined barn opens through
scarring the knees and shins, spattering ink on the knuckles, leaving sores on the wrist
    to time

a robin runs, a squirrel to the Queen Anne's lace-held shadow
and gone

zig-zag the sagged conduits of the phone poles above the mow furrows
oblique to, nerve strands, but not of the field's body
yet sway to the same noontime breeze
and by the try to walk the tops of all these, open

·

the last Bard, the last mantic poet, possessor of the secret, shared, and essential history
    of the whole tradition and its magic
driven to the highest crag above the brilliant torrent of the boundary
time crack raging between the worlds, sunset grandeur of cataclysm sweeping the
    cloudscape away behind
at bay defies the invading army come to exterminate all the Makers

into the disappearance
lost

•

by the light of the full moon and the stars of the Big Dipper as bright as the moon
the commune of workers in the field of vision, in the field of making
harvest the ripe wheat
under the nightiris iridescent waterfall sexual splendor of the trees
to the wheat itself

and in the dark valley beyond
winds the bright river, to

•

at the gate of the West, down the wild iris and thistle-covered, sheeptrack-worn,
    mossbrilliant hummocks to the sea
the Shining Path opens to the Islands of the Blessed and Beyond the Blessed

and the sheep come up close to the sight at the moment of vision
and the steamer and its unpasturing track, and all unwillingness and inability
are swept away

so it is not lost

•

so goes the month of the mother

the maple and the spruce's shadow one shadow
almost touching the white pine's

to the month of the father

to the measuring, across that gap

the young man barechested holding the surveyor's rod moves ahead along the road
    before the woods, beyond the mown enfolded hayfield lines up with the telephone
    pole,
disappears behind the lone
        monumental sumac

•

trumpet vine's orange overhang just at the elbow at the waist
advances again from the last outpost to set the banner, to target
skein-gatherer answering the throw and call of the sightlines
birth nodes the coffee smell's chord
remaking the way

four voices in the dark along that road break into singing and laughter, dance in circles
    on ahead

the dust smells, the bacon fry

body clasping body, across that gap

•

what can be known of the heart any more than of the colloquy of the crows in the
    field out the window

three in a great triangle, walking
and one flown away, and returned, and their calling
or now in the root crease of the field, where they gather and glean
the heart's seed

not lost

•

[2 February 1992]
          for Patrick Doud

The candle in the groundhog's innards, in the rippling of his pelt across the far field
      fled of shelter

stands and burns in the motionless shadow, season cast and lifetime cast

O dig out the scales from the brain!

✪

The flecks of other colors on the worn crayola tips
tip thistle and blood and lymph and what falls and bounces and glitters in the
      lingering smell of baked chocolate
its trunks and foliage, lights and shadows and litter underfoot
and the well, the pool, the verb source, afraid to look into
seen from across the room is what love looks like
the fragments of old wall, the dense branches down over the pavilion, the bright skies
      of the avenue through the window panes in what is open on the sofa
look back through the woods a little, from the fountains down below to the marriage
      and the god's investiture with ring and staff above
across the clearing to the man fallen to the ground, his king serpent about to strike,
      the hood fulfilled forever
the actor and the traitor and the discovery in that conscience
helpless as we are looking on to stop
gather the ashes of, memorialize the renewal of
the skin, the hoodless sportscar, the empty jar, the blue shirt in the sandpile
outside the gate
where the tar workers come down from the roof to the back door and into the kitchen
the smell of asphalt, sweat, and underwear kindled
all, all this we carry away
crusts, betrayal, honor, search, and puzzlement
climbed up on the rocks of and looked down from

and the question asked then is, are you going on home now, and can I come with you
if this, this old leather jacket that is breath can be extricated
and the knob that is being afraid to
turned

✪

Evangel of the Morning, bright messenger
hibiscus, Rose of Sharon, slope of the bungalow roof
whose room still to return to
promise and support of the vacant lot
hair in the wondrous coat and silk inwoven with the wool
the young man into the promise of the concerto
his mother dead in the great foreign city and he left there alone
and the pianist she again but young, and with all grief

[to almost midnight New Year's Eve in Glasgow]

into the dark before the dark before the years
the old pants' velour touch, to the new unknown belongs
as if there were no grown set worry and no undressing out enough
old skin leopard teddy bear witchery of variations memory
and the hat even the feather tango
each nut each sip a look into the ear
incapable smartness, unpredictable calling
old cold metal tumbler the wet lip just sticks to
Coca Cola Lifesavers from before the war accrual
and that soft mezza voce tuba languor and arousal
in the rapt aphasic ear .

✪

Moroni on the play — have you consulted?

brown shoe polish stain on the left middle finger tip and along the outer edge of the
thumb, between excrement and blood

smeared to the forehead, of a residency in a tiny country town of a beginning string
quartet

day care to high school to nursing home, the central corn stalk on the hill of beans and
squash

with its fish and seed, up the spinal column of the hemisphere, the ball game of the
continents

where the directions mesh in play, hole and ear, fiber and hair

become first concert

what play, to be consulted on?

the old grande dame of silk and wool, first dancer once, choreographer of the lost
Pindar once

teacher in the continuance, sun-to-come-up necessary dance with that same necessary
song

a child inherits and knows the obligation to sustain, homage

questions, *have you?*

between the reflections in the water and the incessant tremor, the short sharp intake
of breath at each intensity

each scarred knuckle smeared the same ecstatic shine

a token chocolate nut of ginger that is chosen and shown and put again into the
common pile of mountains

what makes you think you are not in prose because you do not know the continuity?

it is not melancholy, it is not sadness, it is not lament, but the shape and trace of distance

is that release? is that what the concern is about homecoming, about what home is?
itself homage

where some kids have never seen an instrument to play at all, and some adults never
known the means of their production

the black ungained bottom of their unexceptioned conjugal necessity

angel

✪

that after all to walk into a restaurant may be
a wild waste hollow out the way you came you've never been before
great corner between cultivation impossible to cultivate
built up to all day nakedness and coming on the edge of to explore, imbuing
    direction with
the never known about first relatives needing the same sudden tale of getting here
that can't get back except by memory's emptiness
how space and time bulge with so much wanting of
until it is itself whatever direction is, direction as, directionless
except not-here, except all-here

✪

The antiphonal protagonists take pause
pieces held in trust, lost, uncertain how, found or thought to find again at the right
    angles of public places
into the great hidden pageant that is always going on outside the equally uncertain
    conferences of elders, who scold or blame or praise unpredictably
responsibility also to hold, and of another place, to touch our own still carried
    possibility of youth to graduate with these
if he is mingled lure and love, footstep and delirium of love, track of learning in its
    quest, and yet not all attraction instantly, following with fingertips the key
    unlocking flattened blade palooka'd nose, and hair all belted to the waist
she is of the other sight, wise distance, nail pairings, threads of the pawns drawn, what
    animal will be at the trysting place tonight, hair taken and returned, permission
    and allowance, mater ludens, grave and hilarious, eruptive and instructive-patient,
    heart uncloudening
and there is an other older he sure counsellor, and an other younger she sure lover,
    four crossings into the graduation
who is turned to on the high lawns and the hills above, white shirt open to the breast,
    in each absence what history itself is longing for to demonstrate, not with names
    and not with dates, but these, our interinterventions

[transcontinental]

«Rats and wigs'll get you killed»
— Lightnin' Hopkins

«A rat is also a root and a cry»
— Edward Seidensticker

«Wig city»
— Lord Buckley

September Set

For The Wanton Farmers

Mimosa, sensitive, the mime, sweet the feathered tufted coral and champagne crests
    still high up
shirred for a Sunday morning eggs en cocotte in the sweet mimosa heat and to the touch
    immediate
sweet the crusts to enter even the little garden at the back of the station, to feed
kept for the traveller, kept for the fish up the rapids, kept for the mastery of station
the Scottish mail is the Scottish salmon, flown far past
rod cast of all our metal, care not to catch on the high lines, freaked incarnadine
one last dried wheel of fig upright and its blood seeds catch the teeth past to be
    fodder, renew
the extracted life gone on, last this time or this, another mortal entering by its slight
    sip more
telling there to come, *told from* here, that came from *being told* back there
knob to the utter
my who do not fish fish are lithe in and out of the last clothing to nibble the flesh left
    ascendant

532

laugh high lines of the hand up fancy hailing prodigy
out there the first home football game fills the town
in here the same shared inner track is celebration
alchemy is each pulvinus, transmutation of the touch to be like light
a paperclip is the mountain top, and the football game, whistling up there, but to be
    water and its transformation *out*
won in the pines' sound, *lost* in the pines' sound, *sound* in the knobnut leapt for and
    gulped
so for the marriage past, far to the Northland gone
this is the night mail, crossing
                crossed at
                the border

  •

The station is the sphincter of arousal in the brain
empty, darkling, likely to rain
the last year of pilgrimage, to *this* grove
black walnut, cottonwood, honey locust and catalpa
oak and linden, hackberry and Kentucky coffee, hedge and redbud
the passageways of disharmony suspend
the fountain in the well of litter and of leaves
in a desperation nut by nut and sip by sip, husk by husk
to crack open a fissure in the top of the brain
gained up through the soles of the feet and out
spraypaint smell from the patio below
up with the ballbearing rattle at each shake of the can
                      over the roof and gone

  •

So my mother has poured ice water on the table I might have, but only made a ring as
    slender as a tumbler would, rim rung as the rug has been away

The flap of sleeve loose from the sweatshirt cuff and underforearm seam yearns sight,
    ripped and never to be joined again, the so and sewing of who is there to take the
    worndown fleece inside and look back out at every stare

Tondo stare straight down at the table where the company of a meal has been so shared
the hospitality still hangs in the air its solid cube of warmth, exact as every detail
on the tabletop

What are the pools to stare into, binding for the wounds for love, stare-pool hold of
what's to come

•

healing machines
pencils, pens, and crayolas to mark and color with
they draw and shake in the dark, facility
the hands' sudden trembling in the venture of the shoulder to be all hearing nostrils'
peering tongue rimming each shimmering cut dug in the page
and the antitheses and where they have gone
time is the life of the soul as it passes from one state of act and experience to another
and is not outside it

unquiet its faculty that cannot bear to keep within itself all the densefulness of its
possession
dirty the brocade tablecloth of the inheritance and worn through where kept at the
table edge too long, moved back only to fray another fissure
geology of hair, dirt, dandruff, litter, family and love, lees
igneous, intrusions through, sedimentary, metamorphic
spider from the bathmat by the open balcony door to the downpour away
that draws   and in the amber vibratory and compacted of the sap of life
ground to light on each suspended stratum

•

The parable and trump:
pushing the stalled car naked
and picking up along the way enough from the coins piled and scattered all around
to fill the pulledon pants and realize too late
are graveyard honorings forbidden to be touched
the anger is protest not for such a merely personal dumb mistake to suffer whatever
the consequences for
but at the deaths by systematic outrage to put them there

534

Carry always a crowbar in the shoulder bag, lean and bright steel
its intended uses *more apparent than real*
but remember in that passage grave in Sjaelland, crowned with apple trees in bloom,
    we wished we'd brought a light
Tad Palmer suddenly pulled out matches and a candle
he always carried with him, he said, just in case, and with a bit of rope

The anger back and dismissal jeer, "and where the hell have you been all day, in the
    outhouse? and working on what, your *gifts?*"
naked again
        thunder announcing surge after surge of night sunflowers, beside the
      still stalled car their cave painting hanging on the wall in the dark with the passing
      carlights and the streetlamp's cast across to part pathways
stone to be fissure to be

[homage to Richard Lovelace]

There is a redbird eating rowan berries in the leafbare tree
whatever taken from its living source till there is nothing left
leaves such witness in its self-consuming sacrifice
these all-pled falling depths
                  The Gods *that wanton in the aire*
                  Know no such Liberty

blow the heart out with its spume-foam dirt from each tip of the reach, down that
    gutter-neck hiss
to see the self cell once again, more incandescent flame elect than ever since conception
and through the double reinforcing veils of waking and of dream, consume to utter
    blackness at the heart, *pav'd floore, calme Ravisher*

in each afterimage no other landscape that can be known, but landscape after landscape
     nonetheless
and the pictures offered, withdrawn into the other room and shut the door and come
     back out with all the guardian poem places in the palm flashed hold
each winding Law and poyze
                              a warme seate to our rest
wine-red leaves of burning bush, wahoo, and gone
where a bluejay shrieks to-be, insatiate, in the next bare tree

✪

I have a chair in the stair well, just up under the stairs, by the floors-high window, to
     sit in the sun and watch the dust motes drift, the light flux
And I will carry the watch as a seal, burnt in and burnt out of the whirling column of
     extracted lives, and mine

✪

But the cocklight is of the light above, forlorn and of the dog, but of the reach to turn
     the light on up above, and of the light above
O they can see me from the house across the street where the wild pigs roam with
     their big perked ears and look and hear this way
Rich manuscripts that will not be lost but not explained, long to copy and to study,
     grave scrab at the heart embedded, that takes the hidden hadith of Homer for
     their first, for transmission of the heart's instruction

[final exam]

The signs of love again, but with such obstacles, the railroad crossing suddenly
     blocked with heavy traffic, the trash backing up the hillside rivulets, to restore the
     measure of thirst, the mattress of drinking

the signs that out of anger
                                    — I got so pissed off I threw the chalk as hard as I
        could straight through the blackboard to the other year, the white dust
        bullet, it should have been the eraser too, to follow and wipe out the hole
        behind —
                            can come love, the son from anger, the love of the son, to
        transform anger, I who am a son and who love sons
the back way when the trains have let us pass, the snake through the blackboard to
        be the peacock pf arousal in the woods where the sun is gotten off to make
        the woods, black light itself that does not bow down
and the great squash to ride in through the eyes of the widest nightcrack in the
        years, to shine forbidding eating, so we eat each other in its ecstasy
because the boys are talking out loud in the back of the room like back in highschool
ripening seed out of chaos

                    [at the 720th anniversary of the death of Jalaluddin Rumi]

✪

To have a guest, and for this place, and for this food and drink, and for this sharing, in
        the orchard distinguish between marble and its watering
the lordly usage, that does not question when it comes the illusion itself but recognizes
        and accepts it as illusion
for solitude and grieving are also instruments of vision, it drops its tears to take us on
        for, not for our ability
so staring into the world in the river is reflected the world
and if the King and all his retinue pass in the mirror held up in the barbershop to show
        your newcut hair, you do not need to turn around to see, until
the progress of the notorious bumpkin through the minefield of lionhunting golddiggers
        in the purse mirror of the successful one is the window into love not all those riches,
        and of its loss

the keeping of a ladder in the empty central room of the house you can climb up and
      down all you want to any time you want to and no one will ever interfere, an angel
sent agency of revelation, known only in that duration, existing only in the sending
      and the perceiving of the revelation
the repeated mimesis of the pealing of bells, of the crying for the soul
but of that tombeau there is also badinage, radiant wheel, at the one and the same time,
      no less serious, no less playful
shall we not shout and stomp to tell deep grief, and wild fandango celebrate the being
      able to, to be at all

✪

The boys are sitting on the front steps of a house beside the back highway reading
      comic books together
each one separately the same into what the old master poet in his last fragmentary tape
      started to call the Northern sunder reality road share tradition
before the tape ran out, where the vision does, where the comic books end
and they run off around the house to play, each under its kill and its approaching
      ceremony
and someone gets pissed off and yells out "ah I'm gonna go home" "o yeah and I'm
      gonna tell"
or before that this time, the calling home, and being called inside, can concentrate

✪

Would you take the diaphany of ivory and of brightness to be behind the name, and
      power,
and carry into the portraying and then into the writing by the way the ear itches from
      the air
the elephant of interior grace and strength or the bear of insistent nub just by the style
      itself and not by any subject of depiction
an elegy of cradle song for the mother, and that for the nations and for history, and for
      full orchestra
an extended fantasy in meditation for the father, solo, and of the touch
or would that be reversed, or would there be the elephant and bear of crossed arms to
      wonder at hanging not in what is made but in its air, swinging

✪

"Would that I might be rubbed away, like a statue, and given a"
"a more disgraceful body," Helen actually says, as Austin translates her from Euripides
   but what might be returned there, *cloud for a body*, an agalma of wind and fog, of
      constant insubstantiality and dispersal, as her Eidolon itself, named and possessed,
      was made of
into the spirit road of the spirit road, determined only by their passing, not by pavement,
      paramount, or path, but still within the boundaries of the monuments whenever
      they are seen as monuments
the stretch of prairie, cape, and bay shore mansions along the crest of the slope of open
      sward of skin of earth, with stone burial platforms out front, only one the real one
and the other side completely open, with just the feeling of the distance from the line
      as it is a line, from all that is manmade, over
and a single memorial as though a plaque to face back reversal and in cursive backwards,
      but dug down into the earth, a small far flung out sunken garden from each house
that the animal guides and guardians together with their humans, expected but not
      present any other place
here also have their commemoration into the other world, face and face and
      transformation face
cat and dog and parakeet and teddy bear, that in their houses have defined the spirit road
knotted on the other side of the ravine that is the other side of the road, at the right
      angles and obliquities of farewell and departure
so some days crossing the volleyball sand pit the buggerball spiked back and auspicious
      armor of arousal unenclothed
they return us

✪

There is the bare and rich delight of coming back after the long day and long into the
      evening too
to fix a simple mix of canned creamed corn and California dark pinquito beans
sautéing first onion and garlic and chiles, adding sweet pepper and lime juice and cilantro
eaten with sourdough freshly hot but wanting cornbread not tortillas
o my father, I am not ever sure what the terms are of our exchange, and now that you
      are gone, what they become

the corn and chiles and beans are more poignant than uncertainty

the throw rugs and squares of tapestry for seats, you asked about the uses of, like poetry

are spread out on the car where we have talked, to keep on at would be a far drop down
    our mutual staircase

we might make, but I would not try, for in that wood is steel, and other workmen are
    needed in and have already almost come for that

yet if I face you across the table under the lamplight, it is to an old friend and his little
    boy who is next to me

and we build together our unknown animal of curly chocolate tails, we make up as we
    go along, but always with the familiar elephant

chocolate that we do not go behind him, that she not be driven by captivity and relentless
    exhibition into killing and despair and being killed

in the lamplight there is champagne at the one hand, you redecant to offer, and cognac
    at the other, I have poured

they redisperse the spirits in the reckoning, we simultaneously each the communicants
    of the other are behind their graces, at the table we are seated next to, the giant
    sunflowers twined with morning glories have drooped, are withering at the fence

their heads already harvested, their campfollowers still blooming at their feet

and in the cottonwoods not yet turned, the green and the undergreen whirl at the length
    of our petioles

✪

On a winejug tree for a winejug free, wound with the guardian prophetic snake, where
    sundered power holds us divided, who comes to dare

of ouroboros the oros, of abandonment the expansion, and in the very moment of the eye

fluid its meaning, fluid its reaches, but instant the moment

not the plain, not the city, not the fortress height within, but of outside and wild and
    of initiation

sanctuary or dismemberment, where do the loveless find

I took the old, lower, muddied-over sidewalk down along the curbing, under the regular
    walk on the embankment up beside the lawns

no more intending to, but having started down the stairs and turned toward, that was
    the way, on into the corner earth and up by stairs again, the agate ring

of heavy stone the ring itself and oval polished into banded gem on top, and with its
     pebble next to
both there from long past and seen times and times before in the dirt and mulch-dense
     leaves and berries under the mountain ash
now in the path and clear and taken
too small the opening to wear, too thick, a doughnut of red-caramel and cream and
     red, translucent mountain strata weight, and its pebble of unbanded matrix share
in the pocket across the parking lot gravel who also hurrying up behind to gain
     admittance, black centaur beard and satyr eyeball thick
explaining to his ardent arm in arm what is itself the nature of recognition
and altogether of what is before, and of renewal, and of the restitution in reversal
the rock ring jell in the eye of the crow, in the cry of the jay
brought round

The down of stone is speckled and flown
its pale abrupt protective nocturne stain the glitter from the roof unmitigates
keeps the uncertainty of where the car's been parked keeps restless with the celebration
     we know is not really ours
sends out longing, sets out drawing with the natural chalk of the neighborhood over
     each ink line the faint suffusion underglitter of the local dirt
so the kids come up on the porch to take a look at what it's like, hey mister is the mystery
the rock face rendered the red and black currants in their crystal on the dining room table
     remember
we all look in at through the curtains and wish the lights were turned on overhead
following the blue-pink sidewalk centipede of arrow marks around the block
into the pile of honey locust, wahoo, and magnolia leaves trembling as a whole tree
     shakes fallen in the middle of the street

[Homage to Kandinsky and Hartley — composition / improvisation, starting with an affirmation by Hartley]

— and I was a convert to the field of imagination into which I was born

the stable stalltree driver drives so fast up hill and down the stomach and ass almost
    come, and the feats of the wind in the feet

out of the fire above the fire tree line the mimosa bloom bird holds the nine taken
    elephants of the body of its openings up, only the tail and claws and beak, the wings
    are free

beneath each body from gullet to ass and tail and under the trunk and feet and at the
    fringes of the ears the color and speckled opal scales are belly snake of human flesh
    and in thrown flames aloft and all in space around

a stain of use has the sfumato of horizons

roosting places for the power of the energies into which we project the way we analyze
    the world, on the way

and if they had known whales, would they have depicted whales, but did they not know
    and did they not depict, transelemental aspirations of embodiment

she is the one who causes us to cross, but that may be the hall, but that may be the
    driver and his breast and belly

green and of the green, but not of envy, but of the traced residues of other lives, curved
    with the foot curve and with the body just touched into allowing arousal,
    potentiating is remembering

each throws out a line of moment anchoring and faring, circumambulation of the inner
    lake, its old resorts and new adventurings, the werehalls of comradeship, the ring
    auras, processional, the cough, the itch

we carry a photograph around against the breast, of all our lives, three persons we do
    not at first, we only barely start to recognize, and it gets sopping wet through our
    clothes and through harplike through the halls its envelope

and in its drying, the necessary gutter trash of floods, of all the body overflows by
    which we more than live, lodges at the bottom, stuck to the foreground of scrutiny,
    starting to eat away the emulsion and the visages, except the third, above, clear, the
    always who is that the edge does not contain

like some people's x-rays and horoscopes, we pull this out whenever we can and show
    it and ask

the herald of the morn
as though the dog that we had never known before had sighed and wakened in the bed
with us, come back, the candle and the matches, the bit of rope at last for the journey

     •

You see: those skies and colors of the skies and those church machicolated horizons
out from underneath the springs of the holly, the black invigoration vomitory
elastic ilex strength, are the secret of painting of a century ago, that past painted
light now our seen light, but only to make from, not to keep
what has been built is just the circuit of children's elaborate Ponte Vecchios of escape
to the world, the culvert sprung from to the sudden city, each child grown up
almost overnight and hardly recognized until —

you trade again in dreams, finding down between and underneath the sofa cushions,
wondering how long it's been there, become a cottage in the archaic

     •

I thought I saw him shuffling along in Alvin's market, his back to me, pushing the cart,
his almost as tall and just as gray and ashen wife at right angles, frowning and
guarding access away, where I had often seen him, but always alone and vibrant kind
but when I passed it was another who had lost his edge along those aisles, there as
Lord Buckley, still *pushing the mother cart*, the father, the mower, the stroller, the
unabandoned unabandoning child
I on the other hand might just as likely be, alone and whirling with the sauté pan in
demanded unsacramented unrelented fling until the fresh sardines and shallots go
to mush
Cupid stands naked backwards on horseback, his bow unstrung aloft, around the horse's
neck how fast the fingernails grow, some say are hearts in string
and in the other hand a branch of what his toes are also grabbing hold of in the coat,
the autumn almost fruiting rose, the horse's halo aura marigolds
a-prance
love is flung out

as perilously as satyrs dancing on a greased wineskin before the football game, as free,
as full to love, that crystal circuitry not of inheritance but simply gift, but held in
trust as certainly as blood to kin, how long dark moons beneath the nails are
known to be, not one diminished, not one unlost

     •

Where children hymn high longing in the jumpup chalk hawk round the fountain
overflow, until it's washed away and they transported, their age's ancient sag of spine
prelingered in the wing buds' lift and spill
dark as the innards' hidden yearnings masked as picadillo rumblings, to be the tell-tale
in no sensible overhead, yet hold-loam until

     •

And the starter pistol was in the story of a summer research job, all given over to
Spenserian elaborations of the standards of comparison, the institutions of
laudation, because it too revolves, as we do, in the same grandness of just
the ordinary ways of coming and going
for part of the story was that the work also involved finding and documenting the old
glazed-tile ceremonial gates of the university, long since decided out of date and
an embarrassment and buried Trojan layers deep in brickedup side-corridors of
the steam tunnels, but still of heaven possible and of the organ chords they used
to play, processional
Nineveh and lions rampant are not more monumental regnant than these, prairie
turquoise and its high grasses, and the Helianthus gatehead crowning over all, on
into the starry ardors of adversity

                    venite, iterum introite, redite
                    come   enter again   return

[Visitations]

Travelling, travelling, deep within the circuits themselves, not just the circuiting
what in the path passes between the pather and the pathing, or in the reading
and who else, always another, might, always the who else
In the same way the driver told me he thought he was going around and around
    himself in the dark
and the redhead with him in the convertible or the wealthy taciturnity he was driving for
or even the timid fascinated little kids checking him out from the back of the roadside
    stand, and come again
were not the who else
Or your Uncle Bean as Brigadier, he said, looking at me straight, and me to thee
At the same time, between the watcher and the watched there is always another place in
    the process of impinging on us from, aside
while the gut's aside is up and down
And enough, he said, in any case to know it's there, but never enough to be too sure
and not at all the same as stands off to one side and asks, how do you know how to do
    that, you don't know how to do that at all, idiot
But since it is always with us, also ours, holding hands sometimes, lighting a cigarette and
    then not sometimes
but who it is that can keep still
For the true ones are known by their mark, and that I am not ever certain I can tell
O divine luminosities, o fiery tricksters, o other humans alive or gone on, when you
    come, the taste that is real
Or Uncle Bean as Brigadier, though he stood over me, protective, and fixed grave
    houndom's gazed abyss unfathomable into human stare, we share between us
does he bring the certain share, the taste
For even Mary did not know the angel Gabriel when he stood before her as a man
    without a flaw, because she did not recognize the sign
And so at each isthmus, at each petiole you must be careful, and as the sight departs,
    certain only   then, if then, if ever, in the leaving
O if I could only know whether he knows what heart he has possessed, or saved or
    perished or lost to love and left alone to face each certain danger

Now toss the coin of that small song, heads or tails, power on the one side, soul on the
    other, obverse and reverse of what whirl in the telling
no voice for the singing, but in the voice itself the song come out as the color, the rush,
    and then the dying away
The lines as sudden as blood on the fingertip and the scratch it came from disappeared
as lost and hidden in the hair or down the back as Spring gone under in November
    woods, and expectation
And yet exactly there to meet, exactly on the birthday and five years older than was he,
    in the degree of three and three
and play for the meeting a fantasy in Art Tatum for the father, as Busoni's was in Bach
    for his
the trio, "I Know That You Know," or solo, "Begin the Beguine," or Berigan's "I Can't
    Get Started," into the same war, flipped, unflipped
and what the landscape is of each old 78 played until worn out, and past
terrain made peneplain of ridge and groove ground down, too softly intricate beyond
    facsimile to ever map or duplicate
but real imaginal as meetings with our certain dead or those unknown we scan for
    their true seal
But this is land, and music's land played out, and land intrinsicate, into what certain share

Five eggs
on the patio table
weigh
two lemon
yellow two
lavender one
orange in
for days
their bowl and nest
of imitation grass
cold nights have not cracked quiet
as the epilogue of war unfolding

irruptive metaphor against
invisible maintenance
as immanence
a boxer prances
past the dumpster
his tennis ball rolls after
called to to notice
the ball called too
hearing as the eggs
though they do not move
except to yield
the seepages of worlds
plastic translucent
memberment
insanguinate
excapsulate
hyacinth scent
into the under
into the patio
world below
jonquils and forsythia
banks and master classes
to let come out of the grass
the grass itself and who is in the grass
the place in the grass
and the aura
if it is remembered
if it is not all clouded over
the full moon
and the dog in the moon
the eclipse
maybe
the comet
but it is very hard
to go into those rooms

[Instructions]

It is the stranger, it is the strangest come into the dream that is there to tell the dream,
    the dream itself has told
does it, can it, will it, can it not
The golden egg and its molten enamel goo does not say anything
or the tacit four-story truck top holding back from rolling off the roof
only the people down in the street, where the waves and the sands break, call out by
    the finial jar of adornment fallen and come to help
But the egg puts on the abyss, and the fear of falling is the fear of talking
In its other room white moths, a white spider flying, moth lace torn to restore cloud,
    storm, and disperse
The ancient birdheaded scepter found without its wings but known to have borne them
    can unlock doors
and before the door the wakened watch dog has its flat rooftop, its spine scepter needle
    sharpened to alert, but silent
From the next street golf balls are being pitched into open windows out of the secrecy
    of Melville, white par, white worlds aloft, white holes to hope for
and even the garments of intelligence are mistaken for presents taken home to make up
    with an angry spouse
and the chance cork popped displays that frieze of flamey leaves that might be called
    happiness
Which of these is the stranger, which is the strangest, which speaks, which does not
    keep yielding up the very disturbance that would unpack ancestors and the spirit
    itself of the ditch
The seal you seek to speak or need no speaking

The king's seal and the king's reef are in the sky
the sleek head stretched and the solemn imprint
and the ridge furl reached and struck
and the king is generation
Then take up the empery and the dominion and return them

as the rabbits at the salt lick take what is left for the deer
and the long stare back into the woods for the others
The water that is in the sky and the land and the hand
pass on in one direction West with the eagles
and with the spin of blackbirds back against the other
And you are the continuance and the impress and the delivery
and the indication, the in and the from and the pre and the to

.

There are mounds in the dense woods of Northeast corners and all Northeasts
    everywhere
encircling for thousands of years their own reason for being
to the game and its plenty as near the eye and the skin of the eye
as the bare feet to their earth

.

Already at Equinox a carved pumpkin guards the door to the next house
two young men bare skinned attend at one a.m. and leave to light the coming Fall

On the steps there is a cup of leaves just started turning, still turning, overturning flame

rustling in the wind in there, sea surge
to sip the air between crashes on the light shore and returns

From under a different tree, into a different weal

[Borrowers]

There was an English family novel of our parents' generation or just before that
of business and family business and hierarchies of old ritual down the West
She used to talk about a darker side of Galsworthy and his Forsytes, all interwoven
    with Shaw's *Heartbreak House*, as though it were about that music and its jars and
    not alone the same catastrophes
a tradition of reading passed on only in the telling
as once the slow movement of Beethoven's G major piano concerto was the knocking
    of Orpheus at the gates of Hell for Eurydice
teacher and pupil, Romeo and Juliet hiding dying in the scores of the first string
    quartets, sphinxes of mute necessity
She lectured only about the public aspects and the inheritance, the reversals and reverses
we had just our feet to the surface of, as to the edge of a mud puddle and glass looking in
gazing into that complete and silent other universe, the other world of other people's
    other worlds, one day we would be in
She did not say *medieval*, or the hidden story of the Golden Fleece and how it came to
    the West
or the slow migration East and West of the jeweled Falconry of Malta
or of self and more than self and continental self
but in the time search under the sands
an old acid trip remembered as the doubling of reflection lights to step through
it was our estuary, we knew, and that family way

✪

The quiet intricate interior forest of the Christmas cactus and its blossomings bends
    down over the jade tree where the cameo chair seat looks out to the Northern world
what can be seen over the balcony boards, wood rush to meet, contemplation of the
    tops of trees and roofs and the sky lines advancing and receding
If you lean forward far enough you can see almost in the back right corner one board
    with a knobhole through it
the start of a needle down to thread and begin the sewing, the mending and the
    embellishing

and just barely visible over the edge straight ahead at the other end of the compound
    surround
the upper third of a balcony door and the room seen lit the night of the poet's death
    and known there was a sun in there through the dimension
through the leaves and branches into and through the dimension, through what stare
    stares into and through
and drew it, the red life, the thread drawn
deep deep in the zygocactus' cerise and the lobe green the jade tree pine stand reaches
    up through
crows calls, and the plastic shopping bag flapping in the golden rain tree branches
the inner world of iced-over mountain ash berries swallowed, but the birds do not
    swallow them, they talk
saving for much colder weather or too bitter even in adversity and against starvation
The flame blossoms hanging far off in the dark caught woods, and the coleus grove
the discolor the manycolor aura knocking at the door of the kids' migration who live
    down stairs and on this floor
how far a country is college, how far a continent and many countries, talk and return
    and tell
The sun is out today for only about the second time in a month
the cerise fleece guarded in the haunted grove, when the real mystery is the flowering
    itself
the red life out of the green life and back again

[at Rubén Darío's birthday]

Esto es épico y es lírico

One dog jumps out for the big yellow plastic bone, out from the porch of mistings
held back at first by the mystery of mastery, the mistery in a knowledge, just there in
    the seeing of it, and then let loose
and the other bounds out for the tennis ball from the opposite direction
orange liqueur and brandy and one drop of bitter elixir, they meet
and the ball that is not a ball but a rounded shrub of a cylinder, oblation of flowerdom

551

rolls up from their meeting, not bone, not uncurtained, but green and generational

The generosity of dogs, just there in the sight of them, one dog, met and the mass
    more than critical

and the sight more than nova the holding, the bone and the bone absorbed and the
    ball picked up and absorbed

dog life misted out of the greens and the porch of greens

sight was made for, place is made of

[syzygos]

It is great chaos, already forming into flames, and from the inner circles steps an eye

with only ankles and big feet and bigger forearms and enormous arms outstretched

an eye, the only body an eye, the hands on out beyond the flames

the flames the itinerant donkey of destiny placidly but quizzical and a-peel steps out
    through

Have you been astride there, are you come home from that journey out of the deep
    canyon of past life

at the outer edges of the trail and flopping in the dust, he who travels with a cage over
    his head and with the egg to measure by

so tired in the kitchen you've gone to sleep with your head down on your arms across
    your knees

Come to bed, lie next to me, your close-cropped hair against my cheek, our arms
    around each other

the stirring in the loins the tremors along the faults that make the continents

to awaken to the actual absence, to all the other lives we carry face to face and in
    between us

———————————————

The child we were out of the war
the war and the makers of the war
and the anachronism that is time itself
and time against itself
The choice of a life
that we can only make by growing up
that only growing up recovers
To be strangers to the universe
To and in ourselves to stand
Where have they gone
those who brought us here
where have they gone
leaving us alone
and we on after them
and the kids along the way
and come back again
To the empty parking lot and the couple
aunt and uncle
parents' friends
friends of aunt and uncle
who do not take us in
But there is the tent
and the door to the tent
there they have been
and there they will be
and there is no other key
Bindweed flowers in the median shrubbery
dog scratches an ear by the lamppost
by the sofa
lapping water in the hallway
pattern of delivery
pattern of remorse
pattern of remembering
boscage and intarsia of the sky

[tulip études]

Tulips and études   leapings and weavings
they tear their fabric in their eagerness the necessary
know holes know in knowing
the one that is as the other   the other that is as
The tongue of praise and   ready quiet limber and
     boneless   persuader
of the unboned   great red tumbler to hold
the boned and the unboned   overreacher from the new green
overreachers
Tulips and parrots   rocks and gauzes   feathers and
one single feather on the sidewalk to the carpark
pinion feather of a person   not crow or jay or by the river eagle
by the river blood into the underground of blood   flight
that is the breaking of the color   that is the breaking of the flight
Nobody's heard anyone say I'm flying this year   but some are
some wings moiré like curtains they are so sheer
some tongues are so sheer bestowers
I'm flying this here   this sheer
and some tulips may be as dagger and as needle as a cup
as much a work of study as to fly   to break up
loud laughter and delight the sky

    ·

If a turban and a tulip are as together tulle
and neither yet the name itself
if sky is hole conception gives to hide and be alive
can there be a turban of as pointed scales as sharp struck chords
as rum of feathers as of rocks to wear
Always a new part of town not known about before
though always thought was known about   grander and more secret
piano scales and a pause and long held chords practised in a house passed by
the land itself lasting away to its deep hollow

with sidewalks through and stairways back to sky
back of grade school and as deep   as deep as boulders rolled from the ice
You know with a tulip it is a turban and a chalice and a wrapping and a set of spikes
held with a slender knotted thread until it's time to show and opens
it is a flower of town here   that opens
the agate hammer of pride in this part of town   the railroad opens
as this part of town opens   the grander and more secret hollows
and wears their flight of petals in its folds
its wearing in its secret swearing

    .

The year's big red tail sticks out from behind the door   or did   or
this year's little white one
Some people burn their dead flowers to return the sun   some just dump them
some save from the old year's hairs for a brush with this one's
and with one single strand tie and untie the secure knot at the calyx to let fly
the tide of life back up the hollow stalkway out of the underground and back again
And some tulips' aphids are the viral milk cows of unpredictability
carrying and chewing the cud of bizarrerie and breaking
freaking and streaking
to let fly

    .

It drinks far deeper red   blood deeper sea and white and swallowed red
while the depicted heart is tulip scarlet Valentine
but its dark cross its dark stamens and its pistil star are hidden in the cup
its breaking is the rending in the rendering   made true
even if *the god is the place of healing*   and the true
is again and again untrue
Yet the divine drink in its conviction tastes of the heart
and the petals' breaking out of the variegation
The sudden warmth again in middle February brings in certain
Southern-facing and protected beds
the second crocuses and the few first tulips up
to meet that yearning
or it to petal leap and merge

[étude homage, *Religio Medici*]

How we outlive our notions of ourselves
and never know the others in there all along
give them away, become them
only at a stretch imagine
and the stretch is good
the old deep topaz Madeira glow
the pole of the day slowly turns on in its stared down into depths
taste the nigh noon pass!
the tongue decides
better than hands the layers of the day
for the other, I use it but like my Globe
and turne it round sometimes for my recreation
…yet to begin the Alphabet of man

[— and with respects to James Davidson's *Courtesans and Fishcakes*]

He would be the first hour waker from himself
and the right hand again and again gone to sleep
unnumbed
the first story tellers in their adolescence already ask about words that aren't in the OED
    or any other dictionary at hand but certainly are words and wake
First one way from the bathroom the mirror tells and the space between the floors
bird to be flurry, snake to be tail, uncertain space to be the dissolution and solution,
    face to be the trajectories and the passing through
Another way outside owls may be the birds and crows from the snake their plumage
    and their plunge, fire from the hand their fire
The first hour is the hour of falling in love and the waker the way out into the town
    and all its unknown places to live in to look at and want to live in

First they say over and over is to start

He would be the first hour starter from himself

On the cardboard back of an old yellow pad set aside to pack with a young man with
thick glasses says he has come to occupy the house and take over the work I was
about to start myself I said

Socrates says he is the opson eater

along with a brush flourish and a couple of eyelid studies and bills added up from
some September in the red

but opson is in fact the flourish, the relish, the garnish, the fish dish, the made plate
between bread and wine, what is itself the best as hunger is pickle of desire

he himself is the opson

like the passion for fish that weavers have and blown-glass eyes and soft bone tweed to
hang and stir the air and boil desire

On-less, the abundance and the part set aside of all this harvest

and on, of all this harvest, set aside to start with

[Sotto voce]

Hyacinths
in the room hyacinth
smell blood orange
peel bitter Campari
veils and mists
musk and roots
in March
at slow dark
ceneri carefully
ordered not
directed
but to cross the street
is not just to get there
opens

where everywhere
a cloud of little
sawtoothed toothpointed
leaves and boutonnière small
late chrysanthemums
showered and suspended
holds
each banded agate head
of fascination
to hold an egg of agate
in the hand
as hyacinths
in the land
as henbit dead nettles
in forest pinnacles
turn and return
heard and overheard
on the front steps
on the brick walk
talking
football fields
and tomato plants
petunias
and renewals
of the life together
of the songs again
together
the Chance One
and the Chance Two
Tew Tew Baby
the Tao
Breaking Breaking
and the Stonehammer
and the Thundercloud
harmonica and jewsharp
blown bells and rings

through the wrist
better than any
to tell
a golden flicker
glitters from the mud
a mallard
prods
from the pond
one of us
an old clown
on a park bench
gesturing to one of us
the crowd
for approval
to break a branch of lilac
to bear that scepter
to tear asunder
between
and under
and reencounter
now
each nose
a rose
blue opal roses
and red
before an open window
and the loom of light in there
the dipstick of light
in here
into the flowers
in this room
one hyacinth
horizontal to the world
blue violet one
double stalked
rose red and then

white pink again
to the earth
words for the dead
or from
lines that come as close as
but do not
but as osmosis
as the hyacinth smell
and the peeling
here
of the first air

[Ides]

Rings of death   or television rings of death
around not of or in   hearing and doing something else
that tv shows to forget about   for the nights and days of both
    wherever you go no matter
and in the old days we'd have to go over to somebody else's house who had a set
for a special program, a special game, a show, for anything   but used to, all the time
and if they're not home but guests from out of town to have to explain to
not entirely welcoming people who feed off of veiled and varied antagonisms and
    irritations and just their sheer possession of the place
the show is lost or only turned on and not able to follow, even with the happy dog
    come in to join
so with death around the vacancy
and when the owners do come back, and you *do* know them from the many times before
even if neither he nor his new wife nor his daughter seem to care or remember you
and with that much money, all the money in the world, who would have to
it becomes one big big party after all, it usually did
and rings around each other   around everybody
of the temporary and altogether transitional affluence of life itself
when it is the grief you came caring about
and wanting to watch something out of the swallowing up part of the made world
to juxtapose to   and let the forgetting forget itself for a while
but it is never made easy

«Often I reawaken from my body
and inside myself.» Plotinus, II

STUDIES

CUTS · SHOTS · TAKES

a notebook sequence / August–December 1999

After, from, and back to
the California friends

and all the friends

The author wishes to thank the editors of *First Intensity* and *The Pleasure Beast* for first publishing some of these studies.

As in our actual life, or in our dream life, so in our arts or made-up life, in poetry, real and immediate things as well as beings, wherever we acknowledge them in-form us.

But this consonance I seek between actuality and the poem is not easy.

—Robert Duncan

ludus, lūdere may be from the Etruscan
around the humour of life
first-, before-play
as even before the watering
but the watering itself is also part of the play
as it comes glittering down in a braid from above and curves slowly past
is there the flush of fever first on plants that are ill
the sudden hectic of flu or of rhus oil on the naked skin in the green
the baptism of what is *said* in the fire
quick tongue   flick that   blisters still
locust drone in out of the heat

✪

études of massive block sonority
the sound of a cello saved from the baggage hold and caught
just before it hits the tarmac
the walk not to the paradise but the old home gardens garden
even if that's just our same old dump of a place and still to get there
sunk not to oblivion in the center of the river of fucking
but the importuning of intentioned and unrecognizable strangers
to set back the night or set it forward in the light
where inside the hyacinth vine the she-cardinal hops in and out to find

✪

mirrors that reflect backwards of how mirrors should reflect
however long before they give it back
are very thick and no less than new green leaves on the mountain ash
new birdseed bells on the balcony edge
with their twin ties aloft like antennae waiting for days and days to be strung up
the sapling door at the end of the room
is wound around the wrist too tight
too tight the night wrist bound

the wounds to be protected cut off and let loose above the door
full moon into the grove
the lintel black as night blood or black laurel
does not reverse the image
or the dresser mirror's blue self with the nose curved as the moon curves
the dark moons under the fingernails that tell black blood
and do not reverse the self let back
do not let back the self let back
but wait as long and thick as leaves and as late

the window shattered out into the storm lets in the storm
lets in the flood and its redfronded palm trees
lets in what waits at the end
lets out what waits for the end
in this room right now that takes all that has come before and waits
it's time to go home
the father time the mother space
but all these people here already are
a room as vast as presidency and as invaded
the father space the mother time
that are not home but orders of perception
as home itself is an organ of perception
lets in the rain that music makes
lets out the tightly woven carpets of the rain
knows at the end whose redfronded palm trees are they?

the orchard ground runs uphill from the road on out from under the trees to the high
        hills and the valley
there used to be a doghouse here, kids played in, gone with its spiders
now the dogs live in the screenedporch shack
dozens of them waiting around the bare yard and the car
the travel is theirs

568

✪

nobody knows everybody who will be there
one is the *River of Fire Drip*, one the *Pyriform Octopus Slake*
one is the *Autumn Abyss*, one the *Icicle Sonorous Stone*
there is a blackblue satin glow in the blood brown lacquer glaze
that does not melt even to the tongue or the hot finger down the strings
each flamed abyss trembles on its stem and turns about to fall
each pale new hoot refreezes all that has melted
and the ladder is set here, drop resonant by drop

✪

it is not always possible to get The Snake That Binds The Book
to come back and bind the book
not poisonous but recalcitrant
doesn't bite but might

✪

patchouli from Mark and Janice's garden, and a big freezer bag of herbs, four plum
    tomatoes, one quite ripe goldenyellow globe, a couple of jalapeños
Pogostemon cablin/Pogostemon patchouly, Stachydoideae/Lamioideae of the Labiatae/
    Lamiaceae, along with mint, thyme, oregano, savory, and many others, including
    the henbit dead nettle
leaves intensely redolent of the volatile oil, and indeed looking very nettleish
next to the turbid, the dregs-filled vin santo, Tu Fu's muddy cups lifted
fingers smelling of wet basil, flat parsley, thyme, rosemary, oregano, sage, all rubbed
    together
from the last of the store-bought parsley a crushed ladybug falls
whose dots dot the heart
here in the season of falling leaves to meet you once again
and from the branch of patchouli honor the departing oil of life, the departed harbingers
whose wings are eyes, whose elytrons are ours
the balcony door open, the first really flawless Autumn evening, but the air conditioner
    not off yet, not turned enough and lasting, yet

crickets, Dale and Hoa said were far more in evidence here than in Austin
and *dragonflies*, at 9th and Vermont, hovering over the traffic at the stoplight,
      twice recently, even the same one?
later: Cyrus, crossed paths with on campus, tells that male dragonflies hang out
      around places like flagpoles and crossroads felt prominent to attract mates
so the snake doctor where our movement's densest

✪

there is enough sarcasm in the world already without excavating more
but Prokofiev's Op. 17 *Sarcasms* still have charm to restore

a pizza is delivered 11 a.m. next door in its scarlet bumbleshoot to cure
a midweek hangover with whatever leftover beer

inward the bird is blue in its crystal body light the *macbenac* of jay to cardinal to
      catbird and return
even overheard in the distant backyard over the telephone behind the overt long
      report the password given again proved true

✪

along the grain of marble where the leaves grow slack and start to drop
the Autumn cascade in the stone pulses blue as breathing under its skin

✪

but the sun stays covered still, and when will the wind turn
the locust by the dumpster not gone yellow yet, itself a great vein in the rock that turns

✪

the sidewalks are all dried after the rain
except for the dark soul shadow around the dead squirrel
splayed out as though supplicating the concrete

fur of the spine ridge fur of the tail curled up along the spine ridge frayed up rat-gray
      and gnat-thickened
yesterday late afternoon a few yards away it was sitting in the bare dirt head bent down
      to the earth
bitten in the neck or by the quickest plague or simply the heart gone dropped in
      mid-jump
carried in the night play by the same catch and turned around
so now to face me

last night I saw my father and wasn't sure he wasn't still alive
sitting knees up reading in bed and all absorbed as I was in what is in what is not lost
a moment the face fedoraless in the photo made just before he left for the war
a moment some kid in a t-shirt and backwards baseball cap studying for an exam
the face as the hat as the bed as the body of vision as the tense as the death
gone to me

so you leave the car and set out on foot for help
after the kids in their expedition
the little finch-like birds with orange beaks and cheeks, gray and white and a dark bib
      border, unlike any North American species
chittering at the edge of rest
and come back later the same day and the car's gone and the field's plowed and built
      up and the vegetable stands that weren't even there before full of contentious
      sneerers insinuating complicity
you know all about it just as well as we do and you're acting like you hadn't got the
      slightest idea
the bounty of somebody else put some place else and nary word one about where the
      car's gone
even if returning brought an armful of graygold roses flameflared who thought this
      was their field and kept that glory in their odor
orange as pumpkins, and their claws
and finding a front porch down the road to get up on to out of the rain

✪

into the month of the Pumpkin
to be varied, air and embellishments, arie antiche
pensive as of another era in its own
pondering even in its vigor onwards the passing of time and its own other time

leaving behind an old pair of wornout levis in the grass by the road, been there a long
    long while
pockets empty but for a few odds and ends
a marble or two, a couple of pebbles, some smashed links of a chain, a nut, a foreign
    coin (how did it get left?), faded matted ticket stubs
all that it mattered to life to keep always along

✪

the new moon, Venus, Regulus together
vivid when first up at 6 a.m.
noon calls the glory hold   how?
walk out in and memorize
the memory of sheer bodily absorption
still not enough
as brilliant as they were
as brilliant as the day is out
again in the season of departure
and of having come

✪

there is a part of town I haven't been to since before the war
not to the quiet dialogue but the contemplation passing quiet
before another journey
sending regards but not acknowledgements

✪

the hyacinth vine's overflow is cut back from the fence top
an old fugitive tear found in the corner of the eye from its past time its past things to
    cry about glitters and goes as the vine goes
entirely inside
there are still rooms under the canopy in the purple pods and beanlike blossoms of
    the eyefolds
in October in the visitors' time and the rooms gone under everything
in the lablab in the deep eye of the simmering

✪

what are the *216 existents?*
two more than the classifiers
twice the round of counted prayers
and in the categories of apparition beings
the greater governings into which their vaster presences are apparent
the golden centers of the chrysanthemums
as appropriate to their power as the mind shaken by love
whether he comes down in his new red t-shirt
or up from their incandescent cloud
storm down out of the North
or in the quietest eruption
devastating the deepest roots
while the light vine that sways along the patio fence
gives way and carries
riding the new rooms out of the old
leaving this divan where we meet
for the departed the departed return to
for the newly come never known each other before
still come back to
and the clearing and the marestails afterwards still breathing
and the smell of Autumn dense as the smell of naked skin
this gathering this assembly house this house of documents
this place of writing on its own fabric

of spending the night on the way home
of finding each other where travel's dimensionality is the interchange of distillations
can you make up a water of life that will not taste the same but be equivalent
how?   what would that be?   to trade?
first offered a drink and turned it down and then ashamed come back
asleep in the window seat
which of us comes nearest
these meetings and these questionings around the place not spoken not made up not
    made yet not set down not taxed not harped on not angered at
but wanted between us
at the point of rest that still wants everything to come to come
no rest
slant light catching the scattering of the cottonwoods backlit
the strongest grip the scattering of it backlit
prescription tallies carved along the long sides with the sequence of healing plants and
    match
the outer air where the hands hold, the ground
the wood the sky

in Alvin's parking lot he played me the one side Benny Carter ever recorded solo on tenor
Black Lilacs or *Lilac Nocturne*
made privately in Europe in the late 30s and kept private
made where he heard Lawrence's secret *Oranges* and kept secret there too
and told me you couldn't even get that much any more
the satellite failed and lost and only this echo left
he had a lot of packages in the back that looked like boxes of wine bootlegged into
    other boxes, and all these cassettes and faceless CDs
and one track of Hawkins just as rare and no name to it, he never sounded like that
    again, high and mezza voce clear
when you hear something like that it sends me to the mountains
where the snows have come early and just in patches and the black rocks are exalted
calling for that kind of breathing listening
and the aspens against the evergreens

or if you can't, and I can't, here the bronze amethyst chrysanthemums
drunk from the color, no matter their antidote
steel topaz the air, to the heart of the blossomings and back out again, carved in the carrying
and slowness more charged than season can unfold

✪

I knew the patoo in the night
knew of the patoo as the patoo is of the night
not what the patoo is
but what was there
Mother of the Moon

✪

my shmoo gourd is blackgreen on cream speckle-striped
and does not need cutting to be jack light of the ripening
it sits up bigger than a pumpkin's pussums
snout stout hard meditative bright in the night
and guardian amethyst amethyst guardian
promising   promising   promising   promising

✪

on that estate there is an indoor pool in a pavilion rather like the tennis casino at Newport
no, not for swimming, not so deep, but with banks of sea sand piled up, groined with
      wood and leather and handforged stud nails
and not to carry a candle across to keep it lit, though that might be done
the uses as variable and unpredictable as whether or not to have whiskey in your iced tea
      and against what season
but to stare into, to contemplate, to bathe the gaze in
certainly to circumambulate
you can't go in the one door and out the other without traversing two sides
and two sides draw you all around, and all around, the long way
it is the pool of the long way

✪

Plotinus wrote: «Often I reawaken from my body to myself: I come to be outside
    other things, and inside myself.» [*Enneads* IV 8,1,1, the version by Michael Chase
    in his translation of Pierre Hadot's *Plotinus, or The Simplicity of Vision* (University
    of Chicago Press, 1993), 25]
which when I first read it I thought said: «I come from being outside other things to
    being inside myself.»
which is the existence that is a call
there is a conviction that if you jump up and down off and on the curb long enough
    with your feet held tightly together
you'll fly
others have been convinced that perfect immobility for the exact number of days or
    months — and the number varies —
will turn your eyes to emerald
and with emerald the immobility will be limitless vibration everywhere

✪

is that made according to the President's regulations, she called out to us as we came
    from the woods carrying the foldedup banner
take a look at it, I said, and threw it open and up like a giant shortsleeved sweater, as
    high and spread as wide as the maple we were standing in front of
o I haven't got time for that, she started yelling, I haven't got time for it, I haven't got *time*
pushing right up into my face, screaming, you silly sonofabitch, what the fuck are you
    doing that for
and slugged me or started to slug me, and I caught and threw her arm back and pushed
    her away
and two guys came up and tried to calm things down, and very quietly the one her
    brotherinlaw said
she's sort of crazy man, but don't worry about it, she's not really any threat, ever since
    my brother was killed in the war
and we spread the big striped wool banner out on the grass and started folding it up
    again to put it in its plastic carrier
and she said, down on the ground helping us, they see a lot of the details OK, like the
    orange juice and the lemon stripes

576

but not the big picture, not the stretches of what they do, not the flag, not the flag in
  the flag

✪

and who lie down with in the dark
an old highschool friend I never wanted to but who knows
and only just my wanting or not wanting
come in the night but come to me
or gone to

✪

Dale Hawkins is dead, that day, the 24th, in Topeka, where he'd been a fireman, battalion
chief, retired — a year older than me, I hadn't ever known or didn't remember — failed a
grade? it could be, though not very likely — or rheumatic fever? some faint memory click
of that? — but we were in the same grade all along? — I'd just a day or so before been
thinking about him in grade school, wanting the recipe in an old chemistry handbook I
had from my brother, for rose water, to make some for his mother — intense request,
pleading, remonstrating, "come on man, you promised, it's for my mom" — AA member,
Little League, Boy Scouts, the *Fort Scott Tribune*'s obituary of last Friday tells — one
more to earth o'ergiven of childhood's friends — as birth month ends — the dark time of
the year — and what tales of the dark time here? — first Christmas cactus buds just start-
ing to open Dale and Dale — and Dale Barney and all the taunts growing up because
of Dale Evans — the far West side of town, Dale Hawkins, less money, Ab Wood, Jim
Hegge, Carmen Lewis, Oop Hood, to my nearer West side, big house, doctor father —
or Dale Barney's East side, and railroad father — and the closeness with Dale Hawkins
not kept up as we went on into high school — and he into the Navy after graduation,
married in San Diego, and then Topeka and the fire brigade, children, grandchildren —
those who can tell you about yourself when you were young, or you about them — fewer
and fewer, one by one — the closed-in self, the expanded self —

  •

last night my mother died again, and as suddenly and as without any time for leavetaking
and a basketball rolled into the yard and on into the backyard from across the street
and was followed in retrieval by a high-school age kid, and all of it very important

and there was a Viennese stepmother, "very Vienna," though my father had not remarried
    her
that Emporia might somehow be Vienna
—I *had* talked to Denise Low in Alvin's parking lot that evening, and she's from
    Emporia, but her trip had been to New Haven—
didn't enter my mind till writing this, and still is not clear how, even remembering the
    Peking-Vienna restaurant Roi Jones and I passed in NYC decades ago — "man,
    they've bracketed the continent!"
the actual stepmother is from Emporia
has she gone to Europe? it might very well be, by the night net transmission tells of
    hills and dales
"boy, I sure do miss my mom," Billy McReynolds said to me in 4th grade, turning
    around in his desk hollow-eyed
mighty Muthos is a mother and reaches farther than continents to transform
even down the dark side of climacteric as deep and far as ever in 4th grade
or further back than that from across the street into the backyard after what, a
    football, a baseball, a cat
"she's ours, she's Milky, you give her back"
the older boys who come to the gates from the East and out of the West and from the
    Center still to go into
she is with

if I can be the young man who went with that expedition long before I ever knew him
and was their navigator with as much certainty as his own life was not
if only for one long evening finding him lifting himself to be someone more
haven't I kept that yearning since before I was born and his

[For Ed Dorn — 2 Apr 1929 – 10 Dec 1999]

in the far back pasture animals have lined up in lament
dog goat pony horse and beyond them
a cow in its astronomical agility
a real dog and pony show
giving tribute back on their hind legs
musicians at the window
lacking the cock his call
the show the world

along the fence rows in with the hedge apples
the night winter cray bushes are in bloom
the cray?   what are they?
that is their rhyme

✪

when Robert Duncan wrote *tide* on the blackboard he spelled it *tidd*
and through the letters his hound not his cat stretched out
combining leap and lying down

where the trees are bare but the air between them filled with black saturated leaves
dripping clatter   can't you hear them?
surging with the moon

✪

certainly what you bring away is more than yours
each instant still as a fire alarm
or a corridor-counting country-longing out from under the sub-urban blues
no hunters in the snow come out of the woods
only one guy bent over under the hood of his months-dead pickup

leaning so far his underpants show above the levis
nervous and alone, constantly looking around
from one of the Northern river counties, longing home
but not enough to go there yet

✪

when I went out at 9
to buy a Sunday *Times*
and extra presents too
there was a white compact sedan
parked next to mine
engine going couple groping
in a tight embrace
and the woman in the driver's seat
still there still clenched still just as tight
when I got back
45 minutes they'd been at it
an hour easily and more
from on before
and the motor running all the while
but o baby o
it's so
cold outside!
o give me some
o Christmas cheer!
o light the year
to come!

✦

surely the goose boy the gander tender and all the creatures
deserve better than half-frozen ponds and the yard gone gunk
North calls North but not to fly
and who will give it to them?

the hard work home is the hard work home not home to come
and only a foxy dog for a companion
and it too gone before too long
too hard too hard the landscape to the landscape through

+

standing in that line in Borders
exploding I think I was here first, you just got in front of me
well I'm sorry, I didn't mean to
well it sure looked like you did
and a Merry Christmas to you too, though I'm sure you won't have one
o you take your cut where you will

impatient irritation and anger
over and over given way to and shown
these last days of the ending year
the discipline of care
not kept
kept the care of true exchange
not nurtured
ill the use of self and others ill
at what?
edaphic
edaphic what?

light a candle for us all
for the goose boy and the goose yard and the geese gone
and the foxy dog gone
and all gone everywhere
for care
be patient for
as I have not
for what?
to care

✪

the day's the year's walk to come
to search a mystery in your own face in everyone's
o spirit, I'm too old
wouldn't it be better if I just went home to bed?
o no
the rituals to turn around and upside down
to free from the bonds of all the rest of the year and years and days
even if just for the blinking of an eye to start to last
light the temenos of a candle
of a light lit and it
long looked at
and through it
a boy there or who is it in a hooded cloak
bringing fulfillment, *telesphóros,* or is it
the fulfillment-bringing *year,* or through it
the gods also become sharers in the city
having their own plots of land
now only spaces around a light
that
intimate
that
edaphic link
that
terra in
in terra
pax
:
to be
continuously
interested
:
for you will need it

Monica here for dinner, first return since going East late in the summer — Meaux-mustard-breaded chicken breasts broiled, penne with the last of the recent fresh tomato and garlic sauce, Brussels sprouts sautéed black in butter with lemon, salad, ice cream, a Chilean Veramonte merlot, then Germain-Robin — and with the gin before, a big dent made in the chexmix pillow bag, big enough for the heaviest head of dreams, and now and then a white filbert, elephant by elephant — she'd heard George and Chuck read at St Marks two weeks before, talked with them afterwards, especially with Chuck about Parmenides, and her own *Thurageneia* — send it to him, I said — as the year ends, send — and ran into Kyle downtown that afternoon, he and Cyrus and a carfull off to Chicago for the Millennium Turn —

we looked up *hysteria* in the *Oxford Classical Dictionary* — and straightaway spilled wine across the top facing — the myth of the wandering, the errant womb — know how that's been used as excuse and instrument of repression — yours, theirs, ours — mine, I said, as freakout likely as any — our migratory collective suffocation and resaturation — but I'm a man, I don't have one, *really*, who am I to talk — who *am* I to talk — yet the site of making does move, and does release, and is repressed — calls like the sunray calls, to find —

because a fire is there, to search the yearend with a wand as flexible as hazel in the eye or wheat or branch of juniper or only breath of wine — a sestina with the end words never said, just heard and known, tacit as reiteration and as measure is, and always on the move —

hail, *Born of the Door!*

in the Winter light is the carrier
carrying the medium
thick, glossy, sticky, aromatic
smelling like an artist's household
speeding up and slowing down
as dense an intervalic as wet leaves

or newspapers for the wind
to sop the zinger particles up
like ink light
wearing an old overcoat and a cap pulled down
the Rapids in the Fall, and Raven in the Dark
the Green Silk and the Pearly Pure Tone and the Scorched Tail
with a mail of just bills and tearup ads, not even the hometown newspaper
all in the Silence of Every Valley
but the Black Crane comes and dances through the room preliminary to its dance
a searching of sonorities amongst the chords before the performance
as the *hystera* wanders to search each new birthplace
Dinu Lipatti at Besançon in his last recital, Josef Hofmann in his golden anniversary
    concert
to hear the image first, to find the cast of the music in a few notes before the music,
    to flourish the focus in the fingers
抱 *pao*⁴ to embrace, unfold, cherish, brood, hatch, carry in
the arms, may also mean to bring
the *hystera*, its homophone in the first tone, with the same phonetic but with the
    moon radical, the womb
the carrier
as of 抱 琴 *pao*⁴ *ch'in*² bring the lute, the instrument, the tone, for that must be
    carried with such care
makes smooth, makes lustrous, makes slow to set, makes all reworkable anew

✪

"hello"
"is Eddie there?" or Cal or Ellen or Louie or —
"no, I'm sorry, you've got the very wrong —"
and every time it's for somebody different
at least not after that used kayak for sale again
or from the same phone booth full of desperation anger
but the beginning of the fields is right here across the road and up the hill a little
and in the wilderness beyond those fields, or rather inside them, the rescuers insist
    you give up all your portable possessions before they'll take you out
especially anything to write with, and of course any weapons

mine would be age, which could be easily dispensed with, coming down the rocks, as
     already in itself a liability to survival
or the chainsaw yesterday to cut the doorway shrubbery down to Winter
when it has already come
and the tinsel from the Christmas tree that lay two days where the squirrel fell dead
     in mid-leap last September before it was moved and fooled around with and
     carried off
glitter attracted and glittering where
the aura flowed out of the body and stayed a while, dark and luster-damp, tail still
     curled along the back
indelible call of bare trees
where the woods begin this way
and no sea
and this way
and another
see

the prairie Winter clear bare splendor is so deep
I'm sure I remember North Texas from before I remember
from patch to patch the year is unwoven
and across the gap rethicketed to come
and now remember here: interior with a Norfolk Island pine as Christmas tree, until
     Epiphany
and through it a garden in the wall where two figures suspended are confronted by an
     angel whose back is to us
or is it at the balcony door where the curtains moiré the last sunlight of the year, and
     still, and away
the chalk, the little chalk, the oil, the wax of the little chalk
is cray the crayfish cray?
but that's a mistaking out of OE *crevise*, OF *crevice*, OHG *krebiz*: edible crustacean
made to cray*fish*, cray*feesh*, and craw- and -dad
but *gerbh-* and scratch and crab and crawl and graffiti and diagram and draw
and all

UNCOLLECTED

Poem
for Ron Loewinsohn

Letters come telling it's spring already
in the west — the time of day I come home
to letters, where the sun sets already
in that west, all that the wind blew in

all night and morning, in the dust and snow,
and seeped in under the windows. Has begun its
slow spread to this mountain foot,
up the valley north from Mexico, in the air

east from those coasts — even all the metal warms,
is drawn to, the revolution even might be
thought or heard about, is warmer, and old
sashays out the mountain roads to drink beer, to lie

stripped in the sun, rocks come back out —
even in the yards as the car goes past,
and open, spread open—to draw back to,
metal clinked in the air, beer cans

clanked down those warmed rocks.
You stand up and walk off to go piss in the rocks
and the possibility of any love at all
there where the rocks fall, where the sunflowers'

shadows are,
is all the body ever thinks about,
legs spread in the air, that covers all
that space that rolls to west and surrenders

here its lick and slide to earth —
spring! letters open you all up
and dust along this blowing blown-on dust
the cant of voice off those other hills

that range all the way to love
and love, and back to love again,
spread where the legs are spread,
and letters lie, to piss in the sunlight.

— 20 Feb 1964

The Absence

Where are you in Europe, this year, Christmas tide, Alan?
angers between us kept us silent since April, the blood tide
moves and will not lap restful here beside the mid night beside the west ocean
birds move in the streetlight, gulls along the west sand
in that glow, fog to, horns sound, half way across the world
are you my brother

Strings loosen in whatever lute
fingers get caught in them, in the gut
tangle and tired, come
to cry, head against door jamb, jangles
of trying, doors shut, ignorant flesh caught and alone,
words without talking

Tire tracks in the rain
Some kid running in track shorts in the park
Old words out of Seattle
Grant them peace

— 10 Dec 1964

Photograph

Roses sprout, bloom from the table top,
into the light
band of the window, serapes
on the wall

plastic flower, old
ketchup, water glasses

and you, Sam, sitting across the table, half
out of focus, looking off somewhere
beyond my right shoulder, hand over your mouth

The "Gran Quivira," off Old Town square
in Albuquerque, some time in August 1961

And the light shining on it now, 3 years later,
in San Francisco,
till I cannot see your face, the light band
in that back wall —

is where I enter now? all
gone into the light? the sun
light out now from fog all day

burning my self to even feel it, see it,
as it burned, blazed down in that August in that dust and square

and do we enter there? to
gether, to gather

Where your gaze
goes off

She touches down,
The Light, in the light,
is more the door
than door itself
into the light —

words, senses
on top of themselves,
repeated, the same things
over and over again

She is

Flowers, even these plastic ones,
and ketchup,
reach up
towards

Moment in the photograph, moment of time,
this moment over and over again
upon the instants here —

no one is lost there, all
we who have entered

into Her fire: The Light

— 2 Dec 1964

Evening Poem — 31 Oct 1964

Peace out on the land — even if it's
Halloween, and the spirits out
walking on the land, kids
in their masks, cops — it is so quiet
in the long fogged park
they are gone into the wood, into the trees'
bark, into the grass —
the lake water lights holds
who the lover might be — to see
centuries — in the mirror of my toaster
in the dark kitchen I light a match
and see it go out, burn dark and glow —
the match light in the water —
What lover? I am gone half way already
into the trees' wood or the lake,
Caught blood pumping in the veins of my hand
is the same wave ripple by this shore
here, last night, every night. I would give
away anything of myself, then, and to whomever I meet
or know at all. Love, torn up body,
old jacking off or unable to touch it, unable
to go touch the loved body, it is
finally gone into the mind's back sight, behind the eyes,
kept — while I go on
lost into the things and beings of the world.

.

Halloween — what spirits
but the ones I already know
walk out, and speak, and are seen?
I imagine a room across town,
that is empty.
I see my own empty apartment.

And I go out, as in tomorrow
morning I will go in fact,
tonight into the park, lapped
into the streamed fog,
hanging my arms and walking,
as the eucalyptus leaves hang, the trees walk,
streamed, hung with the fog.

second evening poem — 31 Oct 1964

To set things right —

that I am divided, do not know
any certainty of where I am —

that if the body loved
goes into the mind's back pasture
it is not from fullness and a one with the world,
but from despair

Love holds all over my naked body in the bed
going with the eyes into the trees or grass
never removes

The spirits of Love
fuck in my room
All hallows Eve.
They come to my bed

in the darkness where the eyes can see nothing,
and the body —

"It Takes a Worried Man to Sing a Wearied Song"
—The Carter Family

Pete Pavey's
ford, farm, who made horseradish —
    Pavey's Ford
across Mill Creek — west and north
    in the trees
              dabble
    the feet

Mrs. Clark took me there
first, when I was 4 or 5,
stopped the old Model A
and we waded off the concrete

As she took me
picking dandelion greens
early spring, in the hills north,
on the 7-Mile Loop

May I so easily speak
of remembering,
to her,
if she is not yet dead

        .

Fords,   The Old
Military Ford.
The wide spot
in Buck Run
the road behind
the swimming pool —

someone was washing
his car, a Sunday,
we drove by,
before the war

.

The pastoral
of my town,

behind me, just behind
my memory, just before

I lived — it is
that quiet; the

Sunday afternoons,
the wash, the

birth of me,
come out of.

Movies of Fort Scott
seen in grade school

taken the year I was born.
Talk,

The loam into which
we are born. The grass

is concrete. Peaceful
graze they. The ford in the dark

Lehnhoff and I
pissed from, drank across

and into the trees, out
into the field

we were born in, the bonfire
lights out against the sky

and we stand panting, lost,
in front of it, drunk,

looking into the era
looking into the birth

looking into the moments
before our birth

we carry in us, we
walk across

   •

So I would put my naked body in here, too

Relish of light upon the nipples,
  pared away pooched fat till only muscles left

Where the spread of hair is up the loins, belly, chest,
  vines in the light and shade

  curls
  bleached and out in the sun

  Night of the Christmas week, journey begun
    to birth? alone in the darkness, 3 a.m. or past,
    phonograph slowed down to half, in the window
    drips of rain
      fart, kneel naked to bed

                              take myself
                                        then to this same altar

                              Love comes to
                                        in her same dreams

Naked in the sunlight
lying in rocks, in New Mexico

              balls burned

              face turned red

Glow in the dark

              here, where I place my body

              to be naked and face the other side of the page

              where as this room
                        no one is

    •

Till I wish it would rain in this room, too,
      not just in the streets —

      rain, I would be wet,
      I would have to wear a raincoat

      even here

      Pencils
      Nothing funny

A picture of a man starving to death
   sitting in front of a bank building

Let everything that happens in the world happen in this room as well

 •

In Viet Nam
   already one friend killed—
3 years ago, that far
   undulled, unlost

Vague shiftings to protest,
   downtown San Francisco
on a vacant wall, "Get out of Viet Nam"
   A button on Sam's coat last summer

  It'll be a good place
for the Army to send
   fuckups
It used to be Korea

     Messages scrawled on building walls, "Get out", "Get out"
     Buttons on coats
     The friend sitting in the Abramovitz' living room,
      on his way to Saigon, unheard from since

Rain in Christmas week, the San Francisco hills are green,
lights under the layers of rain, clouds low, come from across the bay
Songs sideways, one Salvation Army band
moving down the street, out of the corners of the ears

then enter night, and wait up all night
for dawn, the clouds too thick to see
more than the slow glow
that spreads

Ache, Old rubber bands
shot, snapped

                 Having entered now that spread field
                      wherein the bonfire burned
                 from the other end
                 in the dark

                                — 20 Dec 1964
                                San Francisco

"The faults along which the tremor runs"
                                — Robert Duncan

The night is finally clear, after weeks
      of rain without letup —

and the day was, I parked in Pacific Heights, at Baker and Broadway,
      streaked was the bay, heavy
      Angel Island, the foliage, at Belvedere
      down into the water

      the colorless golden air, the sun

      and driving back from North Beach, the same way,
      the brief half glimpse of the Bridge
           and the tides slung striations
           under it
               light already on

and in the Presidio ahead of me

the sun looked

and turned down

Night as clear, hangs to me,
        just after midnight
        I drive into the park
        to dump my garbage

.

And as the sun has cleared,
                                myself, back up
        from 2 days hangover, the almost
        migraine seizure of the head,

        in the dark

The smell of the cigarette I've rolled tonight after dinner, the same as the pipe my
grandfather or my oldest uncle smoked in Mississippi, Christmas the war started,
the visits later, the cling in the house.

Trying anything to come to some
whole, some understanding past
listing the instance after instances—these
past few days, the drunk, and the
months here in San Francisco without any
order, that come down to this, tie
the back head muscles into
no knots that liquor or pot
could tie, kick in
alone, or let loose

The nation itself, torn
as much, in all the directions
there are no ways to go in all of, cannot
make — layers, separate,
they become — starved or beyond poverty,
populations, lessons, leagues of, Appalachia —
Viet Nam, without even a clear rancor —
race, disgust, riots in summer to killings to floundered FBI turns in
Mississippi —
the defense contracts, the
Defense —
without accession, mix, or whole

Myself that am a nation, then

Where sunlight shines on, and in that moment of look
        out in the light, air, across the bay,
                            unsundered, happy

But wake up still with the unloosened headache
        racks for any way to go
        all others do not
        kick across

    •

Where in the dark
        fissures of the park
as in the crevices
        of the brain

the mingling shells of
        night and light
meet — in the garbage
        dumped

all who may eat,
          all armies of pestilence
and accomplishment —
          the world pains, stinks colors

in rainbows
          in that trash

7–31 Jan 1965

[Developments from a dream the night of 2–3 Feb 1971]

So Olson did come through Fort Scott
hitchhiking to Denver in the early 50's

with some one of his students from Black Mountain
not Dorn as I had thought but

probably smaller and dark, Jorge
Fick-ish, but not, some one I've never known

they must have come in the summer
and I would have met them

at the Fort Scott Drug, not Land's, I was
only 16 in 1952, say summer, still 15, or '53, too young

to drink beer legally and not
out doing it anyway (only

hard stuff in Franz's car
later) because of the paperback book rack

what little *new* was to be had, or
more conceivably

the Public Library — it was cool
and I went there all the time in the summer

trying to find the answers — maybe
the librarian, old Mrs. Pritchard, no, the one

after her, or the fatter one, introduced us
and we walked to meet

your companion, stopped at the drug store which
after all was next door to The Smoker

pool, I waited on the verge
of some *word* to tell, out of so

huge a certainty
I was so certainly

a poet in myself, but held
it out —

more clearly than I ever have —
however shyly

you saw, certainly, but not
really Daddy, I forgot you

till now, on that ridiculously
small low stool

coffeed moustache
eyes — certainly knowing this now

opens a whole
other Fort Scott —

clear and on off
as they were in Gloucester

8 or 9 years later
when I took the picture

it is not adulation now
and was not so simply then

though I imagine
a drawing-out of me

more than you had time for
and remember less of just how far

over my head you talked
but it only took 2 or 3 words

to hit
but which

however warm the heart
had to be forgotten

in time I had to learn
to love elsewhere

and shut up, and come back
exiled, carrying the map

now in California

.

Last night in my dream I was
trying to tell my father

what the new place was (with
arms crossed relishing how

many drinks I'd had) which
is what the poems were always

trying to do (out of the house
or by the time Olson showed

the whole damn world)
he must have told me to come

to Black Mountain, but that was impossible
then, I had 2 more years of high school, and was

simply too inept in the world, say □
he saw that, but

no, part of it was
to learn Fort Scott's past, to find out

all local dimension, but it was
a gleam deep in his eyes

telling me, tell
the Secret History of your town

get the Secret History
of yourself

•

The thrill of it
was finding out about all those

lines of continuity across the country
that went *through* Fort Scott

on off the world
"I'll be confused all my life"

I said, I couldn't really have said that
then, I felt, you

smiled on off NW past
some recurring Montgomery Ward's windows

ocean, I thought, I must have
talked about surrealists and Rilke

which simply didn't last very long
it was the roads of the continent

we travelled on
what the hell

were you looking for
in the Public Library?

eastern newspapers?
but no, some

fixture of the place
in that scheme, *past* Denver

a facet of that gleam in your eyes
secreted in the library

somewhere locked cupboard
gnosis I'd sought confusedly

Malin later, Judge
McComas in *his* eye, gave

me intimations of, but the thrill
was *transmitted* to me, wordless

was shot straight into my eyes
from yours and sank so far

down out of sight it only now
returns as it went in

but I have lived on all
that radiation all along

did you *say* what you were after, in the library?
Charles Francis Adams, no, that's my

Ralph Richards interpolation, it was
somebody I'd never heard of or since

found out, that might be, as I'd
known already, hidden

in a street…

    ·

…or season, tar
heat blistered in front of Memorial

Hall barefoot past from the library with
The Boys Book of Chemistry an era

I wanted to know of my town as
much as alchemy to make

the same transmutings now
Fort Scott's hidden *flower, gold*

was opening before that war
the Socialist mayor in 1912

the houses showed still
I walked to find out, waited

summer was the season, till
by the time you showed

I was on the way
to *internationale*

attentions, adolescence's
natural surrealism

Fort Scott only cuddled — *that's*
why of course your

radium message glance
had to fall in and *wait*

patience, wow, sitting on that
silly little stool, I'd never known

a mind so fast and far
in such a monumentally

patient body car

.

That drugstore interview so much a part of the mystery
I didn't even remember it when I met you

in Cambridge, Gordon Cairnie's Groiler, Good Friday
1959, come down with Ginsberg and Corso, brighteyed

and watchcapped on the leather sofa, I sat down next to
with *In Cold Hell* in my hands and you asked me, "Where

the hell did you get that" and signed it "Smash
the plate glash window"

all this seems fruitless conjecture
hanging back from the next

step of the adventure
not knowing

•

So as a sunny day, as today
driven clean by the high wind

and very bright
I would walk Scott Avenue toward the high school

the way I always return
going south

up the steps and along the diagonal
sidewalk cut looking for

or the open sentience
very bright for revelation

with no more likely revealed
than I ever had

but to find the nouns, the proper
artifacts of the mystery

still
only more weathered?

deep in the heart
that plunge still offers

no matter how much revisiting, re
twisting, that is what Olson sat

on the low stool turning
into me to say:

jump

    ·

—16–26 Feb 1971

✪

It is not discoverable by one poem
it is a life of insights adding up

and pushing out —just now
I was looking down Wall St hill

toward Othick Park and the Frisco tracks
where the fort was and Hawkins school

off to the left on the bluff—
knowing that's changed, the highway in

and no softball, sunken
giant floodtime bathtub park

Buck Run is concrete
viaducted over

611

and now that first, hidden vista
is the same as any recent freeway access cut

not even the railroad's
ancientness

so the ideal image must include
its own destructions

certainly the hungry
alchemy

teaches me that — but I mean, not
discoverable by one, I mean

to get
the centers of my childhood

and I'm not even living there
is all inner

life?
it's easy to say I saw that all

in his glance, but there he sat
a mountain of transmutings

continuously proceeding
I don't think my life work *is*

to transform Fort Scott as he did
Gloucester

but, to put it on the line *above* the personal
or to say the personal

the *real* person
is only what is, "Measurement is

most possible throughout the system"
as he said at the very

last: "That is what is love"

·

— 3 Mar 1971

[Record]

27½ hours left Berkeley c. 2:30 am after
the girls' housewarming party on upper
most Virginia gave a guy a ride to
El Cerrito eyeing a couple LA sign
left him at The Viking his friend just
leaving caught played one game of pool
in Albany then to Giovanni's for
pizza picked up speed at my place
speed at Carrison cold coffee in a
Mason jar left note for Steve and Merrill on
on the freeway by 2:30 or 20 till 3 south
Ginny & John & Ken & blond
Roger panting but quiet all the way like
Frosty to ride's the thing no matter
where Ann Bernstein's 15 mil spansules
in my belly one for her now over the
Golden Gate railing over the leap to
stay perpetually suspended? allow

the question mark to hang *happily*
over the way south kept ticking in me
as if she rode the lonely roads no longer
alone the events shifting drivers and the endless
seeking interest on the radio eternal news
menstrual soothing strings hopeless
rock fading seeking clarity a little while
driving meditation *about* car yoga *with*
remarkable items from the trans Great
Basin intermountain a 500' orange
semitransparent curtain over the highway
in southern Colorado as a gift like
the Statue of Liberty For America on three
great cables Highway Department spokesmen said
they were concerned about the traffic a
hole cut to let cars through before
they would ok ok in the flow as a
hand toward the dawn later Ginny
and Ken wondered if they heard aright as
if the Oklahoma panhandle certainly in
New Mexico crossing the Nacimiento at
San Ardo wide sand scrub that would be
also new discoverers by simply driving non
stop off into the night without a second thought
but yes again San Lucas coffee the famous
truck stop after King City full of Swahili
speaking elegant young men wrapped in
Taos pueblo Sears Roebuck cotton blankets headed
north in a station wagon but when we left we
were altogether into dawn just up while
coffee the first false called false lighting the
fingers of the hand out of the dark
measuring the cloud fingers lit redbrown to all
red singing the first wild Sunday morning shout
and answer African church call from LA loud

and clear the long birthing river valley long
attacking Atascadero in the speeding reborn
brain advance warning of LA smog finger
up an inner valley off the pass before
Goleta already 130 miles across the Channel
sung the warning LA wired respond
to Helen's on the hill in Summerland above
the sea and freeway constant surf and woke her
up 9:30 as always house of visitors and more
to come basking intently in the sun across
her perfect garden enough lavender for all
the sheets to China stealing the stink
off Eastland's speeches as she read on King's
assassination up till 3 typing her article we
came exactly audience upon the surf of
dawn while tornados answered all our
angers of that stronghold of liberal American
high statesmanship to splinters and more wind
my homeland though my parents' land
an ache no life in California will ever keep no
Eastland is not important enough to call
down the winds of Heaven everyone suffers alike
it is only hopeful as the weather was flawless
that day were we divinely favored? on
into LA by 1 to see Aistrup and Sam's studio and
then to Clayton's dinner salad meat pie and
Haut Brion '62 a bargain he said at
the high and velvet edges through the
tongue despite the salad first the midwest
habit vinegar cutting the tongue before
the wine had had its lingering accumulations speed
neither didn't help sweet welcome talk
and that fine wine and cognac after
the cream papayas strawberries lime
and coffee reading to Oregon by candlelight

into the sonorous walls across Burl
Ives' rejected table built for even
Kelly's tapdance facing the south this reach
still for the deepest corners of the continent
in Enzo's john just now "virginity is
god's way of saying 'hello'" among the lines
across the earth for certainty so left at
8:30 20 till 9 everyone wanting to drive
first Ginny got pissed thinking the even sharing
was now her time right Ken didn't hear insisted
"past the dangerous part of the freeway" pompous too
luxuriant exultant in the meal and reading? on till
out past Ventura quit and the argument and pissed
off came out tight a while John drove
the weariness gripped realized unthinking un
responsive all thinking of theyselves the speed
did not allay saw Helen once again at 10
or half past listened to her read a Langley Porter
patient transcript with his doctor now not
charged with sympathy as first heard funny
in his *klang* for every word he said we left
Helen with her other guests her stories of legalized
castration unbearable toward the long long
night one stop at Santa Maria one in
San Martin the finest old time all night stop the classic
Greek cook all very Army John
and I agreed the cutting vegetables disdainful
and without a slip the stove I wondered why
home ranges were not built like reading
the Sunday comics from San Jose the Mercury
at 4:30 facing the last stretch of 17 up
Hayward Oakland Ashby exit home by 6
washed clean slept till 2 got up washed clean
27½ hours the limerick sneakers layer of America always here co-
terminous but not accessible except by these
entradas

                    for all details forgotten enter here the arbitrary

        arrivals

              noon

                                                    —23–24 Feb 1971

January 1972 — The Recurrence of Beginnings
for Charlie

Walked the acequia madre East of Santa Ana Pueblo, catching the red mud with snow
in the boot cleats, caught ourselves by the bare cottonwoods caking the air, mooed at by
some attentive cows, eyed attentively by some quiet horses — "the white one's my favorite"
— tall dried sunflowers caught in the hair, walking past, heads down — caught between
Snake Rock with its attendant lava steps down from the Jemez, and the Sandias, with
the River and the redthread appletree branches in between, in our sandwich — and so
caught, so made a catch by this hand of land, so that we were as certain of the feeling,
here in the face of this whole landscape, as they were who came here first, the very first
time they came here — held by this little place, this *llanito* — and breathed on quietly for
a little while, half an hour walking talking of Good Evil and Arjuna on the battlefield —
as we held our own hands out to show the palms — "I've got a simian fold, characteristic
of Mongolian idiots" — "this girl who read my hand — I don't know if you're into that sort
of thing — told me I should be more selective in my trips" — held out for the surrounding
heaven to see and enclose

Carrison St, Berkeley — January 1972

Jack Howell's backyard, playing basketball
it must be the time of gray winter day
    after school

Swipesy — A Cakewalk, 1900, Sedalia
the fruit cup took the place of mules in the backyard

as if Penrod's father had come up the first cattle drive from Texas
and stayed

Journal Entry — 28 Aug 1972

At Jenning's Daylight Donuts down the arcade from Moritz at *Town Crier*, Mall's Shopping Plaza, Lawrence, Kansas — here Friday c. 2300 driving with Brodheads, leaving Reno c. 1500 Thursday, driving straight through — I 80 & 70, catching daylight again Rawlins, Wyoming, on to East of Salina (stopped there at Mike's sister's to pick up a crib for John) — Wyoming very green (recent rains, a wet summer, Roy said), green antelope suede hills — the cut of US 287 from Laramie to Fort Collins (by-passing Cheyenne) the epitome Rockies / high-plains plateau / badlands edge cut — Estes Park of Henry Adams & Clarence King almost in view still: very green alpine scattered meadows *cum* breakaway hillocks & chasms, and the snow peaks over all — the Keith–Bierstadt chromaticism rainbow edges on the otherwise altogether blazing sun or black — Denver to Kanorado still a very long and uneventful stretch — at the Kansas border a sudden opening up of the prospect — utter change by Salina: the relief — note esp. the idyllic eternity landscape at Wilson, as viewed from the Texaco station's vista point between town / grove & I 70's elevated monorail access — Salina / Chico twilight sidestreets overlay — fly back to Boston probably Sunday

Malin's new Ware book in hand: "Literature has many examples of multiple
                                         personalities. Some of them are of unusual
                                         interest to both literature and general history,
                                         and each is a special case." (p. 7)

Ware/Mallarmé incisions: *Ithuriel / Igitur*

          Ware: "…The book alone remains.
                        Man builds no structure which outlives a book."

Ware's geographical construct:
   Yellow Paint Creek
          Malin: "the poet must have meant the content of the
                        book." (p. 175)

(A suite of recent fragments — copied out for Ted — 18 Jan 1973)

        Hawkins, McComas, watchers from the dead
        bearers of the living; kindly; at the edge of the dark;
        at the right, not with Death;
        Ware and Frank Reeds, pink and red Cosmopolitan covers
        out of the darkness

                    where they go the catalpa beans cover
   a slow road, even in childhood
            even from old age

                 it barely shows

   and Hawkins who has come only

as one turn of the wheel under the plains

only smiles and shakes his head, does not play
            or cause to play, or say
            anything at all

watchers from the dead, masters of the long play

the hang of hair over the door at harvest time
            and the crisp hair of the floor

and the young who can still hear
            the master wort of autumn

                                        — 30 Oct 1972

            •

H.D. wrote: "What of the other Regents of the Night"

            of the Day —
                        in sunlight or gray
            of this hour, studying the shadows
                        to stop the world

            •

what of the other Regents of the Morning
between sunrise noon and sunset
ruling the hours

            •

…of the Sons of the Morning
and those Regents who give way to Noon
as they follow in the season
made alone between sunrise
and sun risen, other directions…

          : these may be
straight up; taking shadow never sunlight
as shape; the stoppages
of fur; the collapse of numbers
and the mumbling of dreams
not in dreaming;
the wood in trees

in the palm of the hand they hold up
turned to face behind them
to the sunrise;
in the palm of the hand held up to the setting sun
as the Sons of the Evening;
in the palm of the Lord of Noon
up to the zenith; and of the Prince of Midnight
down

the carved air
of earth

                                  — 30–31 Oct 1972

    .

…autumn and the Medford willows
filling the river
filter the yellow
difficult of access
the drift of distance
thrown always on ahead

someone is asking the way to the season garden
for *this* day
not a voice and not pictures
but what was missed in them before
tossing the path ahead

                                  — 31 Oct 1972

•

at the left is turquoise
that in the southwest aridities
sees bluesky oceans
and the islands of the blessed
from such a height continents lie
scattered in an instant on the hand
and in an air so clear
earth is ocean
veins of ocean in the land

the hair is black
the feather bluejay
the hand up bears
the sunrise light
but faces West

•

and at the center, blond
and featherless, only his own
long hair in an aureole

the lapis edge of takeoff from the earth
the lapis
lazuli sawn slab
slung against the chest

cold as the stopper of the world
unstoppered

warmer of the hard
straight-up heart

— 6 Nov 1972

lightning steers all things
　　　　　　　　　— Heraclitus

long ago the inheritance
of the completely foreign country
forseen

over and over
childhood's *brown diamonds*
will not relinquish
the possibility
of telling

the redwood carved
not to be seen
into the belt buckle
less noon
to equal, to cinture
the everpresent wheatfield

the sea, a fiction, certainly
of telling
who can explain
the pavement floor
difficult
of access

out from under the cemetery evergreens
the stone farmhouse pine trees
the edge of the blazing
unfed and relentless

the smooth hollow of the collarbone

grain by grain

　　　　　　　　　　　　　— Jul 1976

[Planks Turned to Marble]

for Robert Kelly, for Ruth Palmer

•

or hear that talk of another life   or looked for in the faces passed

    a swinging alabaster lamp, lit at evening, or today, the air so
    full of a gray silk darkness already before dawn, at waking —
    in the corner where the bookcase doesn't meet the side wall
    and one great oversize folio leans, too big for the shelves
    — and left swinging by being lit

and us, who left?   *all lit up*, from some, long long previous
                                    lickering
                       the crystalline body, showing the spark
                         in the depths

struck us, the vibration barely audible
the resonance from far far away   barely splendid

•

I set out to write a poem, to write *some* thing, for your birthday, Robert — and each try
it ended up a love poem for Ruth — *shared distance* of love you would knowing say —
persistant longing of a life — no glittering of just one leaf on the cottonwood but all glitter,
till just one leaf is left — and do not the last few always go at once, together?

gray silk sky at rising, come out of the NW, but the air full, since last evening, of a SW
eye-gooing essence, even rain does not clear

clouded sight in the glass of the sky, vegetable the very eye, the very paring

many teachings require the closest attention to be paid to the image woken with, and the
first seen on waking — *the goo of the eyes*, and, *I lay somewhere expectant*, simultane-
ously — a few days back there had been my double lying next to me, taking away the
twitching in my right leg, which indeed at waking had been taken away — and just this

night past an argument with an old and close friend, I did not know, and left the car and said I thought I'd better cut the weekend short and head for home, and my aunt got out of the car then, too, after I'd gone on in the house and come back out again, and said something like, *I might give you the clap*, and I said, *not yet anyway!*

was that really equal to climbing the ladder to the other woman's apartment, I argued with over the books that had been left behind, I hardly knew and yet parted with friends, *because* of the anger we shared?

or the equation point the waking, or the remembering, or the tallying, then now later ever? not the telling but the listening, because nothing was heard then, only now is anything heard, and *what* is like the tower on a rock in the sea, and the sun black and flared with red, low, and clouds low, and out of one different cloud, made crosshatched and then speckled red, a deluge descends into the sea, all drawn over the date and day of the week and time, all made of familiar, even over-familiar things, even to the balloon around the vista and the three drops entering at one end and the three emerging from the other end, but nothing at all clear about *where then* or *what now* or *what's happening* as each element was put down, only now even a thought about the order of laying on the ink and the color, and the last touches, black, the last touches, the black certain r*epeated sun* by the margin, leading to those escaping drops?

super-familiar the scene out the window, of the woods beyond the tennis court, and the corner of the next apartment building, and the sidewalk, and the edge of this balcony, and the corner of the patio below — and the cottonwood sapling across the parking, by the bushes, for it trembles and glitters and is a part with me, ever a part with me

I wanted to write something for you, my dear friend, for your birthday — in a confusion of love, or seems a confusion because I do not understand or feel my way clear at all — of those we love and those we have loved and those who love us we can't love back and those we love and can't be with and reach, ever reach to — some vast circling of reaching, around and around, passing the — the *sound*, I started wishing for — *the sidewalk news* in all the faces intertranspicuous, mingling, searching, passing on?

[Greyhound station in DC, c. 1345, bus to Annapolis at 1430]

of the Luminist show at the National Gallery yesterday, *still* the Kensetts haunt the most profoundly, the spectral Newport beach light — *so* much in the show it's hard to hold *as* a whole — but, a definite DC notch cut next to the Henry Adams, and the Bierce — maybe as much in the gilt frames as in the paintings' light and subject matter (not just the Great Vistas of the West — à la King) — and again thought I saw Ruth, as I thought I had in Baltimore — laid on the still more-vivid-than-waking-life dream residue of her from the night before — is that all part of the West, and Light, the Western Light? — or is this morning's visit to the House of the Temple on 16th St (walked right past on the other side of the street looking at that side's old houses in process of being rebuilt, and had to backtrack when I got to U St)'s tour? — «…and there *was* Light»? — *what'll I say,* I instantly wondered, *if it is her?* — «when now it is / the moss mystery / stones accumulate» — some *promise* of the inner space to show forth? — like some weakness of the sight from early on meant no choice of the sea, the Navy, as a life? — still remains, to call up as well a similar incapacity of the heart to see? — or is it the Navy captain standing at the gate for Annapolis, the aging parents he's seeing off, makes it also *to take care of* the lack? — «love, and exploration» — with Kensett on the New England shore, or back in the 10th St studio building in New York in front of a canvas, what would I call it *watching in(n)it castaway* ? — so sought Adams away from fields of clover, turned away in South Sea sands and utter silence, if she had been there, looking at Trost Richards?

— May 1980

言霊

crow talk, woodpecker, brother clouds, brothers *unlimit, invite, your* cliffs, old pogo sticks still *deérhnt, deérhnt, deérhnt,* à Poulenc, for the river reedlets and the eagles in the sunset rising — so dances the snow in Debussy, so the late light of afternoon along the sidewalk edges pencil shadows' comb, so whirls the Gollywog along the knife edge upright, strings of memorial crossroads talent, meeting's cast of hearing's fate to ravel, evening listening, car talk, to exhaustion, out at 15th and Iowa, also the fields, historical gunning's rubber peeled out meet — when is it ever *past* all mistaking, and that old pain of catching sight and thinking, o God, it's, but it isn't — bumper dangle, gravel crunch, glacier scrape, standing in the dusk waiting for advance in the traffic unridden

---

In his essay, "The 'Spirit' of the Japanese Language" [*Journal of Japanese Studies*, III, 2 (Summer 1977), 251–298], Roy Andrew Miller cites three texts from the *Man'yoshu* where *kotodama* and the coordinate term *kotoage* occur. The first reads as follows in Miller's transcription and translation [/ / enclosing portions of text not actually written out but necessary to add according to the reading tradition, «(so-called "orthographic zeros")»]:

«M 2506

1 kotodama /no/	3 Doing evening divination
2 yaso /no/ chimata /ni/	2 On the many-branched road
3 yuge to/u/	1 of *kotodama*,
4 ura masa /ni/ nor/u/	4 The oracle truly foretold that
5 imo /wa/ aiyor/amu/	5 My love would come to me.»

[267]

«This poem has reference to the Old Japanese cult of *yuFugë*, 'evening divination, consultation of the evening oracle.' This cult was itself intimately associated with the *kotodama* concept, and hence the collocation of the two terms in the same text is hardly an accident. The *yuFugë* of the Old Japanese period was a curious form of divination in which a person seeking information about future events waited in the early evening hours on some well-traveled road along which passers-by might be expected to appear: he or she then attempted to overhear the first words that these chance passers-by exchanged upon coming within ear-shot, and used these random utterances as an oracle. (A gloss to M 420, where *yuFugë* is also mentioned, in M 1.359 supplies many additional colorful details of the procedure, including scattering rice in the area and making a noise with the teeth of a comb before the passers-by arrive; but these are taken from a source that is reliable, at the earliest, for the first part of the twelth century, and so should not be cited for information about the Old Japanese period....»

[268]

He then notes that in the line yaso /no/ chimata /ni/, 'on the many-branched road,' yaso, 'eighty,' besides also meaning 'many, multiple':

«involves an etymological pun ultimately suggesting the word yasirö 'cult site,' and particularly to be understood here, in the context of the 'evening divination' carried out in the early twilight, in terms of the ultimate Altaic etymology of Old Japanese yasirö, which is related to words in other languages meaning 'secret, hidden from sight, shadowed.'»

[a footnote at this point gives: «Proto-Altaic *dal- 'to conceal, protect'
Mongolian dalda 'secret, private, clandestine'
Middle Mongolian dalda 'a screen, cover, shelter'
Buryat dalda or- 'to disappear' (i.e., 'to enter into concealment')
Manchu dali- 'to block off, screen off from sight, hide'
Evenki dal- 'cover up'
Old Turkish jašur- 'cover up, hide away secretly'»]

«This is why the 'evening divination' and its attendant procedures took place at dusk; and this is also why it was then — as well as where — that kotodama was to be found in its mysteriously disembodied operation.»

[268–269]

—Mar 1981

[en route KC – StL, c. 1940]

tuning the bowl, playing the bowl — between fire and water, there, between earth and air, here — sand on the prosciutto-thin, glass-hard taut skin of the bowl head, into the patterns that the bow against the edge draws — hair, skin, wood, metal: thickets, hungry from, ahead — I can't hear the young Japanese across from me, with a Vail life ticket on his down jacket zipper, as he reads from his English-Japanese Study Dictionary, only see his lips moving, his right hand gesturing as he murmurs, then jotting in a notebook, the dictionary shifting hands — under the Pentecostal searchlight beam of the overhead reading lamp, in the dark bus, Eastward riding — the rest of the bus ahead of us is totally dark, on into the road world where all the lights move for us — and the *sound* — bent over the empty page, rimming the empty surface of the paper with the wet fingertip of the pen, the edge of the glass of the book, into *its* silence feeling — the *sound* that is all around us, soothing as the icebox in the middle of the night but not from stopping and starting up again — the *sound* of the airconditioning blowers and the tires, an unintelligible, barely audible voice now and again rising above, a faint almost popcorn in the picture show lobby smell drifting, fading, persisting — bent over the bowl to play that history of the old languages that we seek, against the onslaught on great signs, the stations of reflection till we turn out the light

— Mar 1981

[SLC overheard, Howard Johnson's, c. 0510, on to Denver at 0630]

"— no one should eat margarine, because it warms the system — India is a country where they've let philosophy tell them what to do and it's ruined them, cause I know what I'm talking about — in Puritan times, now you know more about this than I do, the father had complete control, he could beat his wife and children whenever he wanted to, he could kill them if he felt like it, and it was allowed, he was absolute authority — course a lot of people say there's nothing wrong with being rich — and if you're going to make your career in religion why shouldn't you be paid for it? — I think the church should help people, but I'm not sure Christianity is so bad — Mohammedism, is just as bad, Buddhism, is just as bad — John F. Kennedy, now, maybe he was one of those avatars — when you only believe in yourself you better be good, I have no structured religion but the mind, trying to get someone to think — people start putting their trust in some leader, just like putting themselves in the hands of a doctor — just think of all those millions spent on Disneyland — however when I was in Europe I always went to the churches where I was, I was more likely to go to a church than a museum, of course their churches, religion is much more austere, much more austere — of course look at the Moonies, I think they're a disgrace, but I don't think you can legislate against the Moonies — and this one is Los Angeles, Armstrong's, what's it called, with that beautiful college and gardens and a branch in England, they only think the original 144,000 will be saved — the son was in an adulterous relationship and was thrown out, then his father let him back in, but that Jewish treasurer became heir apparent, something like that, and the son was out again, and all the members, blah blah blah, were up in arms about the money that was being spent — you can't legislate against the Moonies or any church, you can't even make them pay taxes — and if Armstrong wants to fly around in a jet and the treasurer wants to drive around in three pink Cadillacs, that's all right — but now they've got that law passed in Sacramento, the rank and file can find out how the money's being spent — now that Cardinal Cody in Chicago, doesn't he know they've got that law passed? — I wouldn't miss a bit of it, it's as good as any romantic novel — she went to one of those recruiting meetings, they make you feel *so* important, so she went to the retreat, and this girl, and they really started the brainwashing, and this reporter, was there two or three days, I don't know but what she did feel threatened — I don't know finally how she did get away, I've forgotten all the details, but the other girl stayed, and even the reporter, and she was writing an article, found it very hard to get away — and an emotional gang that was roving the temple got her out of there, and then she said she was so happy to be rescued, all that just pouring in on her, and that was just last week or so — still, if I was a judge and a parent came to me and said they had to quote kidnap their child to get them out, I'd go against the parent, even though it might bother me to do so, if the kid is 21 and an adult and didn't want to leave, how do I know but what they like it? — now L. Ron Hubbard and Scientology, now that's the real Beast —"

—Oct 1981

630

[trash]

what do you see beside the road
one corner, the South side of Ohio at 9th, compacted of cans and pop tops in the asphalt
    hump

to be riddled over

the bran mash sop of gutter litter leaves

to be read to, passing over

the thin at-history haze of winter light along the horizon

still the thought of a series of natural histories — quite still — the erratics, as earlier de-
termined, re-determined, and for certain, trees, especially the hedge, or a group of: hedge,
and cottonwood, and Kentucky coffee, and honey locust — and wahoo, cover in the
woods — this year hasn't produced very much, and what little, thin and dry and scat-
tered, obscure without even the lure of gnomic quirk, if lure, if lair — scatter of bird seed
under the feeder chaff, pecked seed ball in the empty bird bath, the sadness of a squir-
rel holding a nut when the fountain's been cut off between his paws, approaching, run-
ning off, coming back up to the footsteps again — sold long since — or "the sadness of a
bathtub when the water has run out" — and then the glitter in the emptiness of the
woods, the trace, the deep reassurance of an accent at all, and the hope out of -tiness,
-liness, -lessness—will, willed, willed *duh*

beast, or virtue, no, say a ball down the street of all the slurried gutter trash, furry in its
dripping, string, changing seasons every moment as it comes — and then the hedge apples
come back to life again the squirrels have deconstructed to coronas in the woods — in the
streets, thunder of their falling, rolls, drop by drop gathering, gathering, gathering, till
the whole town doesn't eat, it just gathers, and eventually what you see beside the road
is not a town at all, but glitter whirl, at the edge of what is paved, where you always find
the wrapper glitter, too, like silver favors in the graininess that's snapped and thrown
away

"aw, he probably goes around in that old beatup secondhand Cadillac of his filling up
cundrum machines in the filling stations — 'and what's your daddy do?' 'wholesaling and
retailing' — shiiit"

the plain old cement landscape in a fine shared eye, on that long thin endlessly wiggling
petiole, deltoides, a torsion, twisting, twisting, falling and refalling, rise, trace

and if a soul — blessèd
and if no soul — blessèd
and if a soul in embryo — howling, how long o how long to grow up
                not to eat, not for love
                not to write, not for sight
                just rising

                                            — Nov 1980

✪

of curly beechbark oak, iron in the dust, of paper sculpted head
and touch with touch the are they are as though a person poet multiplicity stood near
    to tell
the each their each the deep into the forest other looked to feel
and meet again on all our common loss of looking forward out of heart than want, than
    want of what? 's exactly what is lost
desire of solid scrolly bark to eat desire
to kiss the face within the tree or tree within the face all down the hair
ideal of spirit's reach cut down into a fence and post from leaves unseen the scent hangs
    still

                                            —Jun 1981

✪

midwinter days when the focus stays inside entirely, some yet again different than you've
ever made it before dinner out of leftovers and bare, chance essentials — as the glue of the
turning of the year begins to dry and crack, pages starting to loosen and fall out, the gin

before dinner helps watch, without imitation, and the irritation increasingly an instant answer to its own pointlessness, by that quick anger and regret, to use, as by some new peccadillo — to slow, to enjoy, to thank for, the Christmas cactus blooming once again, the realizing it is loser to Jeffers' birthday than Weinnacht, and from the morning, a book jacket fitting a depiction of the Globe Theater into the cursive script of the title without having to do with words or the letters or their shapes at all, which in any case were not to be remembered — the crucial words, it matters very much to look up, though no one dictionary for them can be found, the crucial words *tenedos* &/or *tendeos* &/or *teneos* are kept stretched very taut and resonant across the rest of the day, without ever yielding up exactly what they mean — I hold the tantra of the tendril's tone — the hypotenuse of containment is the alternate sitar — thin, but tender — lean, but cherce — into the family of love, the lover's home, the body of the lover, and the food, that protect the stretching forth to hold and keep, yet heavy with the rift of predictive judgement and its loss — what is meant beyond etymology, in the shifting and then lost *d*, the delta Δ where the seed and the eye appear and disappear in the history of the singular a-historical event, translated to the next dimension on, not quite totally out of the one before, the equilateral three in one in many more than three in one, the three hermits of the story who pray unceasingly, "You are three, we are three, have Mercy on us"

—Jan 1982

✪

the dog-gazed onion in the palm

o just be faithful, says the stone

and that old grasshopper, molasses-mouthed
that chews and chews and chews

to peel those layers one by
color-blind but nostril-perfect one

the gift of the book, to be so dedicate
of inspiration as oblique of understanding
as the edge of handwriting's legibility
and even then not quit yielding difficulty up

who gazes at the bottled horsehair in the sun
to be eel

— Feb 1982

★

so you come again below the snow fume pallor, with a rush of eos in the throat
path through the woods

tatpurusha of the soul-most curtain

taupe coat under the ridge burrow turn to

rose-line flush kerygma murmur first
back white, to tar in silence

then on the blackness of the crack between the years

years' presences

:

I am a citizen of the state that is haziness in the air and long for the color that is the
eye of love as the body for its clouds

— Feb 1982

✪

to look into the pits of
     and the blank of the word that does not come then
     is its pits, to stare into that whole season of absence in its staring
seed of the seed that is not time
given in time into that
     but what escapes from that black hole
     is the recent angel of awareness
shriven staring, to write awareness

fresh mounted messenger from beyond the turning of the earth's direction, back
dithyramb steward of the guardian of the bear, blazing in the forehead, plough step to
    turn and re-turn the pole
                      stiff is the penetrant of attention
mucoprotein gone down that drain, in the altered work, flood of each single fold of
    the marriage host
from the clothing of adornment, jewel wick in the nozzle of the lamp, stretched toward
    this midden, back
emunctory life, paranomastically answering to the root of being

seek, seed, see't, seen
in the gleam of the sunlight off the top of the yellow Capri parked beyond the dumpster
seized

— Mar 1983

[excercitatio / praecipere]

the night flight is to the chestnut square

I think my mother and I approach death by air backwards to the flare of the pain and
the work of the day

long anima, there is a coil of dark hair about the nacelles of the moment, and that smile,
of course, that does not rest or satisfy

launching and calling back the same small ships of the engines, this ship, this offering
of her food, my mother and I do not take

but stare below us to the square of commerce that has been made with our desire,
coming and going and the tickets being taken, and the low wicker gate at the back
way in, ours

•

the night journey to New Mexico we sit before the trunk of sharing, driving alone is
ahead, and the sharp "don't fuck with my head!" does not share, only the hurt and
the regret

here, now, before it is too late, it is time to unwarp the record

the keys have been handed over to the new tenants and the record laid back in the trunk,
what is playing here is the head whirling on its own grooves

these tests, the trunk itself, the means the character is made stronger, warded along its
ways to be wiser, exercised to hold to autarky to be the sharer

the crystal bowl in the shape of an ark, absence and its gift, distance and its gift, in the
morning light repair the giving again to the woods, to be struck and the clear, held
note played back

—Sep 1984

[sophrosyne spring muse overhang · Memorial Day]

Basil Bunting in memoriam

lift the ragged peony skirts, the rain soak dry to mind, and then that mind to vastness
    shown by its own mind

the then the story all so obvious it's eluded us, and every day to have to tell, so certain
    and so central is it, and so certain that it walks the tops of flowers open

just in time to run out after music in the air and take it, the poets' overhair and rates
    remaking, to pay for back for blood and parentage

and *still* so obvious it keeps *on* eluding, the morning of the poem is not the poem then,
    the then that vastness only to another recreation beaten, the afternoon of the
    hearthonk almost wakes

decoration evening, whatever wreath for memory, at least the meat loaf make!

to share to celebrate, and with the wasp that walks the balcony head down into the
    South, minutely prospecting magnitude

honor the skald who lays the common solid vulgar stones that yield, to hardwon heart,
    cut song anew, kick buggerall, king over self and banner petals flying, into the
    great intensity

for then the Craft, the for for something like *the Glory of God*

— May–Jun 1985

637

I have fetched phoenix papers

✪

[after a gift of poems from Roy Gridley, written while travelling in China, silently left at the door between 11 am and noon, 28 Jul 1986]

The referential is the dear telling. What is remembered or not remembered of the dream is of another life. Memory itself is from another life. Cups, called so simply, are not sufficient to account for their overflow. The things that you want to be quick, the things that you want to be more specific, do not account for the power of their sentimentality, for the cough, for their touching of shadows. A loss, then, if we do not, but *never doubt that the world of men can share this knowledge.*

.

There we have gone off along the railroad tracks into, to school, and stop and dip our feet in the creek, just for a little while, to cool and cool, with our little brothers and sisters. That is the distance, and in that it does not return, memory itself is from so long ago, no matter how long ago it instantly is of. And the try to intensify wreaks the comparison, to keep compassionate.

—Jul 1986

The epigraph and the quotation in the first paragraph are from A.C. Graham's translation of Li Shang-yin's "the Walls of Emerald," in *Poems of the Late T'ang* (Penguin, 1965). p. 168.

[still] call steps — three short odes

rough double cups awhirl and stationary within
turns of the eternal triangle pointing away, seed away, great plain away
a fuzzed nickel above, what's left of a nickel's passing
muzzing July to add up twelve and the year be done
halves all light above — all empty, *into* which comes
as the hung gong hummed after, the *let* light —
and the trunk's thumb more maybe than the nickel's
from the whirl recounted as the cut
spun off and then cut *down into* again and again across the rings
harp V's across harp V's — on over the pass again

cups come from — drink to them with
              here as a great sonore   liquor on one side
                  water on the other   and the light drone
                  dumb to be in the great tambor pause
                  and double soft dum dum
how to be double in the return to?

call them parents, not that they are not
call the sources that you've come from the gossip that you know best
that you know least best of all you have to

_____

now into the undersight, where the bird-fish ship moos its beak to be adrift

that would not rest upon the cottonwood sapling   unstill and still unstill
with the water fresh within it   and the marigold grown beside
but cast out into the greengold   undergreen of sight itself

gold old and accumulated   of anticipation
malleable in anticipation   day be done
and the moss

inheritances   and drawn back still by the love of growing things
and care still regnant here   the sight is from, to share

    •

how much in the other time we still argue love and hate
coins all the leaves, always all unstill
the cottonwood palm arrow on the delicate soul antennae of its petiole
and mine, stacks and stacks, to be released

    •

before he died my father made and still was making on a saxophone
the tone still not right in the pink plastic bore
as here, the burr of the holes too close to their grind

    •

in all of this there is another brother, or uncle untold   unmigrated
from this green thumb of love   love on its flesh of sources
perception's at the edges of
who tell   of instrument and making
and of the man come to the pitches of the cottonwood, and leaving

    •

shadows of thumb and forefinger turn about the ball
to the woodland player and the taut muscles drawn
and the iridescent spider risings

    •

who will walk by after that game and after that party's aftermath
into the coins and the flies alight on tight flesh

or see Homer   piss glitter, September, helmet brilliant
           downhoed to pay the presence back from the woods

．

players with pinochle cards under the shadows
leave their traces across the gravel
twined with the oboe hole around the corner
into the fence boards
felt matted memory   before memory
an upturned 10 of clubs   to beat two heads and twice four limbs
into one person   into the hiding and still hiding around the corner
to jump and be jumped   velvet glitter
of the cottonwoods and the marigold
and the moss, above

----

that is the tree matrix, still, and turning at its reaches
till the petioles are emptied, leaf and petiole to litter, and the emptiness, the bareness itself
reaches, still reaching

but the words walk, and we, hoofing it or however mobile
to the tree's clatter, track

to the pit of the woods' glory
at the viper's pit, warm with the wool of perception
that is the scarf, woven, the track, honey, lean as the wasps' winging it, or the singe
track smoke in the chardonnay, unsought, come back
haunting the ash curl out of the volcano
up the mind's tremble and the spine thrill, erupting
the scarf backtracked and rebacktracked for
found in the darkest pit in the darkest shadow patch of all the night way
instinctively passed on the light side of the first time returning for
lying there full-length in the gutter, undriven over
to lead back to

as we can trek, and roam
and the tree's clatter, still, the lank anchor, magnitude, memory
the soft cashmere, plaid, the burr
the soft smoke berries, remote, and taken to the closest
pit of the body, glory

over those same streets, in another searching, my mother, instinctively I have not been
    able to bear the fullness of embracing
so I have been able to live, embracing, and affirm, so there is this sharing, and we walk
    together
shows me, turning aside and turning aside
the wealth to be had, not to be lost from excrement
how plain it is, dog and avoided, at the end of the street
the gunned gold of the locust, hung, and the still green cottonwood, young, bending,
    glittering, toward it
rising over the meadow darkness lengthening toward us
the edges of workout, where the shit is
the rich black trunks, inside the woods, the sex and dreams at either end
carry clothes to work, my mother knows
with what impatience, with what frenzy of lassitude to live
over the dark avenue that is the boundary of every working, construction digs a canyon
    not to be passed over
that still has to be passed over, we still have to get to the other side of town
and from another, back
its capitol street our barrier transmission

so the scarf, my father, I bought with you circumnavigating Italy
you have my alchemy now, with you
the soft wool strip of tracking I thought I'd lost and went back for to be sure I'd lost
    and then to embrace the loss of, finding
what was at either end?
Jack Healy telling in wonder of alchemy in Chaucer, the wine and cake and glow of
    friends celebrating the first anniversary of wedding, the Red Sox winning in the
    first game of the Series

to the feet's rest at last, 2 a.m., after miles of trekking, and a little ice cream, toasted
    almond fudge
to reclaim naming

—Jul–Oct 1986

[three sets of three — I]

there is from the legs in sleep an exhalation of the light, along the tops of the thighs,
    over the knees, down the shins, up across the ankles, and on off the slopes of the
    feet, a spark out of the tips of the toes, out of the loam of the urgency in the loins
there was and there will be a time when that urgency held in the fluid suspension across
    the room of being is extracted to become the ink of writing, as it *is* the writing of
    being
as the paint that peels pliable from the railing at the moment of leaning over the entering
    and leaving below, burns and lets out the breath

  .

it might as likely be the flow of ink in the pen, dried almost to not flowing, lying open
    under the heat of the lamp
while off finding out why the record's skipped, Chopin's variations on "Non più mesta,"
    into an old and wonderful Ravel "Berceuse"
seek berceuse, but waking — ceaseless, seeking
the soft clack of the rod of the hanging scroll in the slight breeze of passing, Tu Fu's
    A single line of white herons ascends the azure sky incessantly seeking ascension
that is "A Mirror in a Mirror" as the music continues, and the spareness of the principle
    of meeting, that is the total contingency of the moment of recognition
the presence of a silence in the night as the center of a blazing in the daytime, as the
    course of a stream beneath a city strung on the net of its hidden sources
the water of the oboe has heard, or at the outcropping of sheer plain, a fluid elaboration,
    and expectation of the living to be fancy and at the same moment purely and simply
    flowing, the bound and aspiration of carry and descent

•

so for a morning construct the currents of support from what they've left
from night its memories that cannot be remembered, the ache of a hopeless and
    unending desire to ever satisfy, the kind of love you thought your life was past, but
    it is not and will not ever be
it was not the wind but now it is the wind, its corridor
it was not the call or the sound of a passing ball bounced or the sudden laughter
that now at the open balcony determine, as the steps of a yearning impossible to fill,
    how the day can know its origins

—May–Jun 1988

[three sets of three — II]

—We who cannot help the heart, the transportation of a time and splatter that cannot
    be further simplified, that cannot be simplified at all, only for a moment like thirst
    assuaged, or like my mother die in it, or like myself live on for it
—Twice he put his hand on my head, and I, angered at this lighthearted goodnatured
    indifference, refused the gesture, disdained the touch, wanting more
—O the wondrous polished bright as jeweled beads pigskin bolero jacket that we share
    in staring and in wonder, what lining is its other skin, what shape do we shift to
    wear it in, in dreams we know we yearn for here?

•

The song of the meadowlark ascends the grass beside the fence
of a fence that is not fullness   but beyond
the wax to the year   as the black ink stain across the fanning of the pages
has its red edge   is given over
is fumed   and in that farm   is followed out
to cross that field again

•

[broideries on two Sufic dicta]

I was a hidden treasure who longed to be known; therefore I created the world. — profound, in the I of the work, in the heart that knows, that seeks to know the heart, the leaf that seeks the leaf— *Ah! to know if* they *know what heart they have possessed!* — and *those* passes crossed over — it is the staff of desire, through all the rooms of the house, from the foremost closest smallest one, returned to — it is the crate of negation and its exposition, setting it down next to its companion, to the wise workmen, the breeze across the sweating body — the staff of simplicity, that in the depths of the forest of tea sways, the plume of the golden rain tree in its glory, the elaboration, the elaboration, the elaboration — as the wasps come each morning to attend the leaves of the cottonwood sapling, they never eat of but come back to and come back to and come back to, studying, sucking at the margins of exactitude — how pale the skin below the armpit, the least tremble of the petiole, its share — in the heat of the morning leaning over the balcony of that attention, lifting the ribbons of paint with each raising of the palm, there is a scarcity of finite verbs as there is of water, and the rocks below are not even rocks but pumiced lumps of acrylic, in the midst of which there is an actual stone, in the tides of ivy — to spit to, profoundly, the reach is of the moisture out of the soul, to dry, as the cottonwood sapling lifts, the reaching leans on, and with it sways

— Jun 1988

[Rückblick — with the three sets]

The young man, junior high/just at high school age, sits smoking, sometimes on the stone seat at the crossing of the two sidewalks, just above where they descend by stairs, just below where the way from the South mounts to the North — sometimes, as today, on the stairs themselves, facing the West, looking down between his legs, occasionally feeling the back of his left calf, shirtless rubbing his left palm over his belly, chest, and side under the right breast and then up over the nipple and back and forth, and then looking down at where his fingertips scratch along the ribs under his armpit — mostly staring down at the ground, spitting meditatively, aiming at some spot or crack in the concrete, as I aim from the balcony at one rock in the coarse fill below, looking as he does, on through — finishes his cigarette, stubs it out and tosses it away, getting up and going on, smoking here, and to gather the reserve, at the neutral territory's strength of the crossing paths, before going home, down and on outward, as he himself ascends and aspires

—Jun 1988

[three sets of three — III]

The wind down out of the North in the night with the old stories of heroes, into the sea surge, surges in the trees and in the dream time, themselves the grass and the illimitable horizon —

noon, and we cross over that pass as over midnight, at the zenith of attention, the wind up tossing the trees inside the breast, where the locusts sing and insist and lament their brief glory, into the after time that calls to look on everything with care and pain and wanting, patience and compassion, passionate at every moment —

slipping away again late in the afternoon reading in the story of that search for home, over and over, where the wind has tossed the possibility of following as far into the storm of darkness as the leaves lift under light into the sunset their glitter, and away —

and far off there, something that for the moment is called the golden lilac, that is the autumn lilac, and the brightest of all, opens, and from its odor enfolds a moment to be door

•

So with my eyes at the tips of my fingers, or in my hands, Sor Juana says, only to see, what can be felt — *sino tener el alma / como que no la tengo* : no, but I will own my soul / as tho it were not mine — and in the creak of the cane bottom chair, as the seat shifts to write, to address that writing, is that knowing — the wheat of the thick meal cracker, salt and sweet, and the coon cheddar cheese, that my black mask wants after, rubbing the caterpillars soft between the paws, and the wine, unable otherwise to see? — the soul roughed at the unsuspected callus of the palm, and of the mind its nub — caring too

646

much not to, isn't it? Coming back again and again to ask and write to ask? — there is a cascade in the mind that makes each hanging scroll preknown, the neck of all experience, of land its flow, unpredictable delight — and knowing there what still was never known before, returns the touching to its sight

.

Now the great blond red buff up from the fields rises into the grasses, as underspread of winter emergent with the sun's descent and turn — and hear at the table underneath the table cloth's deep green, as clear as in the mountain ash's red berries the bare — as of the hand, its bone — the certain color, kept at the tips, for then the singers go for refuge, and return — as from the principality of the orange, its zest

— Sep 1988–Jan 1989

[study]

the noon pass brings rain, the light's clatter of cottonwood leaves up its same wind
who is sitting at the table in the corner by the way over?
and as quickly the shower is gone, the drops played out off the surface of that quick game
but the return lingers and will always, imminent, rise resistant and insisting, to embrace
you can see for a moment the *hole* in the cuff parting to the wrist
the pulse looks up through at the eye darting back and forth across
the double sight of heart the other fingers interpose to measure
where did it come from? and with it the hair in the screen just at the level of the nose
to touch to bend to smell the privet and the mountain ash

— May 1989

✪

doctor into the night life has its court of poisonings and the play of water
is it the ambivalence of examining, and age, the feel of the lean old man's taut belly
where the dark mammy water has come and gone from, is always seeking?
the golden wine is to the child, that is not true, but minding, that is reminding
here are the galleries beneath revolt, conspiracy, and aspiration
flame-fakery in taking, and money no refuge, money, no refuge
pale doctor, that is a degree of desire and acceptance
how long the hair hangs down and is fastened!
walking flares patience, and obligation, to be patient, yourself, of diagnosis
your hand across the muscles of your own hinges
but over there, in that old guy afraid and contentious
who doesn't know what's wrong with him, but *something* is
the reach of a length of a life down its trunk, leaned up against
the slight tremor of each leaf shimmering, felt for a light, and lit
breath held and shared, and let out

—Jul 1989

[Some March Notes, 1995]

[1 Mar]

Bidu Sayão, now c. 93, was off to the Carnival in Rio, @ to *NYT* bit Jim sent of 22 Feb,
to ride on the Beija Flor club's float in one of the parades, as the central figure (in a replica
of Lincoln Center), not back in Rio since 1977 — "'I'm not going down there as an opera
star now because that was long ago. Now I am going as the queen of the samba'" — ex-
actly so! — 'All people do not die in the same way' 'from one culture to another, at the
crossing of the borders, death changes face, meaning language, or even body' (Derrida,
Aporias) : *horizon* — so Robert Duncan on what is to be declared at death's customs —
the disjunction of the languages the essential beginning reality & actuality, even along

with Walter Benjamin's aspiration to the universal all translations are toward, pre-Babel (and post-, however long — so Marx too) — *is* the disjunction synonymous with their own non-contemporaneity with themselves? — all the *Gespenst* presence/essence — 'Could one *address oneself in general* if already some ghost did not come back?' (Derrida, *Specters of Marx*) — Joseph Smith's illustration of 'Ghost Beckons' from that *Hamlet* of 1804, on the cover of JD's *Specters*, looks like the very impetus of Wyndham Lewis' *Timon* figure?! — and Tyndale now, with the street languages, of what synonymy, non-, unto —

[4 Mar]

H.D.'s *Within the Walls* read through before sleep last night, prose from Blitz London, crossing into *The Gift* and both then into *The Walls Do Not Fall* — indeed *many* redbirds the last few days, now *fierce* with Spring singing — *These, March!* — I walked all night   I don't know how — I wasn't asleep and it wasn't a dream — how I managed all the street crossings, off into that part of town up behind the college to the hills — and someone's had to come into the room this morning and sit on the end of the bed to make me aware of the breakfast fixings, and hear the night story I might have dreamed, uncanny continent!   starting to write it down on the dust jacket of the glot, the call to order in the redbird songs one of us isn't paying any attention to — we four, we instruments of imbrication: husband & wife & one friend who has come across in the night & one who has always been here from the oldest crossing — sausage and squash   big red mottled Italian ones cut long ways   & yellow diced — hey, what *is* that book you're writing on   Yule's *Hobson-Jobson: A Glossary of Colloquial Anglo-Indian Words and Phrases, and of Kindred Terms, Etymological, Historical, Geographical and Discursive*   here, you try it, open it, open it anywhere at random — and the first turn is into the second edition preface, so no, that's not the real text, try it again: KIM   the Kim sacrificial bull it isn't there   it's there, red on its green field, for the Equinox song, for the pull — chthonia — the yak bull and the cowcow waters water all the many turbulences to get here   the jewel at the junction is the jhool clothing of adornment   and that in turn is the tumbling of nakedness over and over its own intimate porches   its leaves with their long footstalks tremble like those of aspens and cottonwoods   quivering attributed to spirits   agitating them   as they do   for it is a religious   and from each drip-tip the wet runs off so rapidly the soul is soon dry   which is, where we grow, of some crucial importance

[18 Mar]

KANU's jazz program ends rousingly with Bechet and Spanier's great "China Boy,"
Coltrane must have loved — Mallarmé's 153d, and the hatchments with the *guttes de
larmes* (so Mackey has it) for JBDM — classical piano practicing somewhere to the North,
but can't tell what — Albert calls to his Daddy outside that he has seen a butterfly "it flew
over the *top* of the *roof* — was there a dead friend's presence in the cleaned and emp-
tied-out apartment, the strange look of a place when the furniture's gone or completely
moved around from where it's been for years, the balance of parts revealed, old lamps un-
draped — as later between wrought iron cage work and thermal mesh underwear — *lâme*
noeud rythmique — the yellow pebble buried in the mud at the corner, hard to bury — the
sequences of a sideshow to make conglomerate the stone holding down the voices disap-
pearing into the distance — a parade of clover, can you see it clearly enough to find the
four- and five-leaf shrieks and squeals of frightened delight? and Darío's tortuga de oro
across the carpet, to the balcony door —

[19 Mar]

The hand is a leaf of a table in its balances, and transimaginal of the photosynthesis — left
hand edge up to and across the breast (it is the ancient sign of penalty and recognition)
to receive the sexuality trembling from each person who comes close   the night runs
of the fuck bootleg   off in the woods, whoever's out there, and there are plenty up &
down the coasts and the streets dense with leaves — she wears a candle lit on top of her
head and the stiff coil weavings all around   he is dark & light in reversal and wears the
stud waiting fearful and delight   for this you'll walk all night or run all night   till
the redbirds start their bell teachers just before dawn   and peal by peel strip the dark
to even cold in hand

From Sylvia Molloy's forthcoming essay on Teresa de la Parra, Jim sent yesterday, quot-
ing from a letter of Parra's to Lydia Cabrera, Sylvia's English translation:

Pienso que cuando tenga "mi caja" voy a declararme en mi patria:
siento patria todo lo que vas a pintar en la caja, realidad idealista sintetizada.

I believe that as soon as I have "my box" I shall declare myself in my
own country. My country will be everything you'll paint on the box,
an idealized synthetic reality.

Tho for its impact on me I would stop before the last three words of the Spanish, and
simply take everything that's on the box, whatsoever, not abstractly qualifying — or
even of course what all *box* might be

[20 Mar]

Equinox — wanting the river Hassayampa, unto not even to care the impinging of brute
hopeless financial fact   but it is not a river of the Plains — 'To understand the fash-
ion of any life, one must know the land it is lived in and the procession of the year.' :
so Mary Austin in *The Land of Little Rain* — if so, here shrunk to the size of the apart-
ment and the trek to the campus and back, in active focussed awareness, little enough
of actual *land*   and of the year?   the seasons, but for the *accumulation* of the sea-
sons?   the solitary and unmitigating campoodie — 'The lake is the eye of the moun-
tain.'   but there are many ojos there — all become figurative in this locus, as even 'the
eye of the sentence' is more actual, or of the sound, the abyss of the mowers, who have
started their long season, ridden and pushed — *my box*, and what painting — (towards
an homage to M. A.)   The coyote is the water witch of the land of little rain, which
begins just inside the brain — equal the days and nights of attention, but not of scav-
enging — to study the neo-Stoicism of Poussin and Virgil's visible darkness may yield
the night ride of sex fest and the showing forth by day of its daylights — the pawing of
even the smallest footprint's worth of wet smell may free the dark mammy water of its
earth, and cutting the hair the moose-named he-gnaws from the daddy-making — and
the stories and the smoke and the smell of the smoke before the smoke and the sage rap
and the piñon, passacaglias — long after it was ever known, the black lover she lived with
who had been her rapist, and he knew too well the desolation of his vine — or behind the
layers of alcohol that are not paternity but where its offices are hidden, as in the men's
rooms of the desert — the offer told of once upon a time a literature job in the university

because of the children's studies and a fluency in Spanish that was not kept up but passed on in the blood — in the coyote's music, the land of survival — smell of celery seed crushed in the palms (for cole slaw) should be remembered in aridity — between the smell and the portent, the well   (Richter's 80th birthday! Salut!)

[22 Mar]

David Rattray's death, 1993   *rites of passage know no end* — to conceive a poem only in terms of its *luminosity*, free agent of light and dark, *quite irrespective of any representation*, from within — the storm broods over all day in the latency of Narcissus before the spring — come with a torch to a place of no electricity, dried cattails soaked in slow oil, an art of lost refinement and sophistication, to be such a mason as ruins necessitate to contemplate — whether the blond angel that smells slightly of chapstick comes directly and points to what must be put down next, or as the undiminished figure of the dead in a voice shifting from kid to kid under the window — as tho bending the will to the hidden impenetrable shape of all things, out there in the yard — offering out of a sack of life not large but free to take from whatever you think you need, its bead work and embroidery of the same monumentality and dense rigor, altogether beyond light and dark

---

[23 Mar]

Melville: 'And prosper to the apoplex'   *'Verge where they called the world to come'* — Maggie Teyte again, to hear with the Povla Frijsh in the same Fauré: "Le secret," "Nell," "Dans les ruines d'une abbaye" — huge planter pots as tall as a man, with full-grown fruit trees in them, on an upstairs terrace — and what are the fetish objects on the trunk of the big tree nearest the road in the grove, someone is lying under reading?   and is the man next to the fountain washing his feet for that?   or the remarkable woman in flowing white robes carrying a loaded basket of laundry on her head, striding away along the road to the right, as tho lifted an inch or two off the surface and scooted against the wind?   or the lovers who have just heard something on the other side of the monument they are now sitting up under? — 'a solemn, deep, still summer's noon' — here the yellow-green raked light of 6 p.m. is directly into the woods — and in another country the trees in the enormous tubs are almost into the last shadow of the day — in the same air

[nostos + kuboå]

for Stan Lombardo

never to forget the return
what is remembered is the future
where does what is forgotten go?
does it go there too?
and the spider in the eye
where it came from?

    •

conversion
the return
to the self   just because
again in the   one person
embrace   says I don't
for carry   listen doesn't
of the most   mean I don't
cherished   listen
the most
cherishing
worlds   good
to be bound   for
of both   you   of both
going   coming
and going   and coming
back   back

    •

the madeup
the unknown
the discovered
strictly from hunger
out of nowhere

word
is it
a word?
it has letters
and the shape of
and their sounds
maybe
it has a radical
and a familiar
possible
phonetic
never together
or heard
you can have
any number of
certainties
about what
doesn't mean
without knowing
what
does
empty
as a dingdong
doodah
it points
not to nothing
but its
zero
to return
to the recognition
without remembering
you have to become
a stranger
to have
a homecoming

— Feb/Apr 2000– Apr 2001

✪

Our backyard pavilion was built out of scrap lumber and very crudely finished, but inside was like a tent to the gap-through walls. Of worn Indian bedspreads from the ceiling and rag rugs on the floor, and a frame-hammock full of cushions and blanket-piece throws, of regency, and next to it a folding camp table that rippled. All shimmering where the old garage had been, and the first driveway.

If you dig down anywhere in this part of town you always find something, and something from long before the town was here at all, but they were.

What we ever turned up, just around the edges, away from the crankcase oil soak, was a chicken skeleton, intact and burnt a bit — and a little medicine bottle with a dropper, half-full of a heavy dark-yellow oily liquid we thought sure used to have been nitroglycerine, for the safe, left there by that uncle Grot from before the other war, supposed to have gone off and been a road agent out of Oklahoma and the Southwest, disappeared into Mexico, called from how he'd written his abbreviated Geo T in the sidewalk cement out front — and a slingshot, with no inner tube left.

For the hammock is in fact the sway, the spirit of the deep, before, come up out of the ground and made to wait, made perfectly still and small, and then grown large enough, once the bedspreads drape their canopy, to let processions circumambulate and praise and play their triumph calls and sing their hymns, a throne. Not the dream, but far to found and take the dream.

And we were ready to remake them all, even our names.

Nov 2000 – Apr 2001

✪

When I was younger in the years of living in Lawrence, in my 40s mainly and the middle of my 40s, I did a series of drawings, only recently come to light again, I'd forgotten all about, of faces mostly and profiles, though also of animals and their attendant flowering plants and those plants' attendants, combined with maps and itineraries, named places and stations, and seasons even, routes and named wrecks, lost buryings, the way

655

there — and the way back was the drawing, the superimposition, the contours' inclusions, all one within the other.

And there were coins too, sometimes the actual metal stuck in, sometimes rubbings, or the drawing as the thread — heads and tails, reign and aspiration, flesh and soul, as the eye.

These were often from my own visage or started with an attempt to render it, wherever ended up, for I have no special talent in drawing, and certainly no training — but just as often were studies from faces in the papers, snapshots of friends, pictures of the old well-known — or bigger than faces, or only a part, like a part of a landscape, become bigger than the land, than its scape, tronies of earth shape — one, for example, might kiss a star.

They came together as a matter of dates or of one date, as of looking for a bill and whether or not it had been paid and on time, or the car registration once, or the rent, and so they were to pay back too, and for time back — to embrace a beaver in a tree, to embrace the tree and whose it was, to embrace each one, dead and gone — for they all crossed over one another, and not just with a gaze but an actual embrace, with an actual return, with the actual and total loss.

Portraits I haven't done so much since, but the maps themselves are iterative and frequentative, like the dining room table and its cloth, into and for whoever sits around it, and who attends around them, and the sign that might or might at leaving be the validation of the exact moment of exchange — the *sugges* broken off in mid-message out of the South that is now known as the form of the return, but not the return.

Given: three shepherds on a windmill tower, their long red and golden fur flying in the breeze, tongues out panting happy at their agile climbing to the top, where the vanes are gone and only the scaffolding left, or the Great Wheel was never there, and they alone the catchers of the wind, the overseers of the oak trees to their ministry, the converters — for the series are all conversions.

Jan–Mar 2001

[Some Notes on House and Woods]

for Gerrit

Buds like lights draw the hunters in from the woods on their way home, to hear a shelter under the trees in the living room, as warm as cerise promises, as promises of translucent lights in plastic gallon milk jugs half-filled with water, of luminosities aflame, encircling the house. But only to stay a little while, glow warm again, have one hot buttered punch with black tea, whole cinnamon and cloves and allspice, sealed, and be on their way. Not a game shot left but a story of the woods and the principals in the woods, hunters of their lore, fur of the lore and their love of the lore, to keep warm by, left with us, enough to line a pair of slippers with or add to the throw for the couch, the coverlet for the bed, hold and keep to the heart, the time again in the dark of the year. Or it is we who come in from the cold and take with us treasures as we depart. So in the house the mysteries of who comes in, who leaves, who stays, who gives and takes, constantly change, and of the woods. Sometimes Kalendar Princes that every creature listens to, sometimes the music itself, the palace, the wandering, the coming back. By that flame consentaneous, the respiration, the reciprocity of hospitality.

·

Love: to hear a song of that kind. If there is a vertical mystery of shadows become the ground, there is one horizontal of leaving a flung snapped handkerchief up the air, to walk away and jump the walls and hedges and be gone. Come as an iridescent light of flight back and forth, itself invisible within its spectrum blaze, too bright to look at long, unidentifiable except as that, to announce the changing of the orders. And the young men in the black t-shirts that come and hang around and say so, ask: what was that other order you called in? and before that? which one did you learn and know till now? and this elaboration to untell, now to tell? such obstacles in reciprocity, reveal?

·

It is the old house before the house of childhood, owned all along and now come back to (as some houses keep their first house within them), and the cedar waxwings from the woods have their wing there too, bring in their gathering, their intense restless congregation and gregariousness, their masks and foraging. For there are houses whose far floors and corridors are streets and groves and open out up hillsides, long ago settled and resettled, not even the occultation and concealment of another geography can keep hidden and not find. The rose panel room, the sea rose tapestry, The Secret History Of The Earth panel, the library whose every avenue opens (books are the city), have their key in music, made mind, made touch, the conversation of the muses and their Love's Dream, the secret way through, that thrills. (And secretly they also joke: the psycho-geography of everyday knife! keep it so close to your chest, to your life, you can tell it and smell it and muse it and never lose it, and all the epiphanic switches and twitches and folds and holds, pockets!)

·

In the last hour of the day the sun comes straight in through the one window of the stu-dio, lighting up the jeweled miniature brassicas, the lavenders and St Johnsworts, the rose campions, mullein pinks, the peonies and lilacs, the nightshades covering the back wall, mullion-intricate, deep-scrolled and deep-carved handgrasps of blue-agate jade against gray forest green, pine and spring and citrine crisp, and olive-lemon under vein, suffused into the polished wood. These are not the gifts we take away, but the gifts take these, as bowls made living.

·

And guides, if you pay attention enough to notice, and are to be shown, will quietly but insistently indicate which way, the first leader in the pink gum tree at the middle of the crossstreets, the nudge and nod to one diner as to a better place to sit in the parlor, and to the parlor, the story, the bass note held, the photo, the candy across the counter, through, the farewell through, family matters, yours when you hear them, even if not your yours before. To the wise café lady in her back garden of purple opal trees, who shows first the bow and then the rise, the hands up in and out fluttering, that call down the fluttering hovering blue jay, in and out, back and forth, in their essential interchange, not the generation of boys or of girls, not the generation of war, but of delight. And the jay not tame, not a pet, called down only by her calling when she calls and when he wants to. And the crows and the cats and the possums and the bumps in the night, called in the backyard, called to the porch, come to the backdoor, are each time they are called and return, in that dimension her calling is in and renews.

·

Old stories, and again: a house by the woods (and the sea is near), and he who comes into the house from the woods (and the woods are the world), and he who brings the house into the woods, and knows both, and brings us both. Poet Scholar of the Western Avenue, reciprocal Poet Scholar of the Eastern Hedge and Fence, Master of Lavender House and Lodge, of Mockingbird Hall of Summer, of Start to Catamount and Return. First met come up the back stairs and in the back door on the Fort, to the family of friends, and the family of friends the family that we have ever made, and the first house known, that overlooked the drive-in movie, that sea.

Now, here, what is the late February doing? Holding brightness up for Equinox. In the care of old photographs from its album, always some, and some of the most cherished, lost or loaned and lost, or unremembered or misremembered in their care, which is the surprise of wonder, there! But some are offered now entirely anew, and only of this moment, now. O Gerrit! holding your birthday up and always surpassing it! And it is held up and you do surpass it. And every other day held up and relished in your sharing with us, and surpassed. And all enfolded and woven in the silent mystery held up.

Companion of Companions, of Everyday, of First Recognitions, of Making, of Love that makes the Household ours the World, makes First Hospitality Renewal, Polypragmosyne of Spirit, beyond Far Reaching, Dearest Brother, Nourisher, Revealer, Magister, Makar, Delighter!

HAPPY BIRTHDAY AT 75! A Grand Salute!

[Notes]

The bearing of tolerance: the knife stab left in the coat kept and worn till threadbare to know again and again. The itinerary of emending the intellect, which is the journey of renouncing the inheritance of all wealth. To become a professor in your own discovery, but of something else. Not the distance covered, but the total lack of anything carried along. A geometric method of politics, about as likely to work as of the passions, yet of that yearning and that rectitude, that invention which can be of glory. Why is stupidity and irrationality so deeply sought and felt proud of, and the doctrine of love become the acme of the inquisitor. A science of effects, the sky from them, a religion which is one, as of light and the ground of all design, all desire. A voice whose method of production will be looked for by linking it with the probable sources that most impress the people who don't understand them at all but like it. Yet as someone who loves to watch spiders fight, and making that happen. These eyes of that mind, give thread, their mirth perhaps, the lens for what vision, the life for it and of it and from it. *To be men not destroyers.* To leave good soup at the door for a birthday, and flowers. For there can never be too much delight, or the giving of it, tacit in compassion.

.

Then there were three dogs that became three birds and flew away, Salt and Pepper and Mustard, out beyond the shadows of the room where the walls disappear. And a transparent cow, though all of fur and flesh and hide. And a face entirely of darkness, impenetrable as the interior of the opened box in the hand that says, What do you desire? And not just the carpet runner that comes into being under your feet out in the street and then into the yard as you approach the front door, nor the figurations in the carpet that are after all alive and rustle and run and jump around and bloom and fly, or the weaving itself that is still going on and talks to you as it throws the shuttle back and forth, and looks up at you and stops and explains the fabric up out of the ground, and the spindles of thread that whirl at the steps, set into song by the wool and the sheep that give the wool. And who is that at the door? The lore. Says, let you in. And as they disappeared, they can return, now Salt, now Pepper, now Mustard, now the Milk, come for the supper stew, for the hunger and the fear and the desperation to escape, for the barking of birds and the phases of the face. To make sure you never forget in your prosperity the misery and destitution that brought you here and those who shared it with you, the compassion that created you. And when you have remembered and have restored, to disappear again.

.

The moon too has its fierce as well as its benevolent aspect, beyond its phases, and carries a knife either way. And the coat, especially when it is turned inside out, has always known this, its flickering heard first far away and only much later seen and recognized. *Artifice is fully a part of Nature.* Your dreams are not your own, your love, your life. *A plane of immanence has no supplementary dimensions.* An impulse, an encounter, a passion. A bright wind of jeweled sustenance, of sun gem, of cloud fire, strung. A completely darkened face, and dressed in a robe of every kind of fur and skin, until the face is in the wind. *That things remain enigmatic but not arbitrary.* A new logic but not reason. Insistent urgencies, small racings back and forth between the points of departure, to build up another momentum of trajectory. Can you turn and turn sadness about itself and re-make its consistency, reshake, reslake what it answers? Tenderly, as with the gentlest stroking, but emphatic. Even though the world of tentativeness is also equally inherent? *The more an image is joined to other images, the more it flourishes.* Until the image itself has no further need for, is no further needed. To seek from enchantment, the demands of the actual life to constantly reverify, the release of invention.

— Nov 20 – Aug 2003

[Feb/Apr 2004]

It's a day of red in the head and gray in the day
cherry the last cactus blossoms fall in the dark
and in the dark fade back dry light to burn
and the snow melts back clear black against crescent bareness

　•

And the clearing, if it is clearing, from the North
comes on in the brain like running out barefoot in it as fast as you can
and shivering, and sliver blue, and back

　•

For it's clear the fits are returns
not rejects, but grabbing the attention first by color, then shape, then small sharp
　　gravings and incisings
closer and closer to another story altogether, but not
but the return
fawn red berry thimbled barrels and clear ore holds
light quick shiftings of the skin of crystal
of the face and back of the hand, in on themselves, and away
watching the guy from across the street drive straight into that enormous industrial
　　dumpster with his doors wide open and the music blaring

and knock the power lines in on themselves, and still walk away, and try to explain it
    all to his friends later, and the photographs
the samaras driven down out of the North in blast after blast, clattering, shattering

[Written on Tom Meyer's birthday, 2004]

Valentine's Day, and the Queen and Valentine of Spades
and there is more to the day than the dismissers in the student newspaper yesterday
    would ever admit, for all its exploitation
the volontyn of strength and tense in winter's spring
rededicate to *chese his make*
so the cards set down, and the dark, and the heart, and the suits, and the turn, and death
acts are passions
this storm is nothing next to my passion
and if it is not to heal some passion of the soul, it's all in vain
the chocolate fades and its cherries and ginger and almonds and orange peel
next to the uncertainty and the arousal and where they start from not knowing
if the night in the night is the night itself
is the day in the night itself as well
the heart in the night is not finding
and finding grasses in the wallet and the curb
and not the first time that light and curb and search
and the night off in the night with just the grasses between the buildings and no walk back
and not getting back
the way
today
heart's piercing to be offered, and its reversing
the tradition of sending by what transfixes and transports
by what transgresses reticence
is it the dark in the Norths and Easts
isn't it in any direction
but most of all the wallet and the curb and the grasses

and the even silly sentimentality and indulgence and its transport
we were afraid of, however lofty and unrepenetrant we pose
to want to be the summons of the resins in them all
the mount and wait, to burn
and from the wallet and the curb make walk and talk the grasses
we who drink under shadows
let the plain leaves that cast the shadows
stay just plain leaves
no matter what crown is made from them and given
live far from that crowning and its hidden enmity
darters
darners
shimmers
skimmers
with desire
to search
into desire
deep
upwelling
unending
engendering

[March Set 2004]

After thinking early on I really also ought to ask him whether he'd been publishing
        anything recently
I didn't, stupidly, and the call ended
and so I'm left with, and circumscription by, continued unmasking
comes March and the first day's strong winds
and the milkweed dried vine and pod still in the cedar shrub toss and stay
and the robins and the chickadees and long earlier the redbirds
the call the toss the unstaying
now rapid figurations now full hands now cards now arpeggios

[RWE, "Circles":] *We grizzle every day. I see no need of it.*
but there is a need   he too saw
it comes in the smallest words   to be its own   so
so to be   *is the sole inlet of*   *so to know*
so to us a Redbird Day is given   a conjuration call
call by call by call

The concentration of the fruit in the eau de vie
its breath the cut clear glass breathing
turns on the silence of everyone who is gone and in the day
the day is noisy   but they   are not   in the day

These short complexed enigma dramas
enacted for the seepage left
stain back through the other side of the mind
the no-stain, indelible
the pants patch frayed at the knee
just itching and scratching
to be speech

Mowers have cut down the blond vegetable porcupine from in front of S building
that it regenerate anew
we hope
but it does not
we keep

Dots of red
Tweertyer   tweertyer   tweert
and the *tur* dark   dark
from which aunt did each diamond come, and when, and what carat
the count in the yard of each bag of mulch

making up for the Spring floods
on your finger
in the early morning the rose in the fire call
the rose coal in the crow cold

　　　•

Silence now of the lilac bushes dug up and just thrown away
from around the old law building
not only their quiet when alive
shared with the redbuds still there
but no bench cries out *Save Our Lilac Bush*
as one once did *Save Our Redbud Tree*, and they were
and now the bench is gone, with the lilacs
and now the redbuds too, for a new steam tunnel
at noon the finches and the redbirds cross talk in their distances
in ours their singing
coming closer and passing and not answering

[written on Chuck Stein's 60th birthday . 23 Aug 2004]

spare, the lablab this summer, no cover, but grown through the fence
the nine dragons' cycle ours, the gaps in, where in in is
how do you get to know dragons, and show them, and so roguish
demonqueller demons, creatures, poor suffering human beings in tatters
gambling, scrabbling for tossed charity, yahhing, their eyes
the great snake watching meditating, all attention, wide open, unblinking
hungry spirits come up timidly, afraid, but very hungry
a court lady riding a deer, lake and landfall transpirant palfrey, post beyond
a pomegranate, ink grapes, an orange, red stubby bananas, August all entering Autumn
they call for my mother who's dead, because her name's still in the phonebook, and
　　　only use her first name
and I haven't had it changed for mine because I'm still alive

hair which is a dark grass grows from the elbows of the dragons
and the gaunt eaten nostrils of the destitute
what was a call comes back again
short quick apperceptions of immediacy that unchange the name
hold high an inkstone for the waiting planetpliant upraised brush
gate gone pond gone cliff gone pinnacle gone back around gone here
a dragon grabs out of the incessant torrent a pearl or what is it
the sun, the moon, the whole light globe hold, the furor in delight
and mud and slime and rain and rain and rain and no cover, no shelter, no refuge
but grown through the fence

[Record]

At St. Patrick's Day, and the Saint's death, plus 1500 and 40 years, by the tradition
to hear the call of the deer, the thicket call, the creatures, the tide call, the call
at a Saturday, plus 1500 and 40 hours, by the reckoning

Ed Dorn came to our motel room, talking to my mother and my brother and me
    remarking on the rare chance it was to see all of us together at once
and then was gone and I after him with his keys he'd forgotten
and after my mother, on before me, and with hers too
and then everyone gone and not found
only a boy running down the street ahead of me, faster than I could ever manage
the good of aging

    .

And when you die, or when you think you're dead, or when you dream you've died
your feet are turned backwards and your legs and loins but not your waist
and your arms embrace your head and backwards too and one of them waves goodbye
    to the air in the air
and the dancer on your belly whirls and reaches to regenerate the sun
and rides your body like a boat curved on into the sun

666

holding all you've ever done up like a ticket from amongst the snakes
and blossoms sway to tickle your navel, the entrance and the exit, the swivel and the
    plug, the cast and the release, and the call

            ·

Crows and redbirds   clear cawing and clear calling
and the quiet of Saturday, the quiet of Spring Break and the students gone and the
    students staying
and the cyclamen fading rosier and rosier from blood-crimson to the tide gone into
    the turning

            ·

A small box on Ed's nose?   a little book?   (knows)   tickets?   the balancing
    and the balance and the keys

            ·

"You will feed others"   "I am the ghost"   and the others are onions
and onions are worlds and worlds within worlds and water and corn
and corn is the hill spirit and the thicket
and long-leaved and long-eared and long-legged
and long gone and come again
and all long a-reach

            ·

And the cyclamen petals back blown back by the wind they nose into
sniff, hound snouts down, ears up, hard on the trace and long and hard a-hold

            ·

Hard, in the calling through

Hail, who is coming through

[Studies]

　·

[on Edmund Waller's 400th birthday, 3 Mar 2006]

> *What Art is this, that with so little pains*
> *Transports us thus, and o'r our spirit raigns?*
>
> —"Of my Lady Isabella playing on the Lute"

and the boys were playing marbles on the street in Fort Scott a hundred years ago
and the police told them they were breaking the law and made them stop
and the boys said it was their right by the signing of the Declaration of Independence
Spring is marbles　　is it still?
so hyacinths reach　　and send abroad
taws and the taw call
and the Sun come down　　Knucks down!
and shot across the ground
into terrestrial collision　　like the stars

　·

[on Elizabeth Barrett Browning's 200th birthday, 6 Mar 2006]

so one tree will send out a branch to join another and be saved
so the rock wall and its climber
elusive records, books
in what other dimensions inter-live
and returning maybe or not staying
and only in the mind keeping
and the memory itself going
flake flaking flaky from the start itself
no way to throw another after to find
and in the far distance in the interstice
another orb coming
or maybe here its cloud

•

[on Benito Juárez' 200th birthday (and J. S. Bach's 321st), 21 Mar 2006]

that this one house could carry two whole families
interpenetrant and withdrawing simultaneously and then be gone
but an ascendant stage of other things as mysteries
no more understood but undergone
than who would the life the next night be stayed with
and how get there and be here again
as lying across slabs of yellow stone
to stare close into the henbit in the snow
pink purple tongues of woods
and in the degrees of Spring
in the degrees of families we've made
rewelcomed   certainly rewelcomed
lifted and let fall   and got up and gone on from
and rewelcomed ever
as slow in the slow slow afternoon we are

•

[*a Nocturne of the day* – James Huneker]

In the vanguard of the army they carried 100 or more tubs of flowering trees
and wherever the camp was made, instantly was laid out *the garden*

•

Did Christ *hear* the rotting dog carcass *sing*
as he bent near to admire its shining white teeth

•

Out of the *preternatural occupation* of not or *concealment*
and the *persistent forgiveness* against *incessant malice*

In the middle of the day the smell of peanut butter and mayonnaise and jelly brought
     out a small spider from under the chopping block and the blender
a puff of breath, a puff, and it rolled into a ball, recovered, and hurried back where it
     had come from
bringing and receiving luck and renewal

     .

The wolf spider, hunter of the night, trapped in the kitchen sink and its porcelain slick
     unclimbable sides
took quite a while to rescue, since it hid much of the day in the garbage disposal drain and
     kept trying to get back there
at last brought out with a big plastic spoon and set down between the icebox and the
     sink counter, and away
saving, and the day saved, and again

     .

You might own a pair of such great lichen screens
one of the rocks, one of what grows on them
dyed with their pigments, translucent, illuminant, through
and at the centers, they turn

[plain lines . versos sencillos]

To look for the turn
in the night
in the day
to the curtains
from the hawthorn thorns
for itself
or not only
its meaning
or only
its return
its soak
its sake
its suit
its seek

•

The squirrel in the hawthorn
the redbird
to run in the night
and remember

•

The day is all a-drip
and refreezing
all glitter dripping
one bud that may open

•

Can you see the hair on the moon
where the dog was
the hair in the branches
where the moon is?

[Homage]

You will not always walk in the rain
on a May morning
or see the iris in bloom
before you give a final
on a campus where you were young and took them
longer ago than you will live after

The text of this book is set in Adobe Jenson Pro
designed by Robert Slimbach.
Design and typesetting by
Jonathan Greene.